What People Are Saying About
Chicken Soup for the Golfer's Soul . . .

"It may not shave strokes from your game, but it will make the ones you take a lot more enjoyable!"

Tim Finchem
commissioner, PGA Tour

"This is wonderful medicine! It reminds me of how important it is in life to be able to laugh at ourselves and the importance of win-win relationships. The combination of golf and *Chicken Soup* is the perfect prescription to inspire your spirit and soothe your soul!"

Robert Dedman
chairman of the board, ClubCorp, Inc.
author, *King of Clubs*

"*Chicken Soup for the Golfer's Soul* speaks to golfers like no other book. It reminds us of why we play the game!"

Jerry Tarde
editor, *Golf Digest*

"These stories remind me that golf really is the greatest game. *Chicken Soup for the Golfer's Soul* is a must-read."

Michelle McGann
LPGA tour player

"The stories in this book show that golf is a stage where many of life's dreams—and most of its lessons—can be played out in the most insightful ways. I enjoyed it thoroughly!"

Jim Ritts
former commissioner, LPGA

D0009587

"The common thread of golf binds us together more closely than almost any other favorite pastime. The people, places and feelings we experience through the game come through in shining colors in this wonderful book. If you want to get the most out of golf—and life—get this book and read it!"

Juli Inkster
LGPA tour player

"It's nice to read a refreshing book of real stories written by real people who wake up every morning and put their pants on one leg at a time—just like everyone else."

Tom Lehman
PGA tour player

"Keep and read this book that celebrates the game of golf in such an uplifting and positive manner. It should be required reading for all golfers."

Jim Colbert
senior PGA tour player,
co-chairman, senior PGA Tour for the Cure

"I had such fun with this book that I want to share it with all of my golfing friends. You can't go wrong with *Chicken Soup for the Golfer's Soul.*"

Nancy Haley
CEO, TEHĀMA

"Thank you for bringing *Chicken Soup* and golf together. What a great way to put this wonderful game into a perspective that may be quite different from our own. I plan on using your stories to share insights with my students, and for myself when I need an attitude adjustment."

Mardell Wilkins
president, Western Section LPGA,
teaching and club professional division
Teacher of the Year, 1996 and 1998

"This fine book manages to combine wonderful golf stories with many of the best human qualities we all want more of in our lives. I enjoyed it thoroughly."

Dan Quayle
vice president

"Reading this book confirmed my faith in the inherent goodness of golf and the people who play it. Also, it cured my cold."

Ruffin Beckwith
executive director and CEO, World Golf Village

"Each story will touch your heart in some way."

Liz Comte Reisman
editor, *Golf Digest Woman*

"This book represents a fantastic collection of entertaining and meaningful golf stories that players of any level can appreciate."

Bob Murphy
senior PGA tour player

"A lifetime of great golf stories in one book. I really enjoyed that the book embodies the soul and spirit of this great game."

Rick Smith
renowned instructor and architect,
president and CEO, Rick Smith Enterprises, Inc.

"Golf truly does imitate life. I'll never look at the game the same way again."

Pearl Sinn
LPGA tour player

"This book will make you laugh and cry. Like the sport of golf, it will evoke every emotion inside."

Ann Ligouri
author, *A Passion for Golf,*
Celebrity Musings About the Game

"To perform at your best requires inspiration. To win in competition requires awesome will. *Chicken Soup for the Golfer's Soul* is the well-balanced meal of future champions. Great tales that will satisfy the victorious reader."

Bruce Warren Ollstein, Captain "O"
super coach and author, *Combat Golf*

"A wonderful collection of stories that celebrate golf's beauty and virtues. . . . There is no doubt the game is a great teacher!"

Steve Cohen
president, The Shivas Irons Society

CHICKEN SOUP FOR THE GOLFER'S SOUL

101 Stories of Insight, Inspiration and Laughter on the Links

Jack Canfield
Mark Victor Hansen
Jeff Aubery
Mark Donnelly
Chrissy Donnelly

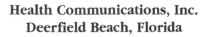

Health Communications, Inc.
Deerfield Beach, Florida

www.hci-online.com
www.chickensoup.com

We would like to acknowledge the following publishers and individuals for permission to reprint the following material. (Note: The stories that were penned anonymously, that are in the public domain, or that were written by Jack Canfield, Mark Victor Hansen, Jeff Aubery, Mark Donnelly or Chrissy Donnelly are not included in this listing.)

The Many Lessons in Golf. Reprinted by permission of Rabbi Marc Gellman. ©1998 Rabbi Marc Gellman.

Only One. Reprinted by permission of J. G. Nursall. ©1998 J. G. Nursall. Originally appeared in *Golf Journal.*

Lost and Found. Reprinted by permission of Greg R. Bernard. ©1998 Greg R. Bernard.

The U.S. Open. Reprinted by permission of Bill Pelham. ©1998 Bill Pelham.

In the Pink. Reprinted by permission of Ernie Witham. ©1998 Ernie Witham.

The Golf Maniac. Reprinted by permission of Nancy N. Winthrop (copyright holder for Stephen Leacock). ©1998 Nancy N. Winthrop.

A Day at The Tradition. Reprinted by permission of Christine Clifford. ©1998 Christine Clifford.

(Continued on page 375)

Library of Congress Cataloging-in-Publication Data

Chicken soup for the golfer's soul: 101 stories of insights, inspiration and laughter on the links / [compiled by] Jack Canfield . . . [et al.].
    p. c.m.
    ISBN 1-55874-659-5 (hardcover). — ISBN 1-55874-658-7 (trade paper)
    1. Golfers—Conduct of life. 2. Golf—Moral and ethical aspects. 3. Spiritual life. I. Canfield, Jack. II. Title: 101 stories of insight, inspiration and laughter on the links
GV965.C4735 1999   98-54998
796.352—dc21   CIP

©1999 Jack Canfield, Mark Victor Hansen

ISBN 1-55874-658-7 (trade paper) — ISBN 1-55874-659-5 (hardcover)

Publisher: Health Communications, Inc.
              3201 S.W. 15th Street
              Deerfield Beach, FL 33442-8190

Cover artwork "The Challenge" by Scott Medlock

With love we dedicate *Chicken Soup for the Golfer's Soul* to the millions of golfers around the world. Your passion and spirit for the game help keep golf and all its history alive for generations to come. We also dedicate this book to Patty Aubery, vice president of Chicken Soup for the Soul Enterprises. We are so grateful to have you in our lives and are thankful for all that you have done to help with this project. Your uncanny ability to see only the good in people and your willingness to care inspire us all to be better human beings. We love you!

Contents

Acknowledgments...xv

Introduction..xix

Share with Us..xxi

The Many Lessons of Golf
  Rabbi Marc Gellman, Ph.D., and Monsignor Tom Hartman..................xxiii

1. THE FIRST TEE

Only One   *J. G. Nursall*...2

Lost and Found   *Greg R. Bernard*...8

The U.S. Open   *Bill Pelham*..13

In the Pink   *Ernie Witham*..17

The Golf Maniac   *Stephen Leacock*..21

A Day at The Tradition   *Christine Clifford*..25

I Hate Golf—I Love Golf!   *George Bush* 28

A Candle in the Wind   *Peter Jacobsen with Jack Sheehan*...........................33

Turning Back the Clock   *Betty Cuniberti*...40

2. GOING FOR THE GREEN

Plimpton to the Fore   *George Plimpton* 44

There Is No "I" in Team   *Dave Sheinin*..50

The Magoo Caper   *Harvey Mackay*...53

Beat the Pro   *Susan D. Brandenburg* 57

Golf Balls *Sam Murphy* 59

Walter Won the Honors *Frank J. Haller* 60

A Special Rapport *Paul Daugherty* 63

Life on the Back Nine *Rich Radford* 66

Living the Dream *Gary D'Amato* 71

Requiem for a Milkman *Tom Callahan* 74

Golf and the Caddie at Royal Troon *Jeff Kahler* 78

The Day Mr. 59 Bottled Lightning *Nick Seitz* 81

3. SPECIAL MOMENTS

All the Good Things Any Man Should Be *Nick Price*

  with Mike Stachura 86

Ike, Mamie, Spiro and Me *Clint McCown* 89

The Day I Met the King *Peter Jacobsen with Jack Sheehan* 98

The Price of Success *Terry Todd* 101

My Best Friend *Andrew Galanopulos* 102

Butterscotch *A. J. Daulerio* 105

Last Will and Testament *Lorne Rubenstein* 109

Babe in the Woods *Tom Turley* 112

The Lunar Golf Shot *Alan Shepard as told to Carol Mann* 115

The Special Gift *Adel Guzzo* 118

The Caddie and the Unspoken Understanding

  David Owen 120

Divots *Don Wade* 122

A Golfer's Best Friend *Bud Gardner* 124

Yesterday's News *Brad Brewer* 128

Every Golfer's Dream *Jay Golden* 130

The Brand New Golfer *Stan Reynolds* 135

Playing Through *Sondra Sue Ward Elder* 138

Rub-a-Dub-Dub *Tommy Ehrbar* 139

Slicker Sam *Frank Christian* 142

4. GOLFMANSHIP

Straight Down the Fairway *Dave McIntosh* 146
A Lesson I Will Never Forget *Davis Love III* 150
Payback *Scott Hipp* 152
Playing It Down *Leonard Finkel* 156
We Play 'Em All *William M. Bowen* 158
A True Gentleman *Hugh Baldwin* 160
Play It as It Lies *Sam Snead* 161
The Day I Cheated *John Meyers* 163
The Clutch Putt *Ken Robertson* 166
The Difference Between the Scots and the Americans
    Don Wade 170
The Gentle Hustler *Bob Brust* 171
The Compassionate Golfer *Carla Muir* 175
Victory for the Golf Rats *Rabbi Marc Gellman, Ph.D.* 177
A Practice Round for Life *Debra Moss* 179

5. GOLF LINKS A FAMILY TOGETHER

The Collection Basket *Jan K. Collins* 184
Remember When *Bud Gardner* 186
Being There *Don Didio* 191
Way Above Par *Harrison Kelly* 194
Divorce, of Course *Gordon W. Youngs* 198
The Ace Man *Mitch Laurance* 201
Early Retirement *Todd Behrendt* 204
Mom Hits the Links *Adam Bruns* 207
Silent Swing *Betty Cuniberti* 210
One at a Time *Larry R. Pearson* 213
The Substitute Caddie *Melissa Lehman* 217
Angel's Flight *J. G. Nursall* 220
The Law of Maximum Irritation *David Owen* 227
Father and Son *Alf McCreary* 230

Return to Inwood *Bradley S. Klein* 235
A Measure of Love *Judy Walker*..240
Dad's Magic Clubs *John Keating*..244
Her Mother's Presence *Tracy Hanson*..250
A Sudden End to a Love Story *Dave Kindred*............................253

6. OUT OF THE ROUGH

Just One More Time *Giles Tippette*...260
The Drive of a Champion *Jack Cavanaugh*................................266
On His Own Two Feet *Ken Bowden* 273
Close to Home *Bob Phillips* 277
A New Perspective *Melissa Russell*...280
Taking a Swing at Stress *Steve Densley* 283
An Embrace in the Bittersweet Middle *Jimmy Roberts*.............286
Lightning Strikes Twice *Bruce Nash and Allan Zullo*
    with George White...289
A Wing Grew Back *Jay Gearan* 291
The Healer *Michael Konik*..295
Happy *David Field*..300
The Benefits of Being King *Rich Mintzer and Peter Grossman* 303
A Humble Beginning *Patty Berg*..304

7. THE NINETEENTH HOLE

Putter Devotion *Karsten Solheim as told to Gina Bridgeman*..................306
Maybe I Need a Crystal Ball *Ernie Witham* 312
Riders *Arthur Berk* 315
The Man Whose Secret Was a Secret *Jerry Tarde* 316
Brush, Brush *Steve Minnick* 319
Zen and the Art of Getting Over the Water Hazard
    Micki McClelland..322
More Help Than a Guy Needs *Walter Bingham*.........................326
The Clown Prince of Golf *John Feinstein* 330

Golf Carts Do Not Have Four-Wheel Drive *Ernie Witham* 332
Fifty Ways to Enjoy Golf More *Mark and Chrissy Donnelly* 335
De Profundis, Homo (About Some Deep Stuff, Man)
   Frank J. Haller 338
He'd Give You the Shirt Off of His Back *Don Wade* 341
The Secret *J. G. Nursall* 342
Enjoy the Round *James Dodson* 347

More Chicken Soup? 355
Supporting Golfers Everywhere 356
Who Is Jack Canfield? 358
Who Is Mark Victor Hansen? 359
Who Is Jeff Aubery? 360
Who Are Mark and Chrissy Donnelly? 361
Who Is Golf Digest? 362
Contributors 363
Permissions *(continued)* 375

Acknowledgments

Chicken Soup for the Golfer's Soul has been a refreshing new direction for us. As with all new journeys, we received unexpected help from many caring people along the way. We were given expert guidance by people who know more about the game than we ever will. But most of all, we were given the love and support that is so important in a project of this magnitude. We would like to thank the following people, without whom we could not have completed this book.

Patty Aubery, thanks for your tireless support and understanding. You have played the role of our most valuable caddie, guiding us around the hazards and keeping our aim true.

Bob and Jan Donnelly, your unflagging love and support have been more important than you know. The ripple effect you started goes on and on.

Nat C. Rosasco and the people at Northwestern ProSelect Golf Co., for your belief and support of the book from day one.

Jeanne Neale, thanks for always being there! Your well-placed calls and caring words of encouragement got us through some of the most difficult times.

Patty Hansen, you are a guiding light of friendship, love

and encouragement. Thanks for being such a great Chicken Soup role model. Thanks to Elisabeth and Melanie for your friendship and hospitality.

Georgia Noble, thanks for opening your home to us and giving us your support. We love you. Thanks, Christopher, for inspiring us with your free-spirited and carefree approach to life.

Bob Carney at *Golf Digest,* your wisdom and friendship have helped to keep us in bounds and in play. Thanks for believing and seeing the potential. You embody what this book is about.

Liz Comte Reisman at *Golf Digest Woman,* our chance pairing on the course led to some wonderful and unexpected results. Thanks for your help and persistence.

Jerry Tarde and the outstanding *Golf Digest* team, thanks for your commitment and enthusiasm.

Melanie Hauser and the Golf Writer's Association of America; your members' contributions added some great stories and even better writing to the project.

Scott Medlock, Wally Buchleitner and your teams, thanks for the creativity and the stellar cover art. It's a pleasure working with you.

Jim Ritts, thanks for your belief in the project from day one.

Leslie King and the communications staff at the LPGA, thanks for your support and efficiency.

Lorne Rubenstein, that fated meeting at the bookstore and your subsequent support have been a real gift. Thank you.

Len Stachitis at the First Tee, your belief and help were invaluable additions to the book. Kurt Knop at CaP CURE, thanks for the eleventh-hour creativity. Steve Cohen at the Shivas Irons Society, thanks for the last-minute assistance.

Heather McNamara, through your eye for detail and

your incredible knowledge of the process from tee to green, you have been a real team player.

Nancy Mitchell Autio, thanks for all of your help in the permission process. Your ongoing support is much appreciated.

Leslie Forbes, Ro Miller, Veronica Romero, Teresa Esparza and Robin Yerian at Self-Esteem Seminars, thanks for providing the support and possibility to focus on a project like this. You may be behind the scenes, but you're definitely appreciated.

Laurie Hartman at MVH & Associates, thanks for minding all of the very important details that help us focus on the big picture.

Peter Vegso, we thank and honor you for your heartfelt desire to make a positive difference in the world. Because of you it's a better place.

Terry Burke, your team's contributions and your personal excitement for *Golfer's Soul* made this a particularly fun project to work on. Thanks for everything.

Allison Janse, your attention to detail and expert guidance through the galley process is appreciated more than you know. It's comforting to know you're on the other end of the line with us.

Bob Land, thanks for the expert editing job. Your insights and improvements helped make this a better book.

Larissa Hise and Lisa Camp, our book looks better because of you!

Kim Weiss and Larry Getlen, thanks for all of the excitement you generate. Your belief and commitment shine through in all of your communications.

The entire Health Communications team, your professionalism, dedication and teamwork are an inspiration and much appreciated.

A very special thank you goes out to the many people who took hours reading and grading our top stories. Your guidance and feedback were invaluable: Diane Aubery, Bob Carney, Christine Clifford, Bob Donnelly, Bud Gardner, Rose Greenman, Amy Fanelli, Brad Halfon, Tom Hazard, Paul Holcomb, Leslie King, Barbara Lamonico, Linda Mitchell, Todd Mielke, Jeanne Neale, Bob Polivka and Liz Comte Reisman.

We also want to thank everyone who submitted the thousands of stories, letters, poems and quotes that we reviewed for possible inclusion in the book. While we weren't able to use them all, we were touched by each and every one. Your stories provided us with constant encouragement and reinforcement that we were on the right track, and gave us additional guidance as to how best to touch the golfer's soul.

Because of the scope and duration of this project, we may have neglected to acknowledge people who have helped us along the way. If so, please accept our apologies, and know that you are appreciated.

Finally, we want to pass on our love and gratitude to everyone who has had a hand in helping us bring this project to completion. We couldn't have done it without you!

Introduction

Golf is life in a fishbowl. Anyone who has ever stepped up to a crowded first tee knows this to be true. Golf's ability to teach us many of life's most important lessons through entertaining true stories is what inspired us to collaborate on *Chicken Soup for the Golfer's Soul*. Golf has the ability to make us more of who we are, or provide us with a place to experiment with changes.

We compiled *Chicken Soup for the Golfer's Soul* hoping to capture the mystery and wonder of this game through stories that will inspire you, provide you with insights into the game of life and leave you with a whole new level of appreciation for the game of golf. This book is for anyone who has ever enjoyed the game, from a scratch golfer to a weekend player, from a tour pro to a fan watching a tournament on television.

Each story in this book was written by someone who was transformed by an experience with golf. Perhaps some of these stories will leave you with a new perspective on how to deal with adversity on the course, or inspire you with others' triumphs over staggering physical and emotional obstacles. Perhaps other stories will give you a new appreciation for the level of integrity that the game requires or help you deal in a more productive manner with those who bend the rules. Perhaps other stories will remind and reassure you that, although golf challenges each of us at different times, we are never alone in our pure enjoyment of the game.

With insight and eloquence, the stories in this book show why golf is such a wonderful metaphor for life. For instance, sometimes life reveals itself in the serenity of a beautiful sunrise shining on an untrodden, dew-covered green, creating a feeling of oneness with nature that transcends the entire round. Sometimes it's the feeling of sheer adrenaline that comes from hitting that perfect shot—the moment when it becomes clear that all things are possible. Sometimes it's the pure frustration that drives us to the brink of giving up altogether, only to be renewed by the hope of a successful comeback the next time out on the course. At other times, golf forges a connection to friends or family, and still other times golf takes us on a journey inside ourselves.

As these stories demonstrate, golf can be the most powerful of teachers. It teaches us to be accepting, forgiving and humble. It teaches us when to press hard and when to relax and enjoy the moment. It gives us the opportunity to explore and develop virtues such as sportsmanship, honesty, courage and persistence. When we are open to it, golf can teach us many lessons that we need to learn. In this way, golf shapes our character long after we have left the course.

We offer this book as our gift to you. Some stories will make you laugh. Some will move you beyond words. We hope that all of them will open your heart, inspire you to new levels in your golf game and in life, and become a treasured companion on your journey. And may you get out of golf all that you put in to it.

Share with Us

We would love to hear your reactions to the stories in this book. Please let us know what your favorite stories were and how they affected you.

We also invite you to send us stories you would like to see published in future editions of *Chicken Soup for the Soul.* You can send us either stories you have written or stories written by others that you have liked.

Send submissions to:

Chicken Soup for the Golfer's Soul
P.O. Box 30880-G
Santa Barbara, CA 93130
fax: 805-563-2945
e-mail: *stories@canfieldgroup.com*

We hope you enjoy reading this book as much as we enjoyed compiling, editing and writing it.

You can also visit the *Chicken Soup for the Soul* site on America Online at keyword: chickensoup.

The Many Lessons of Golf

Golf teaches that we all have handicaps . . . and that hardly anybody knows what they really are.

Golf teaches that the best courses are the ones that hardly change at all what God put there to begin with.

Golf teaches that although there are a few people who are honest in golf but cheat in life, everybody who cheats in golf cheats in life.

Golf teaches that even though we need strict rules, we also need a leaf rule.

Golf teaches that even people who wear green pants deserve some place where they can go, get a little exercise and not be laughed at.

Golf teaches that even though you probably don't have a shot at being the best, you do have a good shot at being the best you can be.

Golf teaches that both success and failure are temporary.

Golf also teaches that success is a lot more temporary.

Golf teaches that although practice does not always make us perfect, no practice always makes us imperfect.

Golf teaches that no matter how good you are, there is always someone better and that person will usually find you and tell you.

xxiv   THE MANY LESSONS OF GOLF

Golf teaches that when you are good you can tell people, but when you are great they will tell you.

Golf teaches that although patience is a virtue, slow play is not.

Golf teaches that even though the best golfers have the most chances to win, the other golfers have the most chances to improve.

Golf teaches that, on some dewy morning or some golden afternoon, with the sun warming the world, we can find ourselves walking through an improvised meadow and realize we are not searching for the little white ball, but for a moment where the world of nature and the world of play are one. And then in the dew and sunshine we can understand that even though we can make a ball perfectly white, only God can make a meadow perfectly green.

Rabbi Marc Gellman, Ph.D., and
Monsignor Tom Hartman

1

THE
FIRST TEE

Golf, after all, is probably the universal sport.

George Low

Only One

Norma Halstead was a slender fifteen-year-old in the summer of 1941. Her father, Grant, was the professional at the new Fresno Municipal Course located on the banks of the San Joaquin River. She and her parents lived on the second floor of the clubhouse, high on a hilltop overlooking the river and the first fairway. It was a simple time and Norma's life was filled with many things, but especially her love of golf.

Summer days in Fresno can be unmercifully hot. Norma would frequently rise before the sun, complete her chores, and then tote her canvas bag off to the first tee for a solitary nine. In the early morning a fine mist often rose off the river. The first hole, which plunged down the hillside from the clubhouse, appeared milky white. Norma was relatively new to the game, but her father's instruction was evident when she cracked a drive off the first tee and watched as it carried out and down into the mist over the fairway below. Norma loved the game and her life at the river's edge.

On one particular July morning Norma set out for her round with no more than the mere expectation of a good walk in the country. As she teed up one of the three Dunlop balls given to her by her father, she remembered his admonition, "a good golfer never loses a ball." Her father's word on matters of golf was gospel, and Norma dreaded the thought of ever asking him for more golf balls. But this morning her drive bore true through the mist and landed well down the first fairway.

Billy Bell designed the course. Grant Halstead convinced the city fathers that Bell was the man to draw up their first public course, and Bell's execution was flawless. It soon became known as the "big Muni" and was the site of many exciting city championships. The real challenge for Bell was in designing the first three holes in the limited space available. The first hole, a long par-4, stretched down the hill from the clubhouse and out along the riverbank. The second was a short, well-bunkered par-3 running up a hillside to a bowl-shaped green. The third hole paralleled the first, with its green chiseled into the steep embankment looming over the river. The design of these three holes, now obvious for its simplistic elegance, was considered impossible. But Bell's talent for the simple yet elegant solution was evident throughout the course.

As Norma approached her ball in the first fairway she could hear the distant whistle of an early morning freight train. The tracks ran the eastern length of the course and at the river's edge crossed a great trestle. Soon the train would be rumbling by the second hole, clattering north to Modesto, Stockton and Sacramento. It took Norma three strong shots to reach the first green, and she holed out with two putts for a personal par.

On the second tee she selected a long iron. Her father's simple wisdom told her never to fear any club. Swing them all the same. But most of all, he would say, "Trust your swing." As she took a practice swing, she thought only of mimicking her father's graceful style. He often said to her, "Imagine someone is taking your picture. Try to look pretty." It was easy for the young girl.

The train was just rumbling past the wooden fence posts lining the edge of the course. Norma's concentration was complete as she rocked into the ball. To her delight it soared swiftly on a line for the round green. Norma hoped for par on the short holes and tried extra hard to reach the putting surface. She was a good putter and could often get down in two. This looked like a good shot, landing at the front of the green, right on line with the flag. She picked up her bag and began climbing up the hill to the green.

On hot days players would often dawdle at the back of the second hole, where two big pine trees spread their limbs and offered momentary shade. The bowl-shaped green easily collected shots, but because it was a small green any tee shot more than ten degrees off line would ricochet off the hillside. Accuracy was rewarded. Norma knew the secret to this hole was to take plenty of club—and trust your swing.

As Norma reached the top of the hill she was unable to see her ball. The train, now well down the track and over the trestle, sounded three short hoots of its great whistle. Norma looked to the back of the green, expecting to see her ball nestled against the collar. It wasn't there. She laid down her bag and began looking closely at the ribbon of rough at the back of the green. Slightly exasperated, the realization began to sink in that she may have lost her first golf ball. She imagined her father's brow creased with wrinkles of incredulity, mouth gaping, dumbstruck by his only child's shameful loss.

It must be here somewhere, Norma thought. She began to walk to the front of the green on the chance the ball had not bounced forward as she had first thought. Then, as she walked past the hole, she looked down and there it was. A hole-in-one!

Though she was only a novice, she knew that a hole-in-one was a terrific golfing feat. She knew her father would be delighted. His broad smile and gleaming eyes filled her thoughts as she reached into the cup and extracted her ball. She wished her father had seen it. She wished her mother had seen it. She wished anyone had seen it.

She finished her round of nine and walked to the steps of the clubhouse, now washed with the warming rays of the morning sun. She looked up to the porch and saw the face of her mother. Not wanting to sound too excited, she said coyly, "Oh, Mom, I hit a really good shot today." Her mother, having been saturated with stories of golf from the time of her first meeting Grant, was prepared to patiently attend to yet another exploit on the field of glory.

Suitably braced to receive the laurels of her triumph, Norma announced, "Yes, on the second I hit a shot right into the hole."

Her mother scanned the horizon, looking out across the course as if she were taking inventory of the young trees sprouting along the fairways. Her mind was on the baking of pies, cakes and chili for the day's customers. While Grant ran the golf shop and taught lessons on the range, Norma's mother ran the coffee shop. Everything was fresh.

She turned and looked at Norma's shoulder-length brown curls, and noticed beads of sweat at her temples. Finally she said, "That's very good, dear. Be sure to tell your father. Now come inside and get out of the sun."

Norma was somewhat disappointed with her mother's reaction. Certainly there was meant to be something more to this. She must have announced it wrong. Trailing after her mother as they walked into the coffee shop, Norma said, "No, Mother, I mean I hit the ball into the hole with only one shot. A hole-in-one!"

Norma's mother put her arms across her young daughter's shoulders and guided her through the coffee shop, and then gently sent her off in the general direction of the golf shop. "Yes, dear, that's very good," she repeated. "Be sure you tell your father."

Norma's frustration only grew when she announced her triumph to her father. They stood alone in the golf shop. The slight fifteen-year-old was dwarfed by the muscled pro. Grant's most impressive features were his massive hands and bald head. His steady gaze could be stern, but most often his eyes sparkled with the spirit of Christmas.

In a solemn tone Grant said to his child, "That's very good, Norma, but you have to understand something. It's not really sporting to say you've scored an ace while playing alone. You see, without a witness ... well ... we'd have jokers coming off the course every day claiming to have done one thing or another." Grant then wrapped his arms around his daughter, gave her a gentle hug, and said, "Just remember—trust your swing and you'll do fine."

In days to come, parents would ponder the psychological injury such a disappointing reception might inflict upon the young willow. But 1941 was a more realistic time, and in some ways parents were not so concerned with sheltering their children from the harshness of the world. They were more intent on preparing them to live in a world of both evil and good.

Norma thought little more of her triumph. She had learned that in addition to the Rules of Golf taught to her by her father, there were other rules. Rules that were only learned by experience.

Two weeks later a postcard, addressed only to "Head Pro," arrived at the clubhouse. Grant received the card and his thunderous laughter could be heard throughout the clubhouse. The card read simply, "Congratulations to that young lady who aced the second hole. What a beautiful shot." The card was signed, "J. C. Wade, Engineer, Southern Pacific Railroad."

When Norma heard the ruckus in the shop below, she came down the staircase from her bedroom and was greeted by her father and four members of the men's club. Her father's booming voice proclaimed his daughter's victory as Norma read and reread the postcard in disbelief. She smiled broadly, and with due modesty finally accepted the conqueror's wreath.

She was about to go back up to her room when her father spoke. "Now dear, fetch your piggy bank. You owe us all a drink."

Norma sensed she was about to learn one more of golf's unwritten rules.

J. G. Nursall

Lost and Found

They say golf is like life, but don't believe them. Golf is more complicated than that.

Gardner Dickinson

From the satchel on my office desk, forty ungraded compositions whispered at me in grammatically incorrect urgency. But after two days of torrential rainfall, a radiant sun enveloped the local greens in a golden Sunday embrace. After a quick shower, I was off for a lone round before trading in my pitching wedge for the proverbial red pen.

The attendant at the clubhouse greeted me with an only slightly disgruntled countenance; rising early to watch others play golf is apparently not without its limitations. The sign-in sheet indicated only one other gentleman had begun his round. Good. The golf would be quick, private and unhurried.

After sticking my wedding ring in my front pocket for safekeeping (it causes blisters if I leave it on), I astounded myself with my first drive, a sweet whistle down the center of the fairway. I lovingly replaced the head cover on my driver.

By the sixth hole, it was becoming increasingly apparent, even given my poor math skills, that I was having the
round of my life. Not that Tiger Woods has to worry just
yet; after five holes I was one under, thanks in part to holing a slippery twenty-footer.

Addressing my ball, I peered down the sixth fairway, a
beautifully designed par-5 that loped around a kidney-
shaped pond fronted with flowering water plants and
cattails. Poking around with his ball retriever was Mr.
Early. This is what I dubbed him, unable to recall his
name from the logbook I had hastily scribbled my signa-
ture into less than an hour ago. Hair whiter than a freshly
opened pair of tube socks, with a posture that suggested
firsthand recollections of the birth of the game, he did not
notice my growing impatience on the tee box. Finally,
rationalizing that I was playing too well this morning to
actually hit him (and feeling the ever-increasing weight
of those essays bearing down on the remaining hours of
my shortened weekend), I teed off with a shank that
would make Sir Murphy and his Book of Laws proud.

Old fart, I grumbled to myself, thrusting the ill-fitting
head cover over my driver. Eager to make the turn alone,
I promised myself not to engage this feeble duffer in conversation. Trouble is, in my disgust over the missed hit, I
had failed to track my ball with any degree of precision.
All I knew is that it had sculled somewhere near where
Mr. Early was still searching.

"Quite the morning, isn't it?" he asked as I approached.

"Yeah," I said, avoiding direct eye contact. Old folks are
like animals, I reasoned, they can see the weakness in
your eyes.

"We seem to have lost ourselves in here somewhere," he
said, waving his ball remover over the tangled grass in
which we waded.

Just as it seemed I was destined to spend my Sunday

morning chaperoning a member of the geriatric unit around the links, I spied a dimpled sphere buried deep in the rough.

"Here I am," I said, reaching for the first thing in my bag. A rotten stick would have done.

"Are you sure?" he asked. "I was hitting a Titleist."

"Me too," I said, rolling my eyes in exasperation. Or was it a Top-Flite? Who cares, I finally decided. The ball was mine.

And I was gone.

But the image of the old man staring at me as I made my way around the lake kept me from concentrating. My game suffered. I grew angrier and angrier.

Following another chunked drive, I slammed my driver into the bag, resolved never to grip its evilness again.

My iron game left me as well, literally. On the thirteenth hole, I went to my bag to retrieve my 7-iron, only to find it was not there. I groaned, realizing what I would be forced to endure. Mr. Early was still behind me, and most likely in possession of my club.

Unfortunately, he was gone. Apparently, nine was enough for him this fine Sunday morning. Probably off to church, I steamed, heading for the clubhouse, my round destroyed.

The clubhouse was still empty as I entered, the overhead fan doing little to cool me off. The attendant gazed at me with that same sleepy boredom with which he had greeted me earlier.

"Did anyone else come in here?" I asked.

"Older guy? Head of white hair?" he asked, yawning.

"Yeah," I said. "Did he leave anything behind?"

"Yup. Said you'd be looking for it. He set everything over on the bar."

"Everything?" I asked.

"Look, it's on the bar. That's all I know," he said.

I walked over to the mahogany counter, the clicking of the cleats ringing in my ears. There on the bar was the cover to my driver, my 7-iron and a golf ball. Reaching for the ball, I felt my face flush red. Top-Flite. It even had my personalized markings, three dots with a permanent red pen. Then I noticed a drink napkin amidst my returned equipment. Set in the middle, shining as bright as the day on which my wife had slipped it on my finger, was my wedding ring. It had fallen out of my pocket somewhere on the golf course. A miracle itself that he had found it. Even more astonishing that he had somehow known it was mine and to return it, with everything else. My throat tightened as I raced for the parking lot.

Mr. Early was just pulling out as I skidded to a halt in front of his car. I slowly made my way to the driver's-side window, which he was already rolling down.

"My stuff," I said. "You returned my stuff. Even after . . . the ball . . . your ball . . . I stole your ball."

"Let me see it," he said, gazing up at me.

I almost ripped my pants digging for that ball I still had in my front pocket. With shaking fingers, I slipped it into his palm.

He peered at the ball, turned it in his gnarled hands and sucked on his teeth. After a long moment, he reached the ball back out the window and said, "Nope. This isn't mine. I was hitting a Titleist 3. This here is a Titleist 1. You keep it, son. You found it."

In a daze, I retrieved the ball from his hand. "But my stuff, you found all the stuff I lost," I stammered.

"Not everything," he replied with a slight smile. "Not everything."

"What do you mean?" I asked.

He put his car in gear and eased it forward. As he rolled up his window, he said, "You lost the one thing even I can't get back for you, son. Go read the napkin on the bar."

And then he was gone.

Back in the clubhouse, I made my way to the bar. Turning the napkin over, I read in Mr. Early's scrawled handwriting the following words:

YOUR TEMPER

Greg R. Bernard

The U.S. Open

*How would you like to meet the top 143 people
at what you do each week in order to survive?*

Bruce Crampton

When I was seven, my dad introduced me to golf by
taking me to Houston's Memorial Park Golf Course to
watch the gentle giant who strolled the fairways of professional golf. It was there that I first laid eyes on Arnold
Palmer and his swashbuckling style of playing golf. I was
mesmerized by his charisma. I told my father that I
wanted to be just like him! My dad saw that I had every
chance to succeed, and twenty years later I was blessed
with the fulfillment of that dream.

But as good as I was, I wasn't nearly good enough to be
an unqualified success. I struggled and persevered, but
fell short time and time again. More than anything, I
wanted to play in a major championship and experience
what that was like. It took me eleven attempts, and ten
straight years of disappointment, before I finally qualified
for my first U.S. Open Championship in 1979.

Qualifying was a rigorous test of thirty-six holes in one

day, usually played in one-hundred-degree heat, with
only a couple of players from a very strong field advanc-
ing to the championship. For every golfer who ever
dreamed of playing golf against the greats of the game,
competing in a U.S. Open was always the pinnacle.

After so many failures, simply qualifying to play one
Open was almost more than I could anticipate. Expectations ran high and hope eternal. I couldn't wait to get on
the plane, fly to Toledo and drive to the course. When we
finally drove through the gates of Inverness Country
Club, the relief and the emotions of the moment brought
my family and I to tears.

I played well in practice, but once the Championship
began, my game deserted me when I felt pressure the
most. I started poorly and finished even worse to miss the
36-hole cut by only two shots. My wife and parents both
walked every step of the way, in some ways living my
dream vicariously. It was a huge disappointment to come
up short, because we knew that I might never have
another chance to play in a U.S. Open.

On Sunday, while waiting in Chicago's O'Hare Airport
for our connecting flight home, we saw the opening
moments of ABC-TV's national broadcast. Jim McKay's
opening oratory was so stirring that I saw my father
moved to tears. He turned to me, almost embarrassed by
his emotions, and said, "Next time, make the cut for me for
Father's Day." The moment was particularly poignant
because it was Father's Day and the U.S. Open histori-
cally ended on Father's Day every year. "I promise I will
next time, Dad," I assured him, holding my breath and
hoping against hope that I would have one more chance.
Deep in my heart, I knew it was a long shot.

Despite my retirement from full-time competition the
next year, my prayers were answered in 1981. I qualified
to play at Merion Golf Club in Ardmore, Pennsylvania, for

my second (and last) U.S. Open. Once again, my family joined me to share in this special experience, and I brought along my best friend, Sam Irwin, to caddie for me. My expectations were low, and more than anything I was just hoping to play well and have a great time.

McKay described Merion as a lovely old dowager. It was a traditional course, built in the early 1900s, relatively short by today's Tour standards, but laced with thick rough, deep bunkers and lightning-fast greens. She was a mighty test despite her length. But most intriguing to me was the history of the great course. It had hosted other championships, including the U.S. Amateur Championship where Bobby Jones had defeated Bobby Cruickshank to win the final leg of the Grand Slam.

This time I started well, shooting a solid round of 73, despite a triple bogey at the fifth hole and bogies on 17 and 18. My score had placed me in a position to make the cut, yet none of us dared speak about it for fear that it would play too much into my psyche the next day. I had not competed in almost nine months, and my nerves and confidence were just too fragile. Besides, I was having fun for the first time in years, just playing for the pure enjoyment and not to put food on the table!

The second round started well, too. I played the front nine in even par before bogeying 11 and 12. As I came to Merion's brutal finishing holes, I knew that I would be tested like never before. I was hovering near the cut line, and one bad shot could end any hopes of playing the weekend. I managed to par 14 and 15 without difficulty. A good drive and a 6-iron to the green at 16 left me with a monstrous forty-foot putt with more than five feet of break. All I wanted to do was get close enough to two-putt and go to the next hole. To my surprise, my putt wandered and curled its way across the green and into the cup for a birdie! Even a bogey at the difficult seventeenth "Quarry

Hole" left me thinking a bogey at the last would afford me the 36-hole cut I wanted so badly.

I played the eighteenth hole—a long 470-yard, dogleg-left par-4—more conservatively than usual. I used a 3-wood off the tee to clear the quarry wall and to better shape the tee shot so that I could easily make the fairway. However, I was left with a very long iron shot to the green, which I left considerably short. My pitch came to rest fifteen excruciating feet from the hole. I only had to get down in two putts now, but the speed of the greens was so fast that I had to be careful—very careful. When I struck the putt, I knew instinctively that it was struck too hard. My heart leapt to my throat as I looked up to see where the ball would finish. To my relief and almost disbelief, it hit the back of the cup and dropped in the hole for a par-4!

I almost danced to the scorers' tent to sign my card. I knew that my score was good enough to make the 36-hole cut, but I didn't think my father knew. He knew that I had played well and that it would be close, but he didn't dare raise his hopes. I had missed too many cuts in the past by one or two shots; it was difficult for anyone in my family to expect good fortune.

After I finished signing my card and shaking my fellow competitors' hands, I walked outside the tent to see my dad standing only a few yards away. As I walked toward him, I could tell he was obviously pleased that I had played well. He said, "Way to go, Punkins," my nickname since childhood. I could hardly contain myself as I hugged my dad tighter than I ever had. All the years of support and encouragement had finally reaped its just reward. "Happy Father's Day, Dad," I said proudly, two days early. I didn't need to say anything more. At that very moment he realized that "we" had made the cut in the U.S. Open.

Bill Pelham

In the Pink

Laughter is the best communion of all.

Robert Fulghum

I had several choices on Saturday. Clean the garage, wash the car or go to the golf store and waste hours looking at a bunch of stuff I couldn't afford.

It was crowded at the golf store. I like it when it's that way. The salespeople are too busy to pester you, and you can play with the putters all day long. I have won many imaginary tournaments on that little carpeted green.

I was heading to the front of the store to forage in the "experienced" golf ball jar when I saw three familiar kids—mine—coming in the front door. At first I assumed my wife sent them on a search party and that I'd have to clean the garage after all. Then I saw the sign over the checkout stand, "Ask About Our Father's Day Specials." They were here to buy me a gift! Not another Three Stooges tie. Not another Handy Mitt, the greatest car-washing aid since water, but a golf gift. Cool.

I ducked down behind the shoe mirror as they headed toward the golf ball section. Would they buy the Tour

Edition Titleists? Probably not without help. I dashed down the club display aisle and slipped behind the mountain of shimmering red and gold boxes.

"What about these yellow balls?" I heard my youngest child ask.

"Or these orange ones?" my daughter added.

I poked until a box of Titleists fell on the floor a few feet from them.

"Whoa, dude. This whole thing could fall," said my older son.

"Yeah. Let's look somewhere else."

Darn. I followed in a crouched position as they walked slowly by the golf bags and over to the glove display. Perfect. One of those double-thick, imported gloves with the removable ball marker. They walked right by. Okay. Maybe they'll pick out one of those electronic distance calculators or a six-pack holder. They ambled on.

Finally, they entered the clothing section and headed for a rack full of Ralph Lauren Polo shirts. Yes! I could already picture myself standing in the fairway, contemplating my approach shot, while the others in my group commented on my impeccable taste.

"Hey. Look over here." The enthusiasm in my daughter's voice meant they had found the perfect gift. I felt bad that they were going to spend all that money, but who was I to question their immeasurable affection?

"Cool. And they're cheap, too."

Cheap? I peeked through some women's sweaters. My daughter was holding up a pair of pink polyester pants that had been on the clearance rack since day one.

"And we could get this to go with it." My older son held up a lime-green mesh shirt.

I gasped audibly. They looked in my direction, so I slipped further back into women's wear, bumping into the store manager.

"Just browsing," I whispered.

He looked at me strangely and I realized I was holding a pair of extra large women's shorts and an athletic bra. Behind me I heard, "Look. The final touch."

I got down on all fours and stuck my head out. My youngest son was holding up a hat that said "Tee-riffic Golfer" in type large enough to see four blocks away.

"But it's red," my younger son said. "Does that matter?"

"Naw," said my daughter. "Golfers always dress weird."

I watched them walk toward the front, then I turned and looked at the manager. "I don't suppose . . . ?"

"Nope. All sales final. Besides, you'd break their hearts."

I slept in on Sunday. At about nine they marched into the room, placed a package on my chest and said, "Happy Father's Day."

I tore the wrapping slowly, hoping I could muster up enough excitement when I held up that hat. But the package contained only a note.

"Look beside you," it said.

I turned slowly and there on the pillow was one of my favorite putters from the golf store.

"I don't understand," I said.

"Dude," said my older son. "We, like, knew you were there. Your car was parked out front."

"Are you disappointed?" my daughter asked.

"No! This is perfect." I stroked my new putter lovingly. "So," I laughed. "Guess they let you take those dreadful pink pants back, huh?"

Just then my wife entered the bedroom carrying a carefully wrapped package.

"Ahhh. Not exactly . . ."

Ernie Witham

"When your husband left for the golf course
wearing orange-and-green knickers, a purple shirt,
yellow sweater, blue shoes and a magenta cap,
did you notice anything unusual?"

Reprinted by permission of David W. Harbaugh. Originally appeared in Golf Digest.

The Golf Maniac

We rode in and out pretty often together, he and I, on a suburban train.

That's how I came to talk to him. "Fine morning," I said as I sat down beside him and opened a newspaper.

"Great!" he answered. "The grass is drying out fast now and the greens will soon be all right to play."

"Yes," I said, "the sun is getting higher and the days are decidedly lengthening."

"For the matter of that," said my friend, "a man could begin to play at six in the morning easily. In fact, I've often wondered why there's so little golf played before breakfast. We happened to be talking about golf, a few of us last night—I don't know how it came up—and we were saying that it seems a pity that some of the best part of the day, say from five o'clock to seven-thirty, is never used."

"That's true," I answered. Then, to shift the subject, I said, looking out the window, "It's a pretty bit of country just here, isn't it?"

"It is," he replied, "but seems a shame they make no use of it—just a few market gardens and things like that. Why, I noticed along here acres and acres of just glass—some kind of houses for plants or something—and whole fields full of lettuce and things like that. It's a pity they don't make something of it. I was remarking only the other day in the train to a friend of mine that you could easily lay out an 18-hole course here."

"Could you?" I said.

"Oh, yes. This ground you know, is an excellent light soil to shovel up into bunkers. You could drive some big ditches through it and make one or two deep holes. In fact, improve it to any extent."

I glanced at my morning paper. "Look at this," I said, pointing to a headline, "'United States Navy Ordered Again to Nicaragua.' Looks like more trouble, doesn't it?"

"Did you see in the paper a while back," said my companion, "that the United States Navy is now making golf compulsory at the training school in Annapolis? That's progressive, isn't it? I suppose it will have to mean shorter cruises at sea; in fact, probably lessen the use of the navy for sea purposes. But it will raise the standard."

"I suppose so," I answered. "Did you read this article about the extraordinary murder case on Long Island?"

"No," he said. "I never read murder cases. They don't interest me. In fact, I think this whole continent is really getting over-preoccupied with them—"

"Yes, but this one had such odd features—"

"Oh, they all have," he replied, with an air of weariness. "Each one is just boomed by the papers to make a sensation—"

"I know, but in this case it seems that the man was killed with a blow from a golf club."

"What's that? Eh, what's that? Killed him with a blow from a golf club!"

"Yes, some kind of club—"

"I wonder if it was an iron—let me see the paper— though, for that matter, I imagine a blow with even a wooden driver. Where does it say it? It only just says 'a blow with a golf club.' It's a pity the papers don't write these things up with more detail, isn't it?"

"Have you played golf much?" I inquired. I saw it was no use to talk of anything else.

"No," answered my companion, "I am sorry to say I haven't. You see, I began late. I've only played twenty years, twenty-one if you count the year that's beginning in May. I don't know what I was doing. I wasted half my life. In fact, it wasn't until I was well over thirty that I caught on to the game. I suppose a lot of us look back over our lives that way and realize what we have lost.

"And even as it is," he continued, "I don't get much chance to play. At best I can only manage about four afternoons a week, though of course I get most of Saturday and all Sunday. I get my holiday in the summer, but it's only a month, and that's nothing. In winter I manage to take a run south for a game once or twice, perhaps a little swack at it around Easter, but only a week at a time. I'm too busy—that's the plain truth of it." He sighed. "It's hard to leave the office before two. Something always turns up."

And after that he went on to tell me something of the technique of the game, illustrate it with a golf ball on the seat of the car, and the peculiar mental poise needed for driving, and the neat, quick action of the wrist (he showed me how it worked) that is needed to undercut a ball so that it flies straight up in the air. He explained to me how you can do practically anything with a golf ball, provided you keep your mind absolutely poised and your eye in shape, and your body a trained machine.

So, later in the day, meeting someone in my club who was a person of authority on such things, I made an inquiry about my friend. "I rode into town with Llewellyn Smith," I said. "I think he belongs to your golf club. He's a great player, isn't he?"

"A great player!" laughed the expert. "Llewellyn Smith?

Why, he can hardly hit a ball! And anyway, he's only played for about twenty years."

Stephen Leacock

READER/CUSTOMER CARE SURVEY

If you are enjoying this book, please help us serve you better and meet your changing needs by taking a few minutes to complete this survey. Please fold it and drop it in the mail.

As a special **"Thank You"** we'll send you news about new books and a valuable **Gift Certificate!**

PLEASE PRINT   C8M

NAME:_____

ADDRESS: _____

_____

TELEPHONE NUMBER: _____

FAX NUMBER: _____

E-MAIL: _____

WEBSITE: _____

(1) Gender: 1)_____Female 2)_____Male

(2) Age:
1)_____12 or under   5)_____30-39
2)_____13-15   6)_____40-49
3)_____16-19   7)_____50-59
4)_____20-29   8)_____60+

(3) Your Children's Age(s):
Check all that apply.
1)_____6 or Under   3)_____11-14
2)_____7-10   4)_____15-18

(7) Marital Status:
1)_____Married
2)_____Single
3)_____Divorced/Wid.

(8) Was this book
1)_____Purchased for yourself?
2)_____Received as a gift?

(9) How many Chicken Soup books have you bought or read?
1)_____1   3)_____3
2)_____2   4)_____4+

(10) How did you find out about this book?
Please check ONE.
1)_____Personal Recommendation
2)_____Store Display
3)_____TV/Radio Program
4)_____Bestseller List
5)_____Website
6)_____Advertisement/Article or Book Review
7)_____Catalog or mailing
6)_____Other_____

(11) What FIVE subject areas do you enjoy reading about most?
Rank: 1 (favorite) through 5 (least favorite)
A)_____ Self Development
B)_____ New Age/Alternative Healing
C)_____ Storytelling
D)_____Spirituality/Inspiration
E)_____ Family and Relationships
F)_____ Health and Nutrition
G)_____Recovery
H)_____Business/Professional
I) _____ Entertainment
J) _____ Teen Issues
K)_____Pets

(16) Where do you purchase most of your books?
Check the top TWO locations.
A)_____ General Bookstore
B)_____ Religious Bookstore
C)_____ Warehouse/Price Club
D)_____Discount or Other Retail Store
E)_____ Website
F)_____ Book Club/Mail Order

(18) Did you enjoy the stories in this book?
1)_____Almost All
2)_____Few
3)_____Some

(19) What type of magazine do you SUBSCRIBE to?
Check up to FIVE subscription categories.
A)_____ General Inspiration
B)_____ Religious/Devotional
C)_____ Business/Professional
D)_____ World News/Current Events
E)_____ General Entertainment
F)_____ Homemaking, Cooking, Crafts
G)_____ Women's Issues
H)_____ Other (please specify) _____

(24) Please indicate your income level
1)_____Student/Retired-fixed income
2)_____Under $25,000
3)_____$25,000-$50,000
4)_____$50,001-$75,000
5)_____$75,001-$100,000
6)_____Over $100,000

TAPE HERE DO NOT STAPLE

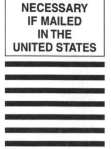

BUSINESS REPLY MAIL
FIRST-CLASS MAIL PERMIT NO 45 DEERFIELD BEACH, FL

POSTAGE WILL BE PAID BY ADDRESSEE

CHICKEN SOUP FOR THE GOLFER'S SOUL
HEALTH COMMUNICATIONS, INC.
3201 SW 15TH STREET
DEERFIELD BEACH FL 33442-9875

‖₁‖₁₁₁‖₁₁‖₁₁₁‖₁₁₁‖₁‖‖₁‖₁₁₁‖₁₁₁‖₁‖₁‖₁₁‖₁‖₁

FOLD HERE

(25) Do you attend seminars?
1)_____Yes   2)_____No

(26) If you answered yes, what type?
Check all that apply.
1)_____Business/Financial
2)_____Motivational
3)_____Religious/Spiritual
4)_____Job-related
5)_____Family/Relationship issues

(31) Are you:
1) A Parent?_____   2) A Grandparent?_____

Do you have your own Chicken Soup story you would like to send us?
Please submit separately to: Chicken Soup for the Soul, P.O. Box 30880, Santa Barbara, CA 93130
Additional comments you would like to make:

_____

_____

_____

_____

B418   C8M

A Day at The Tradition

Blessed is he who has learned how to laugh at himself, for he shall never cease to be entertained.

John Bowell

Several years ago I was diagnosed with cancer. It was the most difficult time I have ever faced. I think it was my sense of humor that allowed me to hold onto my sanity. Like many people who have gone through chemotherapy, I lost all of my hair and I was bald as a cue ball. I always had enjoyed wearing hats, so when my hair deserted me, I ordered several special hats with the hair already attached. It was easy and I never had to worry about how my hair looked.

I have always been a big golf fan. In fact, I have been to twenty-three straight U.S. Opens. At one point during my cancer treatments, my husband John and I decided to get away from the cold Minnesota winter and took a trip to Scottsdale, Arizona. There was a Senior PGA Tour event called The Tradition being played, and that seemed like just the ticket to lift my spirits.

The first day of the tournament brought out a huge gallery. It was a beautiful day, and I was in heaven. I was standing just off the third tee, behind the fairway ropes, watching my three favorite golfers in the world approach the tee box: Jack Nicklaus, Raymond Floyd and Tom Weiskopf.

Just as they arrived at the tee, the unimaginable happened. A huge gust of wind came up from out of nowhere and blew my hat and hair right off my head and into the middle of the fairway! The thousands of spectators lining the fairway fell into an awkward silence, all eyes on me. Even my golf idols were watching me, as my hair was in their flight path. I was mortified! Embarrassed as I was, I knew I couldn't just stand there. Someone had to do something to get things moving again.

So I took a deep breath, went under the ropes and out into the middle of the fairway. I grabbed my hat and hair, nestled them back on my head as best I could. Then I turned to the golfers and loudly announced, "Gentlemen, the wind is blowing from left to right."

They say the laughter could be heard all the way to the nineteenth hole.

Christine Clifford

"Darn! . . . I knew I should have worn a chin strap."

Reprinted from Not Now . . . I'm Having a No Hair Day, *Pfeifer-Hamilton Publishers,* ©1996.

I Hate Golf—I Love Golf!

*I have often been gratefully aware of the heroic
efforts of my opponents not to laugh at me.*

Bernard Darwin

I used to be an 11-handicap golfer. That was before "slope indices," before "soft spikes," before golf carts even.

Today, fully equipped with the latest technology, I am a 22-handicapper going south.

Yes, way back then my woods, crazy though it may seem, had wooden heads. The shafts were of shiny metal. No titanium, no matched graphite, no range of flexes.

The golf balls would smile back when you mis-hit a wedge shot or topped a 6-iron. Slice a 4-iron and you could see the seemingly endless rubber band that wrapped around the ball's rubber core.

I could hit the ball a ton back then. I could get out of sand traps and two-putt greens, too. I have happy memories.

In 1947 I even defeated Chad Brown, a friend at the post office. In the tournament I beat Chad 8 and 7, finishing him off with a fearless, curling fifteen-foot birdie putt. I admit I caught bon vivant Chad on an Excedrin day.

Back then I played in the high 70s.

Today, though I try to play a fair amount, things are different. Chad Brown would kill me. Everyone else does.

I slice off the tee, losing distance in the process. My long irons sting my hands. The ball is seldom airborne. Nor can I chip. Putting? Forget it.

It's not the equipment, for I have the latest in technology. I have four Tight Lies, but mine go straight up. I have great Titleist DCI irons—Black Cats, too. I have Cobras given to me by Hale Irwin himself. I have a big 975 Titanium Titleist driver, also a Taylor Made bubble driver and the biggest Bertha ever made. My high-performance wedges run the gamut—fifty-six degrees, fifty-eight degrees, sixty degrees. I have 'em all. I even have an "Alien."

My golf balls are high-tech. Zylin Covered XLs, Tour Distance-Wound 90s, the Slazenger 420s. You name the kind of ball you like, I've got it.

Sometimes I play with a guy worse than me. He's into all this high-tech stuff. He goes, "I sure like the feel of these new balatas," or "This new baffled 3-wood really works for me." Or "The only putter that makes any sense at all is the Scotty Cameron—that Tel3 is so true. Talk about center cut. I have three of them Scottys—I love the Microstep and the Teryilium insert."

The poor son-of-a-gun hasn't gotten a wedge off the ground in the last three outings and his baffled 3-wood emerges from the fairway carrying a divot the size of an adult toupee. The last time he two-putted a green was when I gave him a four-footer.

He goes, "This new Maxfli Multi-layered Revolution lands quiet. I can just feel the difference on my wedge shots—on my putting, too." Sure, right!

High tech is great. Don't get me wrong. Look at Davis, Tiger and Freddie; but let's face it—high tech hasn't solved my web of problems.

Practice is my main problem. I hate it. I am allergic. I break out in a rash if I go out and hit practice balls. I can't help it.

Putting is the worst part of my game, followed closely by sand play and chipping. A good friend, a guy who supported me as president and was respectful back then, put it rather succinctly last week when he said, "George, you stink."

Anyway, a couple of weeks ago out at Muirfield—a course on which a guy like me should be forbidden to play—I invoked the "no-laughing rule."

My playing partners agreed—"Okay, no laughing."

I put them to the test. In one sand trap I flailed away four times, before going in the pocket. I found brooks and eddies that Jack Nicklaus didn't even know existed when he laid out this monster.

Things were dragging for me. I was thinking, "Why do I need this? I am seventy-four. I have a boat and a nice wife—why this torture?"

But then on the sixteenth I hit a perfect 9-iron—long and straight with a lot of spin on it. It stopped but six feet from the hole. My partners were ecstatic. "You're back!" "What an effort!" "You pureed that one."

But then came my turn to putt. I admit my attitude was negative as I lined up for my downhill putt. I pushed it off to the left. It gathered speed as it ripped past the cup, stopping about six feet away. But I had another six-footer to make coming back.

I jabbed my second putt. It took off like a cruise missile. The direction was great. The speed was wrong. It lipped the cup and was whiplashed violently off course. Four and a half feet still to go for putt number three.

I froze over the ball, my long putter wagging like a vaulter's pole. I came back slowly, and then literally shanked the putt. As it careened off to the right, the "no-laughing rule" was broken. They didn't mean to hurt my feelings—for fifteen dreadful holes they had been careful not to. My partner knocked away my remaining four-footer. "A gimme!" he says.

As I have done several times before, I decided right then and there to give up golf. I hate it.

But after a two-week moratorium I was back.

Playing with our Cape Arundel pro, Ken Raynor, I felt inspired.

The first nine was bad—the chipping and putting betraying me.

Then came the magic. On the par-4 eleventh, my drive was fine. I then topped my 5-wood shot—a scorching grounder that stopped sixty yards short of the green.

I pulled out my fifty-six-degree Cleveland Classic-588. My swing was surprisingly smooth. The "True Temper" shaft gave me that velvet feeling. I felt the grooves gently spin the ball. I felt the "touch" of my Tour Distance-90. It feathered on to the green—landing like a butterfly. Breaking gently to the right, it meandered sixteen feet, right into the hole.

Golf? I hate it, sure, but I really love it.

I'll be on the first tee tomorrow at 6:50 A.M.

George Bush

CLOSE TO HOME JOHN McPHERSON

Designs for golf's new oversized drivers
have begun to spiral out of control.

A Candle in the Wind

There's a lot of levity and joy that goes with being a professional golfer, not to mention the many privileges afforded those who achieve success at the top levels of the sport.

But it would be misrepresenting the whole experience of the PGA Tour to imply that the men who compete out here are somehow exempt from the pain and sorrow of everyday living. Like all the players, I'm reminded from time to time that what we do every day—often with the solemn demeanor of heart surgeons—is nothing more than a game, and that the genuine business of life takes place outside the ropes, far removed from all the lights and cameras. This story is about the real world.

Peter and Paul: the two names are linked together all the way back to the Bible, and when brothers just two years apart are given those names, comparisons are inevitable. As much as every parent aspires to equal treatment of all their children in a good-sized family, it's impossible to ensure that each child gets his full share of attention. In Paul's case, I think it was difficult, because he had two very active older brothers to follow and to be compared against. David and I were both athletic, and involved in golf and other sports. We were both sports editors of the high school paper and took part in a number of other school activities. We made friends easily and had a relatively carefree time of it.

Paul, on the other hand, didn't care much for sports and was more introverted by nature. He had to listen to friends and teachers constantly asking, "Why aren't you like your older brothers?"

As the third boy in the Jacobsen family a lot was expected of Paul, and he just couldn't or didn't want to live up to it. So he went his own way, and, as too often happens these days, he eventually fell into problems with drugs.

As we got older, Paul and I drifted apart. We still loved each other and stayed in contact, and I would hear from his friends that he was proud of what I had done in my career, but it was difficult for him to express that pride directly to me. It was very important to Paul that he establish his own identity. He didn't want to stay in Portland and have to be pestered with questions about being Peter's brother, and why Peter missed that five-footer on television last week, and all the other burdens that David and Susie, my sister, put up with all the time.

So he moved to Los Angeles and got a job as a graphic artist, and did some modeling on the side. In Southern California he could be just Paul Jacobsen and have his own life. I thought it was a courageous thing to do, and I admired him for it.

However, there was a certain tension between Paul and the rest of the family that wouldn't go away. When my wife Jan and I would go to Los Angeles each year for the L.A. Open, it seemed that Paul was usually too busy to come out to the course to watch me play. It was his way of telling me that his life was much more important than coming to a golf tournament, and I understood. We would always talk on the phone when I was in town, but that was about it.

When Paul was twenty-six, he just blurted something out in a phone conversation with me. "You know I'm gay, don't you?" he said.

And I told him that, of course, I knew, and that it was no big deal to me. Although I was surprised that he had told me so suddenly, I was glad for him that he could get it off his chest. It meant he was coming to grips with his life and facing who he was.

Paul's problems with drugs and alcohol grew worse through the years, and it was not uncommon for us to get phone calls from him at three or four in the morning. These would start out normally enough, with "Hi, how ya doin'," then quickly deteriorate into bouts of ranting at us about all the problems in his life. He would get irrational and start calling us names. Mom and Dad would get the calls, or David or Susie, or whomever he could reach on the phone. He was using a lot of cocaine during the day, and drinking vodka at night to come down from it, and just hurling himself around on this emotional roller-coaster.

It got so bad in late 1987 that we checked him into the Betty Ford Clinic in Palm Springs. Thankfully, through the good work of the people there, Paul got clean. He seemed to be getting his life back on track in 1988, when I got the phone call that changed everything.

It was August 24, the day after the Fred Meyer Challenge. Mom called to say that Paul had been admitted to the hospital with pneumonia. Jan and I were immediately concerned that he might have AIDS. I called Paul and he sounded upbeat and said he thought he'd been living on too fast a track and needed to slow down and rest. He even talked about moving back to the Northwest. However, by the next week, when I was in

Toronto for the Canadian Open, the news was all bad. Paul did, in fact, have AIDS and had been admitted to the intensive care unit at Cedars Sinai Hospital. I was worthless in Canada, and withdrew after shooting a first-round 79. My mind had never been further from a golf course than it was that day.

I flew back to Portland, and Jan and I caught the first flight to Los Angeles to be with Paul.

I had heard from friends that Paul's weight was down, and that he had not been in good health for a while, but seeing him in the hospital was a shock. I hadn't seen him since we'd checked him into the Betty Ford Center eight months before, and it was obvious that his condition was critical. He had lost a lot of weight and was extremely gaunt. In hindsight, I think Paul had known he was seriously ill for months before he was tested, but his fear of learning the truth was so great that he put off going to the doctor. By the time he was examined, he had full-blown AIDS.

Despite his drug problem, Paul had always stayed in shape with regular exercise, but now he was so thin and pale. He had lost more than thirty pounds off a slight frame. It broke my heart to see him. I told Jan that we better put all our plans on hold, because we really needed to be with Paul.

An especially vivid memory is of walking into his room and seeing him hooked up to a respirator. He looked up at me with terror in his eyes. Then he wrote something on a pad and handed it to me. It said, "Peter, you can do anything. Please make this go away."

My eyes filled with tears, then Paul put his arms around me and hugged me real tight. It was the most powerless feeling I'd ever had. Here, my kid brother was telling me I could do anything, but there wasn't a damn thing I could do to help him when he most needed it. I couldn't find anything to say, and I started to cry. I finally choked out something like, "Paul, we'll do everything we can for you."

The poor guy was just so scared and desperate. I'll never forget that look in his eyes.

I stayed in his room for several hours at a time, and we all took turns being with him. Then we'd return to the hotel, catch a nap and go back. Just the third day after we'd arrived, Paul took a horrible turn for the worse. He'd been fighting the respirator, which, of course, he needed to keep breathing, and the doctors had just started using a paralyzing drug on him so that his body would relax and he'd be better able to fight the pneumonia. Then he suddenly slipped into a coma.

We went home that evening, aware that the end was near. It was September 5, just twelve days after I'd been told of Paul's illness and only a week since he'd been diagnosed. I was sound asleep when something unusual happened. At exactly one-thirty in the morning, I woke up suddenly and felt a fluttering movement inside my body. I asked Jan to turn on the light, and I told her that Paul was with us.

I said, "He's inside of me."

"Are you all right?" she asked.

I was oddly at peace. I told her that Paul had come there to tell me everything was okay, and that he was fine. I also told her I just wanted to lie there for a moment and feel the spirit of my brother, because that's exactly what it was. Paul's spirit was with me, and it was comforting.

I remember the fluttering movement didn't go away— it was almost like butterflies inside of me—and then I faded off to sleep. When I awoke the next morning, Jan asked if I remembered waking up the previous night, and I recalled it all perfectly. I told her Paul had come to visit me, and that he was finally out of his pain, but that he had left something with me.

That morning I called one of Paul's close friends, who lives on a farm in the state of Washington, and before she heard my experience she told me that she had been awakened the previous night by an owl that had flown down and landed on her open windowsill and started to hoot into the room. An owl is universally regarded as a sign of death. I asked her what time it had happened, and she said one-thirty.

Later in the day, I talked to Paul's roommate, and he said that the dog and cat had been going crazy all week without Paul there, and that the animals had been keeping him awake at night. But at one-thirty in the morning, they had suddenly calmed down. He said he felt Paul's spirit had been with them.

It's extraordinary that three different people who were close to my brother—one of them a thousand miles away—felt his presence at the same time.

When we went to the hospital, one of Paul's nurses told me that his vital signs had dropped sharply at one-thirty in the morning. "In my opinion, he has left us," she said.

Paul never came out of his coma, and he died peacefully later that day. He was thirty-two years old.

The sorrow of his death was eased for me by the certain knowledge that he'd visited me. Paul had said something to me that night that I remember distinctly. "Peter, you're okay just the way you are," he said. "Be nice to people and don't let anything get you down." And then he said, "Go out there and win. Just go out there and win."

Our family struggled for quite a while after Paul's death to make sense of what had happened. I knew that all I could do was try to honor his life by carrying forward with the message he'd given me: just to be myself and go out and win.

While I hadn't won on the PGA Tour since 1984, I had been close on several occasions. I'd had something like seven runner-up finishes in the past five years. But I won the Isuzu Kapalua International in November 1989, and then, in a victory that was extra special, I won the Bob Hope Chrysler Classic two months later, playing the final round on the PGA West/Palmer Course. Coincidentally, the last round of golf I'd ever played with Paul was sixteen months before on that very course. My dad was also with us.

I struggled with that realization the entire last round. I was paired with Steve Elkington and Mike Reid, and had a two-shot lead, but I was also wrestling with vivid memories of playing the Palmer course with Paul and Dad. Every time my mind would wander and I would think about Paul, I'd hear him say, "Don't think about me. I'm fine. Just go out and win." That thought carried me all day.

When I birdied the last hole to win, David, who had come to Palm Springs for the week, gave me a big hug, and I said, "I sure wish Dad and Paul were here to see this."

And David said, "Paul saw every shot. I think he helped you keep that last 3-iron on line."

Peter Jacobsen
with Jack Sheehan

Turning Back the Clock

Golf dispels the myth that the older Americans have to be less active or competitive. Ask any middle-aged golfer who's been bested by some- one his parents' age. I speak from experience; on the links, youth offers no advantages.

Dan Quayle

The bounce has been missing from my dad's step. Illness has invaded his body and spirit. He is eighty. Yet, this seems so sudden. Now I know the ache of the thought: If only I could turn back the clock, just for a day.

Besides his family, my dad has always loved a good joke, the San Francisco 49ers, playing cards and, "best of all," golf. His swing is one of his better jokes—a marvel of mistakes he makes work. "I really synchronized my jerks that time!" he says.

Searching through the misty barriers of age and gender, fathers and daughters sometimes catch only a glimpse of one another. Not us. The morning I quit piano lessons, my mother—the daughter of a music teacher—cried right into a box of Cheerios. She could only watch as I grew more like my father every day. Relatives say when I play cards I even tap my fingers on the table exactly as he does. When I was little, we had "our song." He would sing it, and we'd laugh ourselves silly:

"We belong
To a mutuaaaalllll
Ad-mir-a-tion So-ci-e-ty,
My buddy and me."

Now we are a thousand miles apart in geography, politics and much else. But we are still buddies. We share the most enduring bond of all.

We are golf buddies.

A little more than a year ago, my dad experienced the first of many setbacks in his battle against cancer. All of us wondered if the end was near.

Shortly thereafter, I flew to San Francisco and talked him into a leisurely round at the Olympic Club. I thought just being out on the course would boost his spirits. And there was this other motive: I was playing the best golf of my life, breaking 90 the first time just two weeks earlier.

Once a steady 80s/90s player, Dad had never seen me play this well. I was wild to take his money and win his approval. With the same predatory DNA swirling in our cells, we always played for money. Over the years I'd lost nearly enough Nassaus to reimburse my college tuition. My dad says of this, "Want to earn forty thousand dollars the hard way?"

He delighted in being my mentor as well as my cutthroat opponent. I am convinced his parting words to me will be "Pull down with your left!"

That day at Olympic, I would have to give him strokes. What a proud day it would be for us both, I thought.

Well, he wasn't nearly as excited as I thought he'd be. Our golf date fell on his seventy-ninth birthday. But neither that, my newfound handicap nor a sunny San

Francisco day could summon a smile. We began the round chatting sorrowfully about how his treatment sapped his strength, how he hated never breaking 100 anymore. Then it appeared to me he got down to business. He had 1-putt par on the first hole, while I gasped away with an 8. After that, he started holing out from everywhere. I'd never seen him putt better.

While my score was rising, his jerks were synchronizing. Time after time, he flailed his driver straight up in the air, his body shaking in every direction like Jell-O molds. Before I could even venture a laugh at the sight, THWACK, he'd look up and laugh at himself.

He began trotting back to the cart, urging me to do the same before I'd even completed my swing—just like when I was twelve. "Never up, never in!" he chirped for the hundred-millionth time as I dabbed a dainty putt four feet short. From some unknown place, a laugh rose up out of me.

With an all-too-familiar glow on his face, he totaled up the damage. A 96 for him; 114 for me.

It was exactly like twenty years ago.

Later, above the clouds on a plane to Seattle, I thought of my dad's deteriorating health. I wondered, for the first time, if I'd ever see him again. Then I recalled our game, how bizarre it was that he played so well—and I so poorly—and how much fun it had been. Suddenly, it was as clear as the sky in front of me. On the golf course, on his seventy-ninth birthday, we were given a magical gift. Someone let us turn back the clock, just for a day.

Betty Cuniberti

2

GOING FOR THE GREEN

I have always had a drive that pushed me to try for perfection, and golf is a game in which perfection stays just out of reach.

Betsy Rawls

Plimpton to the Fore

I should have known that the week of the Crosby Pro-Am tournament was going to be taxing when I checked in for the flight to California. The clerk had been very helpful tying the clubs together and encasing them in a plastic bag. It was when he tipped the bag over to see if the clubs were secure that the mouse nest fell out.

We stared at the small heap of shavings and string lying on the floor. "I see that you're ticketed through Monterey," he said. "Going to the Crosby?"

"That's right," I said. "I played it once, fourteen years ago. I'm going to take another crack at it."

"You've really been spending the years getting ready," he said, looking at the mouse nest.

In the first Bing Crosby National Pro-Am I played, in 1966, my golf bag was carried by a diminutive furniture mover named Abe—a somewhat elderly local who occasionally worked as a caddie at Pebble Beach, one of the Monterey Peninsula courses used for the tournament. To my astonishment Abe was waiting for me this time when I arrived to register. He had heard I was coming and hoped I would have him back to "pack" my bag. I was delighted.

Abe felt it would be a good idea if we walked the course, "to refresh our minds" on what the holes looked like.

We started off by following a foursome that included Jack Lemmon. Duffers hold Lemmon in particular affection for his difficulties on the final holes of Pebble Beach, all graphically caught by the television cameras the first time he played the Crosby more than a decade ago. I recalled with relish Lemmon's attempts to make a recovery shot up a steep slope. The ball bounced jauntily up the slope and, as if appalled by what it discovered at the top, turned and hurried back down. We could see the top of Lemmon's head as he shifted about to address the ball a second time. Exactly the same thing happened. The ball bobbed up to the top of the slope, then curled back down. We never saw much of Lemmon himself, just a great deal of his errant golf ball—it seemed to fill the screen with its antic behavior.

As we walked along, Lemmon reminisced about the experience. "The whole mess started when our foursome came into view of the television cameras for the first time. You'd think I'd be used to cameras by now, but when it comes to golf, I'm not. I think I averaged ten shots on each of these last five holes."

Lemmon said that on the eighteenth, as he lay 12 with his ball still thirty-five feet from the cup. He had an elderly caddie whose sense of dignity seemed overtaxed by what was going on. He kept sidling away. Lemmon, down on one knee on the green trying to sight his putt, had to call him out of the crowd for advice. The caddie moved reluctantly until, finally, Lemmon could hear him breathing behind him. "Which way does it break?" Lemmon had asked, over his shoulder. "Who cares?" the caddie muttered.

Now, on the same eighteenth, the famous ocean hole,

Lemmon hooked his drive down onto the smooth, wave-worn boulders at the foot of the seawall that curves along the length of the fairways. The ball remained in sight for an astonishing length of time, skipping and ricocheting hysterically from one rock to another. "Life is an irreplaceable divot," Lemmon said to me mysteriously as he stepped off the tee.

In the Crosby, one professional and one amateur play together as partners from start to finish. This means that even a rank amateur can play in front of the TV cameras on the final day, assuming he and his pro partner make the cut.

Not many golfers go through the stress of the first drive of a tournament in front of a large crowd. It is one thing to start off a country-club Labor Day tournament before two witnesses jiggling Bloody Marys in plastic cups, and quite another to bend down to set the ball on its tee, acutely aware that five hundred people are watching you. The blood rushes to the head. The ball falls off the tee. To start the swing takes almost a physical command of "Now!"

My first drive surprised me, a high slice down the fairway that managed to stay in bounds. I hurried after it, feeling almost palpable relief in getting away from the first tee and its witnesses. After the first round I went with Abe to the practice range to try to do something about my miserable showing. I had not scored a par and had not helped my professional partner, Jack Ferenz.

My second round, on the nearby Cypress Point course, was no better than the first. I spent a great deal of time searching with Abe for errant shots. I had played thirty-six holes without scoring a par. The next day we would be playing Spyglass Hill—one of the most difficult courses in the world. The thought was very much in my mind that I, not a bad athlete, with a golf swing worked on through the years by a bevy of pros, might not achieve even one par.

The round at Spyglass did not start propitiously. My drive moved out onto the fairway, hopping along nicely, but the second shot went off at a sharp angle, hit a pine, then another, and rolled back toward me, ending not more than eight yards away after a flight that might have totaled almost two hundred yards. I stared at the ball as if it were a smoking grenade.

On the next drive I tried to slow things down. The great golf writer, Bernard Darwin, said of Bobby Jones's swing that it had a "certain drowsy beauty." I thought of that on the tee, and slowly, too slowly, I brought the club back. Imperceptibly, like an ocean liner inching away from the pier, the club head slowly moved away from the ball, gradually lifting to the top of the swing. But at the summit everything went out of control. The club head faltered like a paper airplane stalling on the wind, and then it dashed earthward in a cruel whistling swipe. A cry erupted from my throat as the club pounded into the earth a foot behind the tee, bounced, and sent the ball perfectly straight down the fairway for about ninety yards.

"Straight as an arrow," Ferenz's caddie said helpfully.

On the twelfth, Matt Mitchell, the other amateur in our foursome, threw his ball into the water hazard. Of all the indignities that man tries to heap on inanimate objects, throwing a golf ball into the water is perhaps the most hapless. The lake accepts the ball with a slight ripple that disappears almost immediately, leaving the surface smooth, almost smug. "I suppose the thing to do is to think of the ball bloating down there," I said comfortingly to Matt. He stared at me furiously.

As if to make him feel better, on the last par-3 hole, my 8-iron shot described a high parabola and dropped into the water edging the green, stitching it with a little geyser.

"It'll be bloating any minute now," Mitchell said.

The par-4 eighteenth would be my last chance in the tournament to make a par. I hit an enormous hook into a grove of pines. "It's gone," Abe said gloomily.

I told Abe that we had to find the ball. It was my last chance. If we found it, I told him, I would take a tremendous swing and catch it to perfection, whatever its lie. The ball would rocket into the clear open air above the fairway and float gently toward the green. From where it landed, I would hit a delicate wedge onto the green, and then sink a long, curling putt for a par. I would tip my hat gracefully to the spectators. But there was no sign of the ball. My last chance was gone.

When I got back home, I called a place outside New York City called Golf-O-Rama. It has indoor driving ranges that simulate actual golf courses by flashing a picture of each hole on a screen while computers track the flight of the ball. The man said they had the Pebble Beach course. I made a reservation.

Norman Schaut, president of Golf-O-Rama, showed me around. One side of the hangar-like room was taken up with the "golf courses," lined up side to side, each with an elevated tee. The golfer hits the ball twenty feet or so into a nine-foot square screen on which can be seen a color-slide reproduction of the golf hole.

We stepped up on the Pebble Beach tee. "If the computer says you've driven the ball into a water hazard," Schaut said, "there'll be the sound of splash."

I said, "You should have the sound of the waves breaking and the seals barking out there in the Pacific."

Schaut switched on the course. The picture of the par-4, 482-yard first hole at Pebble Beach flashed on. "That's it!" I said. "The dogleg to the right." I remembered the names of the contestants being called out by the starting marshal, the patter of applause from the crowds by the tee and the dryness of my throat when I had bent down to set the tee into the grass—and even here, with the Muzak playing "Deep Purple," I felt my nerves tighten.

I teed up and swung. My drive, according to the computer, was an excellent one for me, 205 yards out. My second shot stopped fifty yards from the pin, and then I hit a lovely, easy wedge, which left me with a six-foot putt for my par. I stepped onto the Astroturf green with my putter. I stared down, brought the putter back, then forward, and watched the ball ease down the line and drop into the hole.

I had the urge to throw my putter into the air. Instead I turned and tried to look suave. Schaut came hurrying over. "Have you got something to say?" he asked, looking at my face, which had broken into a broad grin.

"Piece of cake," I said.

George Plimpton

There Is No "I" in Team

We rather than "I."

Charles Garfield

Bob and Tina Andrews work together like a well-oiled machine. She sets him up on the tee box, steps back, looks down the fairway and says, "Okay." He takes a deep breath and swings, and the ball sails down the left side of the first fairway at Killearn Country Club near their Tallahassee, Florida, home.

They display impressive teamwork. Bob Andrews is totally blind. Tina, his wife, is his "coach," and together they make up one of the best teams in the United States Blind Golf Association.

"The first thing you learn is that blind golf is a team sport," says Bob, fifty-one, who was blinded by a grenade in Vietnam in 1967. "Until you have a coach, you're not a blind golfer. You're just a blind person with some golf clubs."

Bob and Tina were married not long after he returned from Vietnam. He took up golf first for the exercise. "I tried running," he says with a laugh, "but you get tired of taking those falls."

He had played golf as a kid, but he was never serious about it until he became blind. He joined the USBGA, and in 1995 he became president.

Tina is his third coach. Andrews's father did it at first, but it got to be too much for him. Then, Andrews's son took a turn. But he soon went off to college. That left Tina, who isn't a golfer, but Bob actually thinks that's a plus because she doesn't overload him with information. All she does is point him in the right direction.

After they play a couple of holes, it's understood how they do what they do. Or so you think. "Ready to try it?" asks Bob.

You stammer for a few moments, then answer weakly, "Sure."

Until you've "coached" a blind golfer, you can't appreciate how hard it is—and how wonderful it is when things go right. You find that you've never been so interested in someone else's golf game.

Bob holds the club out in front of him, and the first thing the coach does is place the club firmly on the ground, right behind the ball, square to the target. This serves as an anchor. Next is the position of his feet, also square to the target. Then the shoulders. When everything is right, a simple "okay" is all he needs.

Andrews swings, and the ball takes off. "Little fade down the right side?" he asks, judging the ball's path by its feel.

"Yep. Little fade down the right side."

Later, Andrews has about 160 yards, of which about 140 is a carry over water. "What do we got?" he asks.

"About 160 yards, over water," you say.

"Oh, boy," he says. "Let's try a 7-wood." After he's set up, Andrews spends a little more time standing over this shot. He hits it a little fat and it splashes in the water. Your heart sinks. That wouldn't have happened if Tina were coaching. "See, I wouldn't have even told him about the water," she says. "No point in giving him one more thing to worry about. Take advantage of his disadvantage, know what I mean?"

After dropping, Andrews hits a nice pitching wedge over the water and onto the green. You lead Andrews by the arm to the spot where his ball rests, then walk with him to the flagstick. "Fourteen feet," he says. "A little left-to-right, slightly uphill."

Andrews reads his own putts, feeling the contour of the green through his shoes. This seems amazing. But when you step behind him to take a look, you come to the same conclusion: left-to-right, slightly uphill.

You set him up with the putter's face aiming just out-side the left edge of the cup.

"How's that look?" he asks.

"Perfect," you say. But you cross your fingers. His putting stroke is smooth and sure, a perfect pendulum. On its final rotation, the ball ducks into the left side of the cup. Andrews hears the hollow sound of a holed putt. It is a sweet sound indeed.

"Hey," you say as you head to the next tee, "that was a great bogey you made back there."

"No," he says, "that was a great bogey we made."

Dave Sheinin

The Magoo Caper

A great handicap for some golfers is honesty.

Harvey Mackay

Long before con men were immortalized in *The Hustler* and *The Sting*, there was The Magoo Caper. They didn't make this one into a movie.

Here's why.

I started playing golf at about the same age that Tiger Woods did, with a cut-down set of clubs and a doting father to preside over my development. By the time I reached high school I was convinced I could "follow the sun" as a professional golfer.

When I got to the University of Minnesota, the similarities between the Tiger legend and the Mackay legend soon parted company. During my sophomore year, I competed at the NCAA Golf Championship at Purdue University in West Lafayette, Indiana. That weekend I learned that for every good northern golfer—who could practice maybe, at most, six months a year—there were equally talented Southern golfers—who could practice twelve months a year and become twice as good.

So I settled down and accepted my role as a respectable, if not spectacular, member of my college squad. Our coach believed in nicknames. Mine was "Magoo," a nice play on "Mackay," and an accurate take on the Coke-bottle horn-rimmed glasses I wore. My eyesight was so bad I couldn't follow the flight of the ball off the tee without them.

During Easter vacation my senior year, the eight-man squad traveled on their own to that warm-weather mecca, St. Louis, to get in a little practice before the short Minnesota golf season began.

After the first day's round, we all sat together at a beer joint.

"Magoo," said one of the members of my frolicking foursome, "We've got business to attend to. Let's set up the bets for the next day's play. Make it interesting."

Our usual wager was a big-time two bits a hole. But I had a proposition.

"Tell you what. Tomorrow I will play all of you for a buck a hole WITHOUT MY GLASSES. All you have to do is give me a mere eighteen strokes—a stroke a hole—plus, promise you'll point me in the direction of the hole."

A dollar a hole was big bucks then, but they couldn't get their money down fast enough.

Let the games begin.

The next morning we merged the two foursomes and we played an eightsome. No problem. We had the course to ourselves due to a light rain and big wind.

I miraculously parred the first hole. Impossible. The guys went nuts.

I parred the second hole. They went ballistic.

I parred the third hole. Berserko.

Standing on the fourth green, I needed two putts from ten feet to get my fourth par in a row.

"You guys are eyeballing me like a Las Vegas pit boss

studies a guy who has made three straight passes," I said as I lined up my putt.

Suddenly, a big gust of wind came up and I immediately let out a scream.

The wind had just blown one of the contact lenses out of my eyes.

Contact lenses? My teammates had never even heard of them. They had just been invented. I, of course, being Magoo, was the first kid on my block to get a pair.

Hey, I just said I would play without glasses. I didn't say anything about contact lenses.

No go. Hairsplitting legalisms didn't cut it. I shot the rest of the round sans glasses, sans contact lenses.

It was an expensive lesson.

After it was over and I took my licking, I paid off my bets, and we went back to the beer joint to review the day's festivities.

"Magoo, you were right. You were like the guy at the craps table," one of my jolly crew said. "Do you know what happened to him? Just when he was about to shoot his fourth consecutive pass, three dice rolled out of his sleeve. All sixes. That's when the pit boss reached over, pocketed one of the dice and said, 'Go ahead and shoot. Your point is eighteen.'"

And so it was.

Harvey Mackay

"Look, why waste time? I say the man's guilty."

Beat the Pro

You hear that winning breeds winning. But no winners are bred from losing. They learn they don't like it.

Tom Watson

Sam Snead tells the story of a charity golf challenge he played years ago.

A pro was stationed at each hole, and threesomes would come up and bet against the pro individually. Sam was positioned at a par-3 hole and, with one shot to the green, whoever's ball was closest to the pin on the tee-off was the winner.

A threesome approached and the first man said, "Hello, Mr. Snead. I'd like to bet you five hundred dollars that I'll get closer to the pin than you do." Snead accepted the challenge. The golfer hit a good shot to the green. Snead hit it past the green and lost the bet.

The second golfer approached, saying, "It's great to meet you, Mr. Snead. I'm going to make the same bet as my friend. Five hundred dollars says that I'll hit the ball closer to the pin than you will." This time, Sam hit the ball twenty yards past the hole and lost the bet again. He just laughed. It was, after all, a charity event and the object was to raise money and have fun.

The last one of the threesome strolled up to Snead and, with a brash New Jersey accent, said, "You washed-up old man! You just don't have it anymore, do you? I'll bet thirty-five hundred dollars that I can beat you." Sam just smiled and quietly accepted the bet. The cocky golfer hit the ball four inches from the pin. "Now beat that, old man," he said. "You should have put down those clubs years ago." Again, Sam just smiled. He leaned over and positioned the ball, drew back, took a swing and made a hole-in-one. "Better luck next time," said Slammin' Sammy Snead.

Susan D. Brandenburg

Golf Balls

A few years ago I introduced a coworker, Roy, to the game of golf. I outfitted him with a set of my old clubs, including head covers, a bag, tees, ball markers, divot tools and two dozen new golf balls. I even provided him with a visor and a new glove. The only thing he had to buy for himself was a pair of golf shoes.

After a few lessons on the driving range, he played his first round of golf at a company-sponsored outing at Bay Valley Inn, Bay City, Michigan. This beautiful and challenging 18-hole course has water on thirteen holes and is constantly buffeted by winds sweeping in off Saginaw Bay. Not necessarily a good first choice for a beginning golfer, but Roy was bound and determined to play in the company outing.

After a typical beginner's horrendous first nine, Roy turned to me and said, "Sam, I'm out of balls. May I have some more?" I thought my generosity had already reached beyond normal expectations and I replied, "Roy, do you know how much golf balls cost?" Roy calmly replied, "Sam, if you can't afford the game, you shouldn't play."

Sam Murphy

Walter Won the Honors

If you ever felt that there is a wee touch of the spiritual in golf, like the famous book *Golf in the Kingdom* says, let me tell you a true story that may further the notion.

Last autumn, Walter Donoughe, one of my closest friends, was told by his doctors they couldn't cure his pancreatic cancer, but they thought treatments could extend his life and, yes, he could play a lot more golf. He and I were talking all about it a couple of days after he got his prognosis while we were playing the front nine as a twosome. As we sat in the cart waiting for the eighth green to clear, I asked Walter which he would prefer, three more years of golf, or a guarantee of eternity in heaven. He answered immediately that he would take the guarantee of heaven, but he smiled and said he hoped he could play golf there instead of harps. From other things Walter told me over the winter and last spring I knew he had a lock on membership in heaven's best golf club.

We also talked a lot about golf, and how a really sweet swing starts effortlessly, like somebody else takes it back, then brings it down on plane and you hear more than feel the click as the ball jumps off the club. We spent some great hours hitting 5-irons into the net in the bag room as we forgot the winter cold outside and tried for the sweet swing feeling.

Walter kept hanging in there fighting the cancer and was still swinging pretty well early in the spring when the golf committee decided to initiate for July a two-day tournament that each year would honor some member who has meant a lot to the club. They selected Walter as the first honoree. A great choice. He had worked many, many years as a board member and on every committee the club ever had. He won the handicap championship twice, numerous flight and senior championships, and he even won the annual gin tournament twice. A fine man, a good competitor and a great friend.

In the July 5–6 tournament honoring him, Walter and I would have been partners, as we usually were in team events, but he died on June 5. I was invited by, and played with, our club champion, Scott Arthur, who played well enough for us to win it all. But I made sure we didn't as I rolled the ball off the tee, heeled and toed fairway woods, scraped irons right and left, bladed and chili-dipped chips and pitches, and three- and four-putted my way to an agony of double and triple bogeys.

With only two holes left to play, as we headed to the par-3 thirteenth, I told Scott there had to be some lesson for me to learn from these humiliating two rounds, but I didn't think the lesson could be worth it. When we got on the thirteenth tee a hawk was circling high above the green. Scott said it was our last chance for a hole-in-one and he would like one because it was his fortieth birthday. For all the years he had been playing golf he said he had seen only one ace—hit by Walter Donoughe years ago when Scott caddied for him.

With zero enthusiasm I teed up the ball to hit and get it over with, then something strange happened. My 5-iron started back effortlessly like somebody else was swinging it back then bringing it down on plane, and I heard the click more than I felt it as the ball jumped off the club. My myopic eyes couldn't follow the ball but I knew it was hit by that sweet swing Walter always talked about, a swing that I felt only a few times before, at the practice net when he coached me.

Bill Kelley, Chris Vasiliades and Scott started to holler things like "Great swing. . . . Great shot. . . . Go in the hole!" There was a sudden hush, then, "It did! It did! It went in the hole!" Chris grabbed my hat, threw it towards the green, then picked me up and swung me around like a rag. I was thinking, *Please Chris, don't throw me after my hat.*

The screams kept up and were truly sky-splitting, but that hawk was undisturbed. Like the steady pilot Walter was when he earned his wings with the Air Force years ago, that hawk just kept calmly circling the green and was not surprised at all by the miracle that happened down below him.

Now, I don't know how Walter petitioned the Almighty for me, but I know he did. Perhaps he said his buddy down there was getting close to giving up the game, breaking the commandment, Thou Shalt Not Quit. So he took over during his tournament, and before it was too late he arranged to send his pal Frank a message about hanging in there—a hole-in-one. Thanks, Walter, for swinging it for me. Go in peace.

Frank J. Haller

A Special Rapport

They limp when they walk, as if the world is perpetually tilted. Sometimes for them, it is.

Casey Martin hits and rides, hits and rides. When he reaches the greens at Heatherwoode Golf Club, he limps from the golf cart to his ball. The pain in his right leg is throbbing and insistent.

Gina Homan limps. Sometimes, she hops on her good, right leg. When the pressure on her left leg is too much, she'll stand on her right, her hand grabbing the left leg at the knee.

What are the odds? Martin, the pro golfer, has Klippel Trenaunay Weber Syndrome, a rare circulatory disorder. Gina Homan, who is twelve, does, too. Until Martin sued the PGA for the right to use a golf cart in tournaments, Gina never knew anyone else with her disability.

This was somebody like her, doing exactly what he wanted to do, without fear of prejudice. This she had to see.

She came from Minster, Ohio, with her parents and her older sister, to watch Martin in the Nike Miami Valley Open. He spoke to her at the first tee, "How's the leg today, buddy?" and smiled at her frequently during the round.

"What a sweet kid," Martin marveled afterward. "What a trouper."

Gina Homan was quiet and beaming. She didn't say what the day meant, but you knew what was happening behind her eyes.

Here's a funny thing about people with disabilities and the people who love them: They count their blessings. They smell the roses. They know what good fortune is, because they've seen the flip side.

Gina's mother Eileen explained the bumps on her daughter's leg. "Clumps of blood vessels," she said. "We're lucky. She could have that on her face, or throughout her body."

What are the odds? The Homans noticed Gina's over-sized leg when she was about six months old. They took her to doctors who checked her kidneys and heart. They took her to an arthritis specialist. Why is her leg so big? Nobody knew.

An x-ray technician finally made the correct diagnosis. The blood does not move efficiently from Gina's leg to her heart and back. It pools, causing the swelling. Martin shares her disability. He embodies her spirit.

And so Gina was out there waiting for him and following him for eighteen holes. They took a walk together, of a fashion.

The PGA thought the Casey Martin controversy was about carts and unfair advantages and the athleticism involved in putting one foot in front of the other. They didn't know.

It was about giving somebody a chance who deserved one.

Gina Homan might grow up to be a teacher. She's an A-student. She loves little children. She's patient and tolerant, and now she knows she's not alone.

"It slays me when kids stare" is what Eileen says. Gina

can't run or ride a bike. The left leg is noticeably bigger than the right; at the knee, it bows out.

Because her left foot is significantly smaller than her right, the Homans often buy Gina two pairs of shoes, to get one pair that fits. "I'm a little different physically," she says.

I ask Eileen Homan, "What do you wish for your daughter?" She says, "To grow up, find a job she likes and find a person she can be happy with."

At twenty-six, Casey Martin has grown up. He has found a job he likes. About the other, I don't know.

I know he did not ask for special treatment. People with disabilities rarely do. They want what we want, which is a fair shake. If you've watched Martin play, you understand. If you saw Gina Homan—limping, hopping and beaming, courageous—you'd empathize.

Eileen says, "She has a good heart. She's compassionate. She always strives to do her best."

After the round, Martin gave her a hug. If only we all were so disabled.

Paul Daugherty

Life on the Back Nine

Don't get your knickers in a knot; nothing is solved and it just makes you walk funny.

Kathryn Carpenter

The first time I played golf—real golf where you keep score and putt everything out and take it seriously—was in a father-son tournament. I was ten. I remember thinking it would be cool to drive the golf cart. I was right. It was very cool driving the golf cart. Did I already say I was ten at the time? I think we shot about a 65 for nine holes, which is all we played because the attention spans of young golfers really don't allow for a full round.

The golf course I grew up playing, Meadowbrook Country Club, has a 609-yard par-5 that wore us out. I think we made a 12. But I was very proud of the fact that I didn't whiff any shots. And I was hooked. My dad had introduced me to a game that would forever be a part of my life.

It would also test the boundaries of our bond.

By the following summer, I was playing golf every day, which included sneaking onto the course on Mondays, when it was officially closed, and squeezing in three holes on the front nine on Tuesdays before the Ladies Day crowd would make it around to the seventh tee.

I even found what would be the family dog on the golf course that summer. A stray collie mix met me on the third tee one morning and followed me for the rest of the front nine. After I fed her half my hot dog from the snack bar, she was mine.

By the time the next father-son tournament rolled around, I would have cried if I'd shot a 65 on my own ball. I had developed a strong short game and expected my dad's length off the tee to make up for my shortcomings. If he could get us within 135 yards on the par-4s, I could get us on the green. And one of the best things about Meadowbrook back then was there was hardly any water and—except for one par-3—you never had to carry a water hazard to reach a green.

We shot 48, and I was miffed. I rolled my eyes every time my dad mis-hit a shot. I grimaced when my putts didn't fall. I kicked at the grass and mumbled to myself. I had a miserable time. We finished third. I thought we should have won.

That afternoon and evening, I moped around the house like it was the end of the world. This pattern carried on for years because, although my dad and I were both accomplished players, we never learned how to play together. By the time I hit my mid-teens, I was regularly shooting in the 70s. I won the club junior championship when I was fifteen, and the members had to put up with a five-foot-nothing squirt playing in their club championship that summer because the junior champ got an automatic invite.

Life was good, except for when Dad and I would tee it up as a team. We could go out on Saturday and both shoot in the 70s—I remember both of us had 6 handicaps when I was sixteen—then turn around the following day in that hate-inducing alternate-shot format and fire an 85 in an event in which you were allowed to choose the better of two tee shots.

I was so disgusted one time that I putted the last three holes left-handed. Not a word was spoken on the ride home. The crazy thing was that we'd take this act on the road to play in the Tommy Galloway Father-Son at Hermitage Country Club, which was a big regional to-do. Winning the low gross in our age group was impossible because we were bound to make a couple of 7s. We'd always get to the sixteenth tee and one of us would say, "Well, there's always the net. If we shoot 82, they take away our two worst holes."

One time, we reached the par-4 seventeenth hole 7-over for the day and looked like we'd break 80 . . . until we both dunked it into the lake running down the right side of the fairway. It was negative on negative. The problem was, we couldn't learn to accept each other's faults. He sprayed drives and had a tendency to severely misclub himself. I was into go-for-broke golf. By the time I was sixteen and had hit a growth spurt, I figured there wasn't a par-5 I shouldn't reach in two. And I had turned into a terrible putter. My dad fretted over my jab stroke, which was either on fire or ice cold; I, meanwhile, fretted about his desire to play it safe.

By the time I was seventeen, we'd accepted the fact that we weren't much of a team. We were at the peaks of our games—my high school team won the 1981 state championship and I signed a golf scholarship with Virginia Commonwealth University. Dad was as consistent about shooting in the 70s as he'd ever be. But together we were mush.

I went off to school and lost myself in books and knowledge and a hunger to be a newspaper writer. And I lost my interest in playing competitive golf. After two seasons, I was through as a college golfer. There were some memorable rounds, but they were too few and far between.

Meanwhile, we had aged out of the father-son tournament. But a few years ago, Dad called and asked if I wanted to play in the father-son again. Turns out they'd changed the name to the politically correct parent-child and had created an over-eighteen age group.

Did we really want to put ourselves through that turmoil again?

I was playing rarely, and Dad had developed shoulder problems and was playing even less.

"Sure," I said. "Why not?"

A funny thing happens when you reach adulthood. All of a sudden, you can accept your dad's faults because you start to realize you have your own. And why in the world should four hours of golf with Dad be so stressful?

We hit a bucket of balls to warm up, and I don't think either of us hit more than three practice shots on the sweet spot. I would have hated to pick up the range that night; Team Radford had sprayed shots everywhere. But we must have left all the bad shots on the range. We birdied the first hole when I hit a wedge to about ten feet and Dad ran in the putt. Then we birdied the fourth hole, a par-5, when Dad hit a 200-yard 5-wood onto the front of the green, and we two-putted from forty-five feet. By the end of the round, we'd made four birdies. We had some ugly holes, too, but they weren't too ugly. And the amazing thing was that after an ugly hole, we always followed it with a chance for birdie. I remember laughing when I signed the scorecard.

Here were two hacks who had never played well together and they'd just shot 4-over 75 in an alternate-shot format. A lot of the guys I had grown up with, and who had always trounced us as a father-son tandem, had decided to play that Sunday. I scanned my age group's scores—81-77-85-76-82-90.

We'd won? Unbelievable. When we came home with the hardware, Mom also couldn't believe it. For years, she'd had to hear us trash each other for hours after every father-son event we played. Now she had to hear us gloat.

Suddenly, Dad's 220-yard drives into light rough were a thing of beauty. And just as suddenly, as long as my putts went into the hole, Dad didn't care what my awful stroke looked like. We laughed about the fifteen-inch putt he missed on the fifteenth hole, something I was constantly guilty of.

Two holes later, I air-mailed a par-3, something he was more prone to do in the past. The following year we shot 72. By the back nine, we weren't worried about beating the field, we were wondering if we could beat par.

All of that negative energy that had followed us for years had become positive power. For years, we had been in situations where we would ponder whether to play the ball out of the woods or the one that was buried under the lip in the bunker. Now, we were having to choose between a ten-foot downhill putt or a fifteen-footer uphill for birdie.

We haven't played in a parent-child tournament for a few years now. Dad's shoulder became so aggravating that he quit playing and gave up his membership at the club. But I was in the attic of my parents' house the other day looking for some old Batman comic books for my own son when I came across a box of old golf trophies. The first one I picked up was the first-place trophy for the 1989 Meadowbrook Country Club Parent-Child, unlimited age group. The second one was a third-place cup for the 1973 father-son, eleven-and-under. It took sixteen years to get it right. But finally we did.

Rich Radford

Living the Dream

The name jumped out at me from the list of tournament scores in a national golf publication. It was printed in teeny-tiny type, and I caught it only because I'm in the habit of scanning the mini-tour results for past and future tour stars.

I didn't expect to see his name in italics, and it stopped me in my tracks and made me smile.

Darryl Staszewski.

I stared at the letters until they blurred, feeling pangs of nostalgia as I thought about an old high school friend and the paths we chose in life. I felt admiration for Darryl, and maybe a little envy, too.

Staszewski, a graduate of St. Francis (Wisconsin) High School class of '74—my class, my friend—had tied for seventh place in an obscure mini-tour event somewhere in the Northwest. He won $216.

Big deal, you say?

It is, if you knew Darryl twenty-five years ago. As a high school freshman, he stood probably four-feet-ten-inches, and couldn't have weighed much more than seventy-five pounds. By his senior year, he had sprouted to five-feet-six-inches and tipped the scales at about 120, soaking wet.

Naturally, he got teased about his size. His buddies, especially, were relentless with their wisecracks. He took it in stride, mostly, but I'll never forget the day I snatched his driver's license out of his hand and loudly announced, with no small amount of glee, that Darryl was required to sit on a platform to see over the steering wheel.

In terms of teenage insults, I'd hit a 350-yard drive. Darryl laughed with the rest of us, but I noticed tears of humiliation welling in the corners of his eyes. It was the last time I ever teased him.

Darryl was a pretty good athlete, but he obviously was too small to play football, and after freshman basketball— he looks like a waif in the yearbook team photograph—he didn't make the squad as a sophomore.

So he turned to golf.

A left-hander, he swung in slow motion and barely managed to hit the ball out of his own shadow. He practically buckled under the weight of his golf bag. He didn't make the varsity team until he was a senior, and then only as the sixth man on a five-man squad, perhaps as a reward for his perseverance. Darryl played in few actual matches.

Back then, a few of us dreamed about becoming professional golfers, but we were eighteen and full of silly notions. Instead, we went off to college or to work, got married, had children. Ultimately, we fulfilled our destinies in golf: We became weekend hackers.

Except for Darryl Staszewski. He had the determination, the courage and the focus about which the rest of us only talked. Maybe the teasing he had endured made him tougher. Maybe he just wanted it more than we did. Maybe he just had more talent than we did, and it simply took a while to surface.

Not long after we graduated, Darryl moved to California to work on his game. Eventually, he became a club professional, and at some point in the late 1970s, I lost track of him.

Twenty years later, I was in the media tent at the Greater Milwaukee Open when somebody tapped me on the shoulder. I turned around and there was Darryl Staszewski—a lean, athletic six-footer.

He was living near Seattle, but was in town on vacation and had barely missed earning a spot in the GMO field in the Monday qualifier. We chatted for a while, and he gave me his phone number, saying it would be fun to get together and play a round if I ever got up to the Northwest.

And then I forgot about Darryl again until I found myself staring at his name in a golf magazine. It really doesn't matter whether he won $216 or $216,000, whether he finished seventh on the Cascade Tour or won the U.S. Open.

You see, Darryl is living the dream.

Gary D'Amato

Requiem for a Milkman

God does not subtract from one's allotted time
the hours spent playing golf.

Gerald O'Gara

This is the story of a retired milkman named Emil Kijek, who wound up his life in the arms of a friend in the middle of a fairway on a Thursday afternoon.

The setting is southeast Massachusetts, on the rim of Narragansett Bay, where stories this small are usually thrown back. Lizzie Borden hailed from Fall River, right next door; Ishmael and Ahab sailed from New Bedford, just down the road.

As a center of drama, Rehoboth is not quite in their class.

It's a pretty little town though. Driving through, you might take it for hunting country if John Pellegrino weren't there to set you straight. "Shoot my deer" explained the owner of the Sun Valley Golf Club, "and I'll shoot you."

Pellegrino's operation is similarly unvarnished. Starting with the arrow sign on the highway, everything at Sun Valley could stand some paint. The roof wouldn't mind a little leveling. The clubhouse is mostly a bar. But the gray-haired men crisscrossing with pullcarts look well satisfied. The senior rate is thirteen dollars for eighteen holes.

Ron Collett, Morris Dumont, Jack Alexander and Emil Kijek were teamed up that Thursday in a tournament. Collett and Dumont were not Kijek's regular partners, although both knew "Ky" well. Everyone did. "He had a spirit about him, I tell you," said Dumont, a retired piano tuner. "Ky was the type who enjoyed the day better than the golf, who took the good shots and the bad shots as they came, always hoping the next one would be perfect."

Alexander, on the other hand, was Kijek's customary golfing crony and his closest friend. They served together in Hawaii during World War II, though they didn't know it at the time. Kijek had gone in and out of the Army before the war broke out. When it did, he came back as a Seabee, a builder, and eventually saw Saipan.

On Oahu, when Alexander only knew of him, Kijek was also a boxer, a middleweight. He was one of the staple attractions in the Friday night fights at Schofield Barracks, a model of that paradoxical gentleness you so often find in boxers.

His father was the same way. Back in Warsaw, Jacob Kijek had been a weaver's foreman preoccupied with keeping a certain loom operating, the one run by Caroline. Falling in love and emigrating to Pawtucket, Jacob and Caroline raised their boy in the weaving business. As he had been an only son, Emil grew up to have an only daughter, Sandra. Her childhood memories are of spontaneous picnics, Sunday rides and a father whose only rule was kindness.

It was in the early 1960s that he embraced golf, when a cardiologist's first warning gave him four months off. After he retired—especially after losing his wife, Mabel—the golf course became home. He was a good, straight hitter, an 11- or 12-handicapper who held to that number (even as his distance waned) with increasingly better putting. This phenomenon is unheard of in the pros but well known in places like Sun Valley.

As a cardplayer, Kijek was a scratch, a legend at gin but even more partial to "pitch," the working man's rhapsody of high, low, jack and game.

"Deal the cards, old man," Alexander would say. Kijek would smile like a handsome child, and everyone else would laugh. At seventy-five, Alexander was only four years younger, but lately they were telling years. Ky was losing his edge with the cards.

He could still putt. At the first hole that day, he made a twenty-footer for par. At the fourth, he knocked in another. "You're saving us, old man," Alexander said. The day looked bright.

The sixth hole at Sun Valley is a 155-yard par-3. Kijek took a 3-wood.

"He hit that thing so beautifully," Dumont would say later. "It had this amazing trajectory."

"Emil, I can't see the ball," Alexander murmured after a moment, "I think it went in."

"Naw," Kijek said. He'd never had a hole-in-one.

"Old man!" Alexander sang as they reached the green. "Come get your ball out of the cup!"

Dumont recalled, "Ky was really happy, but there was no jumping up and down. He was such a humble man."

After driving nicely at the seventh, Kijek wavered over his second shot. "Emil, let somebody else hit first," Alexander suggested gently. "No, no, I'm okay, Jack," he said.

In the next instant, Ky started to fall, and his friend caught him. They settled softly in the grass. As the others ran for help, Jack said, "Emil, squeeze my hand. Don't stop until I tell you to." But Ky gave him that smile again and let go.

Who was he? He was a man who enjoyed the day better than the golf, who took good shots and bad shots as they came, always hoping the next one would be perfect. And it was.

Tom Callahan

Golf and the Caddie at Royal Troon

If I ever think anybody is better than me, then I can never be the best. I always have to believe I'm the best.

Payne Stewart

My wife and I had planned our first trip to Scotland for more than a year. Working through Scottish Golfing Holidays, we started our week at Royal Troon. I was to play the course in the morning, then my wife would join me in the afternoon across the street on the Portland Course.

This was the first morning of the first day of my first golf in Scotland.

Two things happened that will remain with me forever.

First, we were delayed more than fifteen minutes waiting for Payne Stewart and his group to show up. Clad in uncustomary slacks and regular golf-style cap, Stewart and his group finally appeared and were escorted to the back, or "medal" tees, where they all teed off. Playing with Stewart were three others, the best of whom probably was no more than a 10 handicap. Having already been rebuffed from playing the back tees, I decided to give it another go. The starter, with whom I had been enjoying a long conversation waiting for Stewart's group to appear, said it was impossible—unless, of course, the club secretary gave his approval. He then volunteered to speak with the secretary on my behalf. Taking my letter of introduction, which said I was an honorable fellow from Nebraska who had played in several USGA events including Amateurs and Mid-Amateurs (I have never qualified, but that didn't stop me from trying) and currently holding a 2.4 index, he disappeared into the clubhouse. A few minutes later, a tall, respectable gentleman wearing a coat and tie came to the tee box. Colin Montgomery's father looked down at my five-feet-six-inches, from somewhere high above six feet, fixed me with a Scottish stare I would get to know over the coming week, and asked me directly, "Have you one to waste?" Being fully loaded with far too many golf balls to fit comfortably into my carry bag, I responded affirmatively.

He then said, "Hit your driver o'er that hillock," pointing to a tall mound between the first tee and the ocean. With slightly sweaty palms, and a crowd of twenty-five or so golfers watching, I managed to make a good swing and sent a fine drive directly over the hillock. Mr. Montgomery then turned to the starter and said, in a voice that carried clearly to the surrounding crowd, "Mr. Kahler is a fine amateur from the States and will be allowed to play the medal tees. Everyone else will play the regular tees." With that statement he turned and strode directly into the clubhouse. And I played Royal Troon from the medal tees.

The second event that day involved Payne Stewart. As we were teeing off on the seventh hole, a dogleg-right slightly downhill, the rain and wind simultaneously picked up. Stewart's group had moved off the fairway into two rain shelters on the left side of the hole. We hit our drives, then agreed to also seek shelter to allow the storm to pass. I had hit a great drive and was just a few yards behind another ball from the group in front of us. As we reached the shelter, our twosome was huddled in one shelter and Stewart's group in another. A few minutes later, Stewart's local caddie ran over to our shelter and said a few words to my caddie. My caddie then said to me, "Mr. Stewart would like to know if you would like a small wager: closest to the pin for a pound." I agreed. Not because I thought I could hit it closer than Payne Stewart, but I would have a great story to tell and it would only cost me a pound. Because we were a twosome, and more willing to brave the elements than Stewart's foursome, they invited us to play through as the rain and wind lessened. I hit a career shot, holding it into the wind, coming to rest within ten feet of the hole. As we walked to the green, Stewart's caddie came running out and handed my caddie a pound coin, which he, in turn, passed on to me.

I don't know whether Payne Stewart actually made the bet or provided the pound. The more I have learned about caddies in Scotland, the more likely it was the caddie himself who made and paid the bet. And I don't know how close Payne Stewart hit the ball to the hole; we went on to the famous Postage Stamp eighth hole before they resumed play. But I did leave a ball marker in the green where my ball had been on No. 7. And no one asked me for the pound back later. I use it to this day as my ball marker.

Jeff Kahler

The Day Mr. 59 Bottled Lightning

If you hit a bad shot, just tell yourself it is great
to be alive, relaxing and walking around on a
beautiful golf course. The next shot will be better.

Al Geiberger

Hundreds of men have run the mile in less than four minutes, and a couple more no doubt just started their finishing kicks as we speak. How many can you name? And who is the current record-holder?

We remember Roger Bannister, who did it first and did it for posterity. Talk about the four-minute barrier and you talk about Roger Bannister.

It's the same with Al Geiberger. He became the first player to break 60 on the PGA Tour, shooting a shocking 59 in the second round of the 1977 Memphis Classic. Seven golfers shot 60 on tour before 1977, including Sam Snead, but nobody plunged into the 50s until that one-hundred-degree afternoon in Memphis. Only two players have done it since, Chip Beck in 1991 at Las Vegas and David Duval in 1999 at Palm Springs.

The supremely modest Geiberger is Mr. 59, a superlative his agent alertly copyrighted. You can put it on his tombstone. Tell Tiger Woods if he starts to run out of goals there's always the 59, which Geiberger shot on a 7,249-yard, par-72 Colonial Country Club course that ranked among *Golf Digest*'s One Hundred Greatest Courses.

The tempo king hit every fairway and every green. He made eleven birdies and an eagle, holing a thirty-yard wedge shot. He took but twenty-three putts, the longest from forty feet to start his round; an amateur mathematician reckoned that Geiberger sank 166 feet worth of birdie putts.

I remember Johnny Miller remarking afterward that he never thought anybody could putt that well on those greens. "They're Bermuda grass, which means you have to hit everything very firmly and truly," he says. "And Al had a late starting time, which means they were tracked up. You just don't make twelve putts longer than ten feet!"

The closest score to 59 was 65.

Yes, there's a caveat. The fairways were so patchy after a severe winter that players were permitted to lift and clean the ball. Nobody is quite clear how many times Geiberger improved his lie. Playing partner Dave Stockton remembers that on several shots Geiberger did not need to touch the ball. Geiberger recalls perhaps being helped on one shot, the holed wedge.

The turning point was a snack.

With the field split, Geiberger's round began on the tenth hole, and at the fourteenth events heated up, literally. A fire had broken out in a nearby parking lot, and fire trucks, sirens shrieking, were arriving as cars burned. Then, a friend of Geiberger's, who lived alongside the fourteenth brought him some crackers heaped with peanut butter. The gangly Geiberger fights a low blood-sugar count with frequent protein fixes, and peanut butter is his favorite.

"The heat was making me weak," he said. "I needed a picker-upper, and the peanut butter did it. I played the next seven holes in eight under par."

After he birdied the last four holes on his front nine,

Geiberger began thinking about the tour record for consecutive birdies, which is eight. Shooting 59 didn't occur to him until he birdied his fifteenth hole and his rapidly swelling gallery began to chant, "59! 59! 59!"

He needed to birdie two of the last three holes.

He birdied No. 7, a par-5, with a pitch shot and nine-foot putt, but parred the eighth, two-putting from twenty feet. So it was all riding on the last hole, a 403-yard dogleg-left with a bunker lurking at the corner. Geiberger was a short, left-to-right driver. But the crowd was goading him into breaking out of his conservative nature, and he aimed straight at the bunker . . . and carried it, which he'd never done. His resulting 9-iron shot finished eight feet from the cup.

Geiberger told himself to get the ball to the hole whatever else he did. The putt was left to right and uphill—the type that's easy to misread or think you are misreading.

Geiberger rammed it into the heart of the hole.

Stockton, Geiberger's close friend and winning partner in the old CBS Classic, said later, "Berger came the closest I've seen him to getting excited. He got his fist halfway clenched."

Since the 59, Geiberger's life has taken unexpected turns, some for the better, some for the worse. He has divorced and remarried, lost a child to a drowning accident, undergone major surgery almost regularly and battled financial problems. He's always in the middle of one comeback or another, and yet he's won ten times in ten years on the senior tour.

Today a fifty-nine would shoot his age. Despite a life that appears from the outside to have been dominated by hardship, Geiberger considers himself a lucky man. If that sounds like Lou Gehrig, Mr. 59 is made of much the same stuff.

Nick Seitz

3

SPECIAL MOMENTS

The game has its sensuous pleasures, when you make the perfect swing and execute the shot precisely as you had planned it.

Peter Alliss

All the Good Things
Any Man Should Be

Golf puts a man's character on the anvil and his richest qualities—patience, poise and restraint— to the flame.

Billy Casper

I have to tell you honestly that I never believed Squeek wouldn't be back carrying my bag. Not for one minute. Not until the very end, when he was so sick he couldn't even open his eyes to say good-bye. It's selfish, I guess, but that's what it's like when you lose a friend.

He was diligent and conscientious and humble and simple and honest and all the good things any man should be.

I remember often I would invite him in to share our success, to set the clubs down for a minute and drink a victory beer in the locker room. "Don't worry, Squeek, come on in," I'd tell him when he hesitated. "If there's a fine, I'll pay it."

We shared dinner often, but there were other times I would offer and he would decline politely, saying he had other plans. But I knew he really didn't. It was just his way of stepping back, never trying to take too much.

On the road, I think he was more content to baby-sit my kids and order a pizza. He loved to sit and play with them, and I know they loved him, too. They don't understand why he's gone now, anymore than I do.

For him, the rewards were more private. It was enough for him to get the flag from the eighteenth hole after a win and tack it up on his wall at home.

Doing the job well, doing it thoroughly, that was paramount for Squeek. In our six years together, I think I questioned a yardage only once. Once. That's unheard of.

He was no expert on the golf swing, but he learned what to look for in my swing. "Watch that right elbow," he would say when I was getting frustrated on the practice range.

In tournament play, he always had a knack for knowing the right thing to say, even when that meant saying nothing at all. And he understood the nuances of competition as well as anyone I'd ever met. He would always check the leader boards, and he could see a player struggling long before I would.

"He's feeling the pressure, Nick," he'd say as we headed down the last few holes, convincing me that a tournament still could be won.

He'd never let me get negative. At Turnberry in 1994, I had two terrible days of practice, but he never lost confidence in me. When I said, "Aww, I'm not swinging so well," immediately he pulled me up on it. "How can you expect me to be positive when you start talking like that?" he would demand.

When I asked Squeek at the end of 1990 to come work for me, he said Tom Watson had just asked him the same thing. A few days later, he came to me and said I was his choice. I sometimes wonder how different things might have been for me had that decision gone the other way.

We had one hell of a time together, I know that. I might have won without him, but it wouldn't have been nearly as often or nearly as fun.

The moment that stands out most for me was winning the Open at Turnberry. Squeek cheered me on through all the doubts of that final round. When I had to hit that last shot to clinch it, Squeek was never more positive, giving me the exact yardage and telling me to split the "D" in the big yellow sign behind the eighteenth green. When I had hit the shot and started up toward the green, the walk of a champion with the great crowd cheering, Squeek lingered behind humbly, typically, not wanting to intrude. I stopped for a moment and looked back at him.

"C'mon, Squeek," I said. "Let's enjoy this together. I don't know when we'll get the opportunity again."

If I never win again, I will always have the memory of that walk, shared with a friend.

Nick Price
with Mike Stachura

Ike, Mamie, Spiro and Me

I've never been to heaven and, thinkin' back on my life, I probably won't get a chance to go. I guess the Masters is as close as I'm going to get.

Fuzzy Zoeller

As every player knows, each round of golf is subject to small miracles, moments when probability upends itself in glorious fashion and a thing occurs that shouldn't, according to the odds.

I've had my share of golf miracles, certainly—some good and some bad. I once had a hole-in-one on an unfamiliar course, wearing cowboy boots and playing with borrowed clubs and a range ball. I once came within inches of a double eagle on a shot that hit a concrete drainage pipe in a water hazard. On at least three occasions I have putted out-of-bounds, and twice I've putted into water hazards. Once I even lost a ball on a putt—which I still take to be a true milestone of statistical improbability.

But all these things pale before the astronomical odds of my most unlikely golf experience, one that had nothing to do with the rub of the green or the skill of any shot. When I was nineteen years old, I was the beneficiary of a happy chain of events involving tree surgery, the Civil War and the U.S. Secret Service, all of which culminated, weirdly enough, in my playing two rounds at the Augusta National Golf Club during the week of the 1971 Masters.

It started in the spring of my junior year of high school, when I was able to parlay my considerable employment experience in odd jobs into a better, more responsible position: I became the tree trimmer for the double-decker-bus tours in Gettysburg, Pennsylvania, that bastion of Civil War tourism. My role was to ride the upper deck on the fifteen-mile route and cut back any branches that might poke a tourist in the eye.

A few weeks later, something even better opened up: The Secret Service had been authorized to hire a yard boy/gardener to mow the grass and tend the flower beds on the Eisenhower farm—as well as to care for the General's backyard putting green.

General Dwight D. Eisenhower had retired to Gettysburg after his presidency, partly because of its distinction as a shrine of military history, but partly for sentimental reasons—he had been stationed there at Camp Colt early in his career.

On those days when you ended up standing around with him in the golf shop or chatting on the first tee, he was always a genial, accessible guy who loved to talk golf with golfers. Two of his Secret Service agents, in fact, were picked specifically because they shared his love of the game.

Well, it seemed to me that my bus-tour duties could pass for gardening experience, and I sure knew what a putting green was supposed to look like. I figured I was a natural for the job. So I talked to the Secret Service agents about it, and Herb Dixon, the Special Agent in Charge, hired me immediately. He was clearly impressed by my background in high-level plant defoliation.

Okay, it might have helped a little that my father was one of the agents on the Eisenhower detail and was the General's primary golf partner. But in any case, I got the job. The pay was two dollars an hour. I was in heaven.

Every day there would be stretches of free time, and that's when I would get out my golf clubs and practice chip shots to the putting green. The Eisenhowers didn't seem to mind. On the hotter afternoons, they would even send out lemonade.

The General passed away early one spring, and I stayed on as the yard boy to the end of the summer. September brought new priorities, and I had to quit the farm to focus on my schoolwork. Journalism was my main academic interest, though in the end academics played no role at all in my choice of college. I applied to Wake Forest University because it was the most prominent golf school I knew.

I soon found there was no shortage of golfers around campus. You couldn't throw a 9-iron without beaning some scratch handicapper. Lanny Wadkins was there, and Jim Simons, and later Jay Haas, Scott Hoch, Curtis Strange and a dozen others who could play the game like no kids I had ever seen before. Any one of them seemed to stand an infinitely better chance of being invited to play at Augusta than I did.

However.

I got the call from my father on the weekend before the Masters. Even though the General was gone, Mrs. Eisenhower still maintained their yearly schedule. Springtime always included a stay at the Augusta National Golf Club, in a house near the eighteenth green.

Mrs. Eisenhower didn't have any interest in the game, but she remembered that I did—probably from all the divots I had left in her yard. It had occurred to her, my father reported, that maybe I would like to visit for a few days before the tournament. She had noticed that the course was almost always deserted, so she saw no reason why I couldn't just stop in and play a few rounds. She said I could bunk with the Secret Service agents in her basement.

There were other factors for me to consider, of course. The timing couldn't have been worse. It was midterm, and I had tests to take and research papers to type. I had no choice but to decline the invitation.

Yeah, right.

Ten minutes after I hung up the phone I was in my car heading south. I drove straight through to Augusta.

I arrived on Sunday afternoon and was ushered through the front gate by a guard who found my name on a list. The parking area near the clubhouse had only a scattering of cars, but they were all shiny Jaguars, Mercedes and BMWs—plus a few others so exotic I didn't even know their names. The only Bentley I've ever seen was in that lot, and the only Aston-Martin, outside a James Bond movie. Mine was the only Ford Maverick.

After checking in with my father and Mrs. Eisenhower, I asked about the possibility of rushing out for a round before dark. Here was a setback: Hadn't I noticed it was pouring rain? The course was closed for the afternoon.

But rain or no rain, I knew there must be a practice area somewhere, so I shouldered my clubs and my shag bag and went out to find it.

Only one other golfer was practice-hungry enough to be out that day—a big, sturdy fellow virtually cocooned in rain gear—and I joined him in one of the bunkers. For twenty minutes we alternated shots to the pin, blasting ball after ball until our side of the practice green was white with trails of wet sand.

He finished before I did, but as a matter of etiquette I stopped hitting shots and walked onto the green to help separate the balls. That turned out to be an easy enough chore: most of his were right by the pin.

"You're pretty good with that sand wedge," I told him.

He looked up and smiled.

"Thanks," he said.

It was Jack Nicklaus.

I tried, of course, to remain cool, but it was useless. There was no way I could go on casually hitting practice balls with him, not without risking total golf humiliation.

So I opted for a simpler form of humiliation, pestering him with awestruck idle chatter until at last I drove him from the practice green. Yes, I alone succeeded where thunder and lightning had failed.

I slept fitfully that night, but when morning came I was up with the sun—and the sun, thank God, was indeed up. That morning there were only two groups scheduled to go off: former U.S. Amateur champion Steve Melnyk had a 10 o'clock tee time; I was to follow at 10:15 with my father and another Secret Service agent.

But at 9:45, I experienced one of the most bizarre episodes of my life.

Just as I was walking out the rear basement door, one of the younger agents—a nongolfer—stopped me with the news that Mrs. Eisenhower wanted to see me upstairs. My timetable was suddenly in jeopardy. Still, what choice did I have? I stepped out of my golf shoes and walked up the basement steps into the living room, where a window overlooked the eighteenth green and, beyond that, the first tee.

Mrs. Eisenhower was standing by the window in a big, flowery dress. A man in a suit stood next to her, gazing at the lush, empty course. I hesitated in the doorway, but she saw me at once and called out, "Come in, come in.

There's someone here you have to meet."

The man in the business suit turned from the window smiling, and shook my hand in a very solid, professional way.

"This is Mr. Agnew, dear," she said. "He's the vice president."

I don't remember much of the conversation that followed. I do recall apologizing for not wearing any shoes. I also recall that he talked about the country's need for more young Republicans like me. That struck me as odd, since I wasn't a Republican. I mean, I wasn't anything. I was just a golfer.

I do know he had a lot to say about the grave state of American youth and how we could fix it—hard work was part of it, I think he said, and respect for one's elders, fewer Beatles songs, a less liberal press—but most of the details were lost on me because the longer he talked, the more I wondered why he didn't have anything to say about golf. Didn't he know where he was?

Then came the moment when I failed my generation.

"What's your view on all this?" Mr. Agnew finally asked.

If only I could have told him some inspiring story, maybe offered some brilliant insight into the American psyche that would have set him thinking along some bright new path. At the very least I could have suggested he might want to glance through the Constitution one more time before launching any new projects. After all, Watergate was more than a year away, there was still time to head off disaster; no one yet needed to go to jail or resign in disgrace. But at that very moment, through that glaring picture window my only view was of Steve Melnyk hooking his drive into trees on the left side of the first fairway.

"I'm really sorry, Mr. Vice President," I said, "but I'm next on the tee." By the time Melnyk had found his ball and hit his approach shot, I was back in my golf shoes, shaking hands with George, my caddie.

Caddies were required at Augusta, and they wore uniforms slung with various belts and pouches containing grass seed, fertilizer and soil. You don't replace your divots at Augusta; instead, your caddie re-landscapes after each shot. This was intimidating—I kept topping the ball so George wouldn't have to clean up after me. George talked me through that crisis, and countless others. He didn't keep me out of trouble—no one could have done that—but in eighteen holes he never mis-clubbed me. If everybody in the workforce were as skilled and conscientious on the job as the Augusta caddies, there would be a worldwide Golden Age.

Of course, I was skeptical at first. After I hit my drive on the first hole, George handed me a 6-iron before I had left the tee box.

"How do you know I'll need a 6-iron?" I asked him.

He shrugged as he slid my driver back into the bag. "Tell from your swing," he said matter-of-factly.

"But you've only seen me hit one shot," I pointed out.

He shrugged again and started down the fairway. I followed him to my ball and saw that he was right: A 6-iron was indeed the club.

I was impressed enough to start asking questions—not about my shots, but about George. I couldn't help but be nosy. Here was a true insider.

George had been at Augusta for fifteen years, he told me, and had caddied in fourteen Masters.

"Who's the best golfer you've ever caddied for?" I asked, hoping to get a few juicy stories.

"Best is hard," he said. "Best comes and goes. Right now the man I put my money on is Mr. Charles Coody."

Charles Coody? This was a pretty disappointing answer. Charles Coody was essentially a rank-and-file pro.

"Mr. Coody was my man last year," George went on. "We were right in it, too. Could have won it if he'd done a couple more things I told him to." George shook his head and smiled. "But this year—you just watch. Me and Mr. Coody. That's the team."

I decided not to argue, though it would have been easy enough to rattle off a long list of more likely candidates for that year's green coat. Instead, I asked George what he could predict for a player like me on this course.

"Low 90s," he said without hesitation. "That's the best I can do."

"But I'm a 2-handicapper," I protested.

George nodded his head as if he had already figured that into the equation.

"I'm bound to break 90," I insisted.

"Next round, maybe," he said. "Not today. Not off championship tees. Couple good holes, though. Maybe a couple birdies."

Much of that round, I regret to say, has faded from memory. But certain moments remain. The greens were fast as linoleum, and I shook over every putt. On the 205-yard fourth hole, I hit the green in regulation, then took a triple bogey with a five-putt. On other holes, I found pathways to destruction: I hit into the creek on the twelfth and lost two balls in the azaleas on the thirteenth. But I came back with birdies on the fifteenth and six-teenth, which, even without TV cameras, was the pinnacle of my golf life.

I shot a 92.

The next day I had another crack at it, and managed an 88.

High scores notwithstanding, this was an idyllic stretch of days. I hung around the clubhouse with Phil Walil, the club manager. I walked Augusta's Par-3 Course, favored by General Eisenhower. I met the stern-faced Cliff Roberts, a cofounder of the Augusta National with Bobby Jones, and of whom everyone was afraid. ("Don't annoy this guy," my father warned me. "He'd kick us all out in a heartbeat.")

Then, as suddenly as it had begun, it ended: just one sunny day before the opening round of that year's Masters, I had to pack up and leave. Mrs. Eisenhower, as I said, had no particular interest in golf. For her the tournament was an inconvenient interruption in her routine, a time when her lawn would be overrun by tourists, golfers and television crews. So she had the Secret Service load up, and they all set out for Palm Springs.

I had no choice but to buy a couple of souvenirs and hit the road myself. Everything about the experience had been wonderful. Standing by my car, looking one last time at that stately clubhouse, I was keenly aware I would never play there again, not if I lived to be two hundred.

And for a quarter of a century, that prediction has held true. But oddly enough, I'm not as pessimistic about my chances for a comeback. Something happened that Masters weekend that made me realize just about anything could come true. This revelation came to me while I was sitting alone in my dorm room watching the final-round coverage on a twelve-inch black-and-white television set. The golf world was shocked that year—I was, too—by one more Augusta miracle: A middling pro playing the rounds of his life had somehow walked off with the title.

The Masters' champion that year, some of us will recall, was Mr. Charles Coody.

Clint McCown

The Day I Met the King

I'll always remember how I first met him. It was in my rookie year of 1977. Coincidentally, it occurred at a tournament that has become very special to me through the years, the Bing Crosby Pro-Am. We had the Monday qualifying system back then, and I had missed the first two qualifiers at Phoenix and Tucson. I had finally made it into my first official PGA Tour event at the Crosby and was out playing a practice round at Monterey Peninsula Country Club, one of the courses used in the rotation at the time.

It was late Tuesday afternoon before the tournament, and I had played the front nine and was somewhere on the back side when I noticed a large cloud of dust billowing up in the distance. It was like in the old cowboy movies when there's a cattle drive or the posse's ridin' up on the bad guys, and I knew something important was happening. But I went about my business and, sensing I didn't have time to finish all eighteen holes, I cut over to the sixteenth tee.

As this was my first time on the course, I really didn't know the layout of the holes. I just knew I had about half an hour of sunlight left. So I hit a couple drives off the sixteenth, when all of a sudden, out of nowhere, an incredible throng of spectators emerged over the rise behind me and surrounded the back of the tee.

It was like when the entire Bolivian army encircled Butch Cassidy and the Sundance Kid and aimed their rifles at them. These people weren't armed and dangerous, but they were sure looking at me with expressions that said:

Who is this kid, and what's he doing out here?

And then the Red Sea parted, and who should walk through it but Arnold Palmer himself, The King. He couldn't have been more regal had he been wearing a robe and carrying a staff.

I felt a chill come over me. I was shocked and embarrassed. I mean, here was my boyhood idol, and I'd just cut right in front of him, and hit two balls no less. I wanted to crawl into the ball-washer and disappear. But true to his character, Palmer walked up to me, shook my hand, introduced himself and said, "How are you?"

I managed to squeak out a "fine," although I wasn't. And he said, "Could we join you?"

Now that was the first thing he ever said to me, and it struck me so funny because I was thinking, "Can *you* join *me*?" What I wanted to say was, "Can I have your permission to crawl under a rock and stay there for a day as penance for getting in your way?"

But, of course, I acted cool, considered his request for a long second, and said, "Sure, love to have you," like it was no big deal.

This was gut-check time, even if there was no money on the line, because in addition to meeting my idol for the first time, I also met Mark McCormack, who was Palmer's amateur partner. McCormack was head of IMG, with whom I had signed just a few weeks before, but I wasn't sure he even knew who I was.

Nevertheless, I was determined not to let the situation intimidate me, or worry about embarrassing myself. I've always loved the challenge of golf, whatever it may be, so I looked on this as just another challenge, and a darned good preparation for the coming week. After all, this was just a practice round, so I couldn't worry about future endorsements, or impressing these guys. My goal at that point in my career was simple survival. All I wanted to do was make some cuts, make some money and keep my playing privileges. I was recently married and I wanted to be able to make it to that Christmas and have enough money to buy my wife a nice present.

But back to the sixteenth hole. Arnold hit a nice drive, and I remember feeling good that both of my drives were past his. If I felt a moment of cockiness, however, it quickly evaporated when I snap-hooked a 7-iron into the bunker. Fortunately, I got it up and down, and that eased my nerves. On the next tee, Arnold asked me what kind of ball I was playing, and I told him it was a Titleist.

He said, "You ought to try one of these good balls," and tossed me a Palmer ball. I hit it and liked it, so he tossed me a three-pack and said, "As a rookie starting out, you need good equipment, and these might help you along the way." He was sincerely trying to be helpful, because it wasn't as if he needed the endorsement of an unknown kid from Oregon playing his golf balls.

As abruptly as the experience of playing golf with Arnold Palmer had begun, so it ended. After holing out at 18, Palmer thanked me, wished me luck in my career and disappeared into the madding crowd. When I looked up a few seconds after shaking his hand, everyone was gone. I mean everyone. There was no more Arnie's Army, only Peter's Poltergeists. I had to shake my head to make certain it had really happened.

Peter Jacobsen
with Jack Sheehan

The Price of Success

Success came late for golf pro Harvey Penick. His first golf book, *Harvey Penick's Little Red Book,* has sold more than a million copies, which makes it one of the biggest things in the history of sports books. His second book, *And If You Play Golf, You're My Friend,* has already sold nearly three-quarters of a million copies. But anyone who imagines that Penick wrote the books to make money didn't know the man.

In the 1920s Penick bought a red spiral notebook and began jotting down observations about golf. He never showed the book to anyone except his son until 1991, when he shared it with a local writer, Bud Shrake, and asked if he thought it was worth publishing. Shrake read it and told him yes. He left word with Penick's wife the next evening that Simon & Schuster had agreed to an advance of ninety thousand dollars.

When Shrake saw Penick later, the old man seemed troubled. Finally Penick came clean. With all his medical bills, he said, there was just no way he could advance Simon & Schuster that much money. The writer had to explain that Penick would be the one to receive the ninety thousand dollars.

Terry Todd

My Best Friend

The agony of the final round set in off the first tee. It wasn't Sunday. There was no tournament. It was just me and Matt, my golf partner of three years, not to mention my best friend since the third grade.

We had entered the world of golf as two youngsters with cheap clubs, inspired by our fathers' stories of birdies, three-hundred-yard drives, and near-holes-in-one. For some reason these tales failed to hold true when we played with them.

Expecting to go out and conquer the game, Matt and I were quite surprised (not to mention angry) when we found ourselves humbled by a little white ball. Over time though, our swings became more controlled, good shots became more frequent, scores lower and our friendship stronger.

That summer, we entered a junior golf tour. We soon realized how much we had to learn, and how much we wanted to win. We had been in the game for two years already, and we figured all we needed was some fine-tuning to give our game the extra edge.

We played almost every day after school that year with the hope that the hard work would pay off with victory on the tour next summer. Then we got the news.

"Andrew, my dad's being transferred to Charlotte right after school," Matt said when he broke the news to me. He was moving away following our freshman year and right before the golf season would start. We had only a month left together, so we decided to make the most of it. Golf was the only way we knew how to enjoy ourselves without facing the sorrow of separation. No matter what is going on, golf helps you forget by making you concentrate on the task at hand—beating the guy you're playing with—and that was good enough for us.

We played and the time flew, and soon we found ourselves in what we realized was our final round together. We had tried to ignore it for so long, but now it hung over us. The only way to shake it was to continue the eighteen.

When all was said and done, we finished the game. Our scores were average. He beat me by three strokes.

Matt had to be home so he could wake up early in the morning and head out. We stood at the practice green waiting for his mother to come get him. Finally, she arrived.

"It was a pleasure playing with you." I held out my hand. He shook, and then I half-hugged him, like boys do when they want to be men. I saw him off the next morning.

He played on a tour at his new home, and I competed also. One day, I received a letter in the mail. It was a scorecard and a picture of the leader board. Matt was atop it. He finally won.

Over the years, I received many scorecards from Matt (unfortunately more than I sent him). I keep them in my golf bag for good luck.

I guess the magic of golf isn't the course, or the swing, or the sound you hear when you hit a solid 3-iron. It's the feeling you get when you beat your best friend, or lose to him, for that matter.

And sooner or later you realize that you didn't play every week because you were golfers, you played because you were friends.

Andrew Galanopulos

Butterscotch

It isn't the big pleasures that count the most; it's making a great deal out of the little ones.

Jean Webster

My father did not start playing golf until he was in his sixties. He used to practice putting balls into plastic cups and coffee mugs on the rug in his family room while watching the Sunday tournaments on television. He used to boast about how he had sunk fifteen of these putts in a row. I used to watch him perform these putting exercises and watched his concentrated eye focusing on the mug at the end of the room, taking two or three practice strokes, and then following through with mechanical precision, making only minor adjustments to his swing when the balls would career off the edges of the mug. I did see him make about four or five in a row at one point, but unfortunately not fifteen.

My father did not have the best all-around golf game, but he did have an acute eye for putting. If he had started a little earlier in life, he may have even become a better and more complete player. But, his love of being outside in the sun and the long walks for exercise and the competition we shared on the course, that was what really made him enjoy this game. Nonetheless he would reward himself for any minor victory on the golf course with a piece of butterscotch candy. The candies were not only rewards for him, but for myself or anybody else who played a hole nicely. If someone sank the tough ten-footer from the rough or even just the two-footer to win the match, a butterscotch candy was his way of saying "Nice job." As long as something was done on the course that impressed him, a butterscotch candy was the victor's spoils.

When my father reached his early seventies he developed Alzheimer's disease. His world and my family's were suddenly turned upside down. His concept of time had been wiped out, his memory was fleeting at best and his independent life was soon coming to a close.

In the beginning stages of his sickness, we would still make the occasional trek to the golf course. I did not know exactly what to expect at this point and really just characterized the memory lapses and spatial imperfections as symptomatic of old age. The frustrations of my father's illness combined with the challenge of the game made it a very tough morning.

"Dad, Dad, Dad! This way!" That's all I seemed to be yelling as my father in the midst of disorientation would face the opposite direction of the holes and begin to tee up. I had to physically grab him and turn him in the right direction at some holes. When I put my hands on his waist and turned him around I could feel how lost this man had become and how dependent on me he was. It felt at times like I was playing with a small child who had never stepped on the golf course before in his life.

I remember watching him walk, or better yet shuffle, around the fairway in a half-hearted attempt to find his ball, truth being he had no idea where it was. "Dad, it's over there!" I would yell and point, simultaneously waving ahead another foursome that was playing behind us.

The afternoon seemed to drag along more and more. The fifteenth hole was upon us and I had finally reached the green in about six and was prepared to putt. I had dropped a ball for my father in front of the approach just to speed up our play and let him poke it onto the green. I stood behind my ball waiting for him to chip. He had three weak digs at the ball before it finally scooted onto the green about six inches directly in front of my ball! He wore a little smile as he awkwardly shuffled around the green and waited for me to putt.

We stood and looked at each other almost comically for a few seconds—then I lost it. "Dad, mark your ball!" He still wore a face of delusion and disorientation as he meekly patted his pockets for a marker. He pulled out tees and balls—but no marker. He sensed my frustration mounting and I started to let my impatience seep into my expression.

Eventually he pulled something out of his pocket. I watched him reach down and pick up his ball and replace it with one of his butterscotch candies. He put it down and did not have the slightest clue what he had just done. The candy stood right in my putting line, the circular candy only a little bit smaller than the ball itself, its shiny gold cellophane wrapper reflecting sun and sitting so stupidly on the green.

I looked up at him and he was not even looking back at me. He was just looking around at the trees, at other golfers, wherever. I looked at him and started to laugh. I laughed hard. He looked back at me, then he looked at the candy sitting on the green. He laughed too.

The last three holes we played that day were some of the most memorable ones I have had playing this game. We both still played lousy the rest of the day, but we had fun, and my father and I would both have small awakenings amidst the green. He was freed from the delusions and disorientation of Alzheimer's for a couple of hours, and I was freed from the grasp of taking this game way too seriously.

That would be the last time I would ever play golf with my father, but it was the best time. The game became simple and fun for me again and he gave me that. Now, there are no more temptations to throw clubs or curse out loud or come home after a weekend of golfing upset because "I lost my swing." From now on, I take my time and I have fun—in all aspects of life. I carry a butterscotch candy on me whenever I play golf and even when I realize I am getting terribly frustrated with this game, I reach in my pocket for the butterscotch and remember that day on the course with my father—and laugh. I now enjoy golf and I am better at it. I am a pretty good putter now, too. I sank fifteen in a row in the coffee mug just a couple of days ago. Really, I did.

A. J. Daulerio

Last Will and Testament

Don't be too proud to take lessons. I'm not.

Jack Nicklaus

In his first forty years of golf Jack Nicklaus had but one teacher. That man, Jack Grout, died in 1989 at the age of seventy-eight from cancer.

Nicklaus was only ten when he met Grout in 1950 at the Scioto Country Club in Columbus, Ohio. Grout, an Oklahoman, had become the club's head pro that year. He'd turned pro at fifteen, in 1925, and in 1930 accompanied his brother Dick to the Glen Garden Country Club in Dallas. Ben Hogan, then seventeen, and Byron Nelson, then eighteen, were junior members. The threesome practiced mornings and played three or four times a week in the afternoon.

Grout, Hogan and Nelson took to the road to follow the Tour. They drove a roadster from tournament to tournament, tying their clubs on the side of the car. Up and down the West Coast they went. Grout lasted until 1957 on the Tour, the last seven years while working at Scioto, where Nicklaus's father Charlie belonged.

The elder Nicklaus asked if he could enroll his ten-year-old son in Grout's two-hour Friday junior clinic. Young Jackie enrolled all right; he was the first to register and was always the first youngster on the tee. Soon Grout was asking his young protégé to demonstrate certain points about the swing.

The rest, as they say, is history, where Nicklaus is concerned. He went on to become probably the best golfer ever. And Grout was always at his side. Grout and Nicklaus went over the swing from A to Z at the start of every season. Meanwhile, they became close friends.

In the way of the world, Grout died precisely at 7:45 A.M., on Saturday, May 13. That was Nicklaus's scheduled starting time in the third round of his own Memorial Tournament at his own Muirfield Village Golf Club near Columbus, where Grout was also the professional emeritus. "J. Grout," Nicklaus always called him, and now J. Grout was gone.

Said Nicklaus: "Jack was like a second father to me. He was part of our family. . . . He taught me how to play the game and he's been at my side whenever I needed him."

Grout also had something to say. Item 6 of his Last Will and Testament was handed to Nicklaus soon after Grout died. The document tells it all.

"Having heretofore disposed of all my worldly goods, I have just one final bequest I should like to make. If there is anytime at all in the life of a man when he should make an extra effort to be truthful, and at the same time sincere, I think it must be while he is preparing his Last Will and Testament. What I have to say in the next few words comes straight from my heart.

"Over the course of the past thirty years or so, from time to time I have read in various books and magazines about the contributions I have made to the career of Jack Nicklaus. Since this may be my last opportunity to do so,

I thought maybe it would be well to set the record straight.

"In all honesty I don't think I ever hurt Jack's golf game in any way. To put it another way, if he had not come under my tutelage in the early 1950s I don't see how he could have turned out much better than he did. From the outset of our relationship I recognized that the thunder in his stroke and the courage in his heart were gifts that clearly had been bestowed upon him; and that there was very little I could do to take them away from him.

"I do not mean to suggest that I made no contribution whatsoever to his game. For one thing, I worked him hard (and he seemed to enjoy every minute of it). I made him stand away from the ball with his arms fully extended, and I insisted that he swing hard. Within a few months you could hear the swish of his clubhead all over the practice range when he took one of his legendary cuts at the ball. I made sure that his posture was correct; I fitted him correctly with equipment; from time to time I would check his grip, or maybe the rhythm of his swing. I always tried to encourage him; and in the very early days of his development I made a special effort to explain to him and interpret for him how extraordinary I thought his talents were, and for that matter still are.

"If I made any other worthwhile contributions, which I can't think of now, or if I made any of which I may be unaware, I am grateful that I had the opportunity to do so. There is not the slightest doubt in my mind that Jack Nicklaus is the finest golfer ever to swing a club in the entire history of the game. It has been a distinct honor and great pleasure for me to have played some part in his career. And that brings me to my final bequest.

"To you, Jack Nicklaus, I give my thanks."

Lorne Rubenstein

Babe in the Woods

If I don't celebrate the exquisiteness of each day, I've lost something I will never get back.

Sally P. Karioth

A large crowd had gathered around the first tee by the time Babe Ruth shambled out of the golf shop at the Poland Springs, Maine, resort in the summer of 1940. He was a moderately heavy man, deeply tanned, with alert dark eyes and sloping shoulders. He was immaculately dressed; a woman's fancy bobby pin held his forelock in place. I was a teenager at the resort's caddie camp, made up mostly of boys off the streets of Boston's South End. The Babe had just finished a charity golf match near Boston and had come to Maine for some private time. I had been chosen to be his caddie.

He approached me and handed me a small, square, unlabeled bottle filled with a brown liquid. "This is medicine," he said. "Be careful of it." I tucked the bottle into the golf bag between some clean woolen socks, and we walked onto the first tee.

The crowd and photographers backed off, and the Babe

smashed a booming drive that almost reached the green over three hundred yards away. Throughout the afternoon the Babe, a lefty, hit towering arcs off every tee. But with almost every shot, he let loose a string of profanities in the most unexpected sequence. He was wild. Dangerously wild. We spent a lot of time in the woods and in the rough looking for his rockets. Even then, I lost three balls.

On the fourth hole, we were crashing through the woods alone when he asked for his medicine. I handed him the bottle, and he took a long swig. I sniffed it; it smelled suspiciously of rum.

At the eleventh hole's refreshment stand, an entourage awaited us, including Ruth's wife, Claire. She pranced around waving a lengthy cigarette holder and bussed Ruth with a big show-biz hug. Ruth bought soft drinks for everyone, including the four caddies. He summoned me for more medicine to mix with his Coke.

At the twelfth hole, I stood near his drive in the rough, waiting for the rest of the foursome. Ruth looked out at the distant mountains, the nearby lake and the flag flying atop the antique hotel. His huge face softened, and he leaned close, within six inches. "Gee," he whispered in that gravelly voice. "This is beautiful. So peaceful and quiet. Isn't it wonderful?"

That was the last respite. At the thirteenth hole, the crowds reappeared, and we were once again in the center ring. I'm not certain of the Babe's final score, though I think he finished in the mid-80s with a few "gimme" putts. And I don't recall exactly what he paid me for the caddie fee. In those days, seventy-five cents was the going rate. I do recall that despite the three lost balls, Babe tipped me five dollars, a monumental sum. Then he gave me a short wave good-bye and disappeared into the clubhouse.

An hour later I saw him at the baseball field near the hotel, posing for the cameras with some players. The crowd stood back, clapping, as flashbulbs popped. A small smile was fixed on his muffin face; the mighty Bambino was back on stage, performing for his public. The quiet moment we'd shared at the twelfth hole seemed far off and forgotten. Then he spotted me in the crowd and winked.

Tom Turley

Frank and Ernest

© 1978 Thaves/Newspaper distribution by NEA, Inc.

Reprinted by permission of Newspaper Enterprise Association, Inc.

The Lunar Golf Shot

Have you ever thought about hitting a driver 1500 yards or a 6-iron 900 yards? Or watching a white ball against a black sky with a time of flight of twenty-five to thirty seconds? What golfer even dares dream of these things?

I thought about these things during *Apollo 14* in 1971. You see, the moon has one-sixth the gravity of Earth. That means with the same clubhead speed, the ball will go six times as far and stay in the air (or in this case the vacuum) six times as long!

Actually, Bob Hope gave me the idea of playing golf on the moon, although he didn't know about it until months after the flight. He was visiting NASA one day—Deke Slayton and I were showing him around—and he had an old driver that he was swinging as we walked around the campus. We hooked him up in a moon walker and as he was bouncing up and down on his toes, he used the driver for balance! That's when I said, only to myself, I had to find a way to hit a ball on the moon.

Perhaps people on Earth watching me on television thought it was spontaneous and unauthorized, but it was well-rehearsed and all approved before we launched.

I had planned to use a collapsible aluminum handle, which we normally used to scoop up dust samples, since we really couldn't bend over in a pressurized suit. And then I had a golf pro design a clubhead to snap on the handle, replacing the small scoop. It was a number 6-iron since the handle was about as long as a normal 6-iron shaft. I planned to take the clubhead and two ordinary golf balls in my suit pocket—at no expense to the taxpayers!

I practiced before the flight several times in the suit-training room to be sure I could swing safely. The pressurized suit is cumbersome and I couldn't get both hands on the club; still I could make a half swing with one hand. And, finally, I checked with the "boss" and told him my plan to hit two golf balls at the very end of the lunar stay, only if everything went perfectly up to that point. He agreed.

Fortunately, although we had some problems earlier, everything went just right while we were on the surface. Consequently, just before climbing up the ladder to come home, I prepared to tee off! When I dropped the first ball, it took about three seconds to land, and bounced a couple of times in the gray dust. Then, I improved my lie of course (winter rules in February) and made my best slow-motion, one-handed half-swing. Making a full swing in a space suit is impossible. I made good contact and the ball, which would have gone thirty to forty yards on Earth, went over 200 yards. The ball stayed up in the black sky almost thirty seconds. I was so excited I swung harder on the second one, which I shanked about forty yards into a nearby crater! I decided to call that a hole-in-one, even if the hole was several miles in diameter.

So I folded up the golf club and climbed up the ladder to take off. The two golf balls are still there and ready to be reclaimed and reused—after all, they were new. But the club resides in a place of honor at the U.S. Golf

Association in Far Hills, New Jersey, where all who see it can imagine, as did I, what a 1500-yard tee shot would really be like!

Alan Shepard
As told to Carol Mann

[EDITORS' NOTE: *Alan Shepard was the first American launched in space, in 1961. Ten years later, he commanded* Apollo 14 *and became the fifth man to walk on the moon—and the first to play golf there.*]

The Special Gift

Sean was just a little kid, about eight years old. When I first met him one summer day he wore a Chicago Bulls cap and baggy shorts that needed a belt. He carried a bag stocked with four clubs and plenty of balls. Once when he took off his cap, I noticed he had no hair. He was a lot smaller than other kids his age. Still, he always seemed to be smiling whenever I would see him with his pals, trying his darndest to hit as far as they did.

I played with Sean once in a while. He told me that he always had the best chance when playing a par-3 because he could usually make it to the green.

A year or so passed and I hadn't seen Sean around the course. I had heard that his cancer was getting the best of him. Still, his friends said he was going to try to get out and play a few times before fall.

Sure enough, he was there the following week. My group went out just ahead of him. I noticed that one of his buddies was carrying Sean's bag. "Watch out!" I heard Sean tell his pals. "I feel kinda lucky today!"

Despite his words, Sean was having an awful time trying to drive the ball. He and his friends arrived at the last par-3. His friends had all hit, and Sean was up on the tee.

He brought his club back and hit the ball as hard as his fragile body would allow. It flew up to the green and out of sight. One of his friends helped Sean walk up to the green. It was a tough walk because the green was higher than the tee. I could see Sean searching for his ball as he stopped to catch his breath.

Sean's buddies were looking for their balls behind the green. Out of the corner of my eye I saw one of his friends pick up Sean's ball and drop it in the hole. Then he ran and pretended to look for his own ball. He caught me staring at him and winked.

When Sean finally got to the green he was disappointed because he thought he hit over. Then he glanced in the hole. What a smile lit up his face! The boys looked at each other and said, "You can't tell me it's a hole-in-one!" "No way, Sean, that you put it in there!"

"No, really! Look!" he said. They all acted surprised and as I watched, I thought Sean looked like the happiest guy I had ever seen. I never saw Sean or his friends after that day. But it was then that I learned just what golf should be.

It's not about what score you get or how far you drive. It is about caring for the friends you play with and enjoying the time you have with them.

Adel Guzzo

The Caddie and the
Unspoken Understanding

*Make friends with your caddie and the game
will make friends with you.*

Stephen Potter

Peering eagerly from among the shadows in the far-
thest corner of the clubhouse porch are our new caddies.
They are middle schoolers, mostly. The older ones pick
their teeth with tees and want to double-bag. The
younger ones fuss with jackets their mothers made them
wear. The caddies arrived early, just as the old-timers
were setting out with their squeaky pullcarts. With luck
they will get to spend the rest of the morning earning fifteen dollars and a free round on Monday.

Before last spring, there had been no caddies at my club
for many years. In the 1930s, a man I sometimes play with
earned thirty-five cents a round—sixty cents for two
bags—and he once received a ten-dollar tip from "Light
Horse" Harry Cooper, who was in town for a wedding.

Last winter, our pro suggested we try again. Twenty
kids turned up for training—a good showing in a town

with a population of four thousand. The credit belongs to Tiger Woods, who among other feats has made golf attractive to sixth and seventh graders.

Caddying is known to be morally uplifting for adolescents. They earn wages competitive with those paid to baby-sitters, learn to bounce golf balls on the faces of pitching wedges and meet grown-ups who may one day give them some old irons or a job.

But the real beneficiaries are the golfers. Playing with young caddies allows adults to share the crises of juveniles without passing judgment, something that seldom happens at home. If your own child has a bad report card, you are likely to take it personally. If your caddie has a bad report card you are likely to share a story about a bad report card of your own. A golfer who is willing to listen will hear a lot—about a broken bike, a teacher who's a jerk, a test on stuff that wasn't in the book, a father who's lost his job, a dog that almost died, a mother who is dating someone nice. The golfer responds as an adult rather than a parent. There is the same unspoken understanding that there always is among golfers: What is discussed during the round will not leave the course.

Last Saturday, a new caddie carried the bag of a friend of mine. The caddie was a fifth grader but looked two years younger. The bag was nearly as tall as he was, and on hills he had to lift it by the handle to keep it from dragging on the ground. Rain fell most of the morning, and by the time we finished his hair was pasted flat, his shirt was soaked, his sneakers were sloshing and his legs were flecked with grass. My friend and I exchanged nervous glances over his head, anticipating the fury of his mother.

Next morning, I came out early to play again and scanned the faces on the porch, expecting not to find his. But there he was, leaning over the railing to get a better look at the first tee, his jacket already abandoned.

And he was smiling.

David Owen

Divots

Years ago, the caddies on the tours weren't nearly as professional as they are today. In fact, often they were just local kids without much experience or knowledge of the game. Julius Boros ran into just one such kid.

After hitting his approach to the first hole, Boros pointed to his divot and told the caddie to pick it up. As the round progressed, the boy fell farther and farther behind. Boros, thinking the caddie had become ill, asked him if he was feeling all right.

"Yes, sir, but I was just wondering what you want me to do with all these?" he said, opening the side pocket of Boros's bag, which was filled with divots.

Don Wade

"Let me guess, you and your caddie will be playing the
Water Nine today."

Reprinted with permission by Jerry King. Originally appeared in Golf Journal.

A Golfer's Best Friend

Animals are such agreeable friends—they ask no questions, they pass no criticisms.

George Eliot

Playing a round of golf with a friend is much more fun than playing alone. I learned this as a teenager when I played some memorable rounds of golf with my brother Don and my dad in my hometown of WaKeeney, Kansas. But then, as a member of the golf team at Fort Hays Kansas State University (Hays, Kansas), I quickly learned that to play well I had to practice long hours—alone. That's why I enjoyed our team's challenge and out-of-town matches—because I got to be among friends.

When I was graduated from Fort Hays State, I moved to Russell, Kansas, Bob Dole's hometown, to teach biology and coach at Russell High School. One of the reasons I chose teaching as a career was to have my summers free to play amateur tournament golf. Again, I found myself spending many, many hours practicing and playing rounds of golf by myself. So to break up the monotony, I decided to take along a friend—Mike, my boxer dog—for a few practice rounds.

Mike was a full-grown, powerfully built purebred boxer. Weighing seventy-five pounds, he was all muscle. He was energetic, unpredictable and playfully aggressive. He loved people and begged for attention from total strangers. He did nothing in a calm, easy way.

He was so impatient and rambunctious as a puppy that I taught him to sit until my wife or I fed him because he would knock us over trying to gobble up his food. It was a battle from the start. Finally, he got it. Begrudgingly, he'd sit for five minutes, drooling over his dish, waiting for my "Okay, Mike" signal. Then he'd attack his food like a wild animal.

As he grew older, I disciplined him by extending the waiting period to ten minutes or more, sometimes forgetting all about him. He never touched the food, but after ten minutes or so, he'd begin a mournful howl that prompted, "Okay, Mike!"

Oh, how he loved to run, jump and play outdoors! As a puppy when tied on a leash, he would eagerly sit for long periods waiting for someone to notice him. Then, when you looked at him, he'd jump straight up in the air about ten times, wiggling his whole body with excitement. That's when I thought of the "game."

I'd make Mike sit; then I'd step off about ten paces, pat my knees and shout, "Okay, Mike!" He'd charge toward me at full speed and leap high into the air. I'd step aside, hold out my arms, and catch him, his yucky tongue swabbing my face in delight. As he grew bigger, it took all my strength to catch and hold him.

Then I got a bright idea: Why not take him golfing with me? He'd get some exercise, I wouldn't have to walk him later and I could enjoy a round of golf at the same time. This worked very well for about six rounds. Then one day, an older gentleman about seventy, I'd guess, asked if he could join me for nine holes. I almost said no because of Mike, but then I knew he'd obey me and sit patiently while we hit our shots. So I agreed.

On the first tee, I positioned Mike behind the tee box and sternly said, "Sit!" He immediately sat ramrod straight, poised, tension mounting as he impatiently waited. The older man hit first and I followed. I decided to leave Mike there for a few more minutes, so he could bolt and run hard to catch up to us, a ritual we had practiced many times before.

After my playing partner hit his second shot, we arrived at my ball about 250 yards down the fairway. Just as I addressed the ball, the older gentleman said, "Hey, Bud, what about your dog?" Oops! Concentrating on my game, I'd forgotten all about Mike. I turned toward the tee box and yelled, "Oookkkaaayyy, Miiiikkee!"

He let out a yelp and bounded down the hill toward us. I marveled at his grace, power, speed and galloping fury. When he was about seventy-five yards away from me, I stepped away from my pull cart, so he would not injure himself smashing into my clubs. I knew he expected me to catch him as usual. I'd stopped that long ago. He sprinted so fast on the golf course now that when he jumped, I'd turn sideways, hold out my arms, then pull them back at the last second as he sailed by with a con-fused look on his face. He never quite understood how I could change the rules like that.

Mike was now just twenty yards away racing at full speed bearing down on me. Just then the unexpected hap-pened. The old man, getting caught up in the moment, slapped both his thighs and yelled, "Come 'ere, boy!"

"Nnoooooo!" I screamed, as Mike instantly changed course and blasted off about fifteen feet from the old man, expecting to be caught. He crashed into his chest, knocking him head over heels. Mike was happily licking the old guy's face when I got to him. He wasn't moving. I just knew he was dead.

I ordered Mike to "Sit!" while I nervously examined my dazed playing companion. In a couple of minutes, he opened his eyes. "Are you okay?" I asked, fearing the worst.

"I'm fine," he said. Then, glancing at Mike, he winked at me. "Kind of a spirited fellow, ain't he?"

"Yep," I said. "He's my exuberant golfing buddy."

"Well," he drawled, grinning. "With him along, you'll never get beat in match play."

Luckily, my disheveled partner sustained no permanent injuries. I know because my older friend and I played a few more rounds of golf that summer, but always *sans* Mike.

Bud Gardner

Yesterday's News

During my years of playing professionally and now teaching the game, I have been associated with several PGA Tour greats who have won tournaments and even major events. A tournament win is a benchmark in a Tour professional's career and a memory that is greatly cherished. I have come to notice how many of these champions will designate a room in their homes for the trophies and memories, almost a shrine you might say, to their great achievements. I have also noticed how too often after reaching the pinnacle they don't seem to produce the same results, many times going into a slump and sometimes even disappearing from the leader board, never to be seen again.

Back in the late '80s I had just been hired as the director of Arnold Palmer's Golf Academy and was invited to the Palmers' home for dinner. I arrived a few minutes early that evening. Mrs. Palmer greeted me at the door and graciously invited me into her home. "Arnie is still getting ready, Brad. He will be down shortly." So I asked her if it would be alright for me to get a tour of the "Trophy Room." Ninety-two lifetime Tour wins, I'm thinking this has got to be something to see. She replied, "Oh, we don't have such a room, Brad."

Later that evening, during dinner conversation, I brought up what was kind of puzzling to me since my arrival. "Mr. Palmer," I asked. "Ninety-two Tour wins, that's a lot of hardware. So how come you have no designated trophy display?"

He put his fork down, looked me straight in the eye and said, "For what? That's yesterday's news!"

After a brief pause, he went on to explain himself with that Palmer grin of confidence on his face. "Don't take me wrong, Brad, I have enjoyed every victory and cherish the memory greatly. We even celebrated a little bit after each one. But come Monday morning of the next week, I'm no different than the man who missed the cut last week. In fact, he is probably more hungry than I. So if I am to be competitively ready, I must get my thoughts off yesterday and deal with today. There will be a day when I can take the time to look back. But as long as I want to stay competitive I must never stop and marvel at what I have accomplished, only look forward to my next challenge at hand."

Brad Brewer

Every Golfer's Dream

Imagine that you are an avid golfer who has discovered the "Secret of Golf." The U.S. Open is being played at your home golf course and you successfully qualify.

We see you in the first round
It's early, wet and cold,
You finish strongly for a 74
You were playing fairly bold.

Will you make the cut after two?
You wonder but aren't scared,
A 66 in the second round
You are very well prepared!

You make the cut by a solid amount
You're off the lead by 5.
You are confident, cool and talented
And very much alive.

After eight holes in the third round
Your friends begin to roar,
Three under par at this point
At the tenth you go to 4.

Eleven, twelve and thirteen, however,
Are way out of whack,
Bogey, bogey, double bogey
You're playing like a hack.

But you're two under par on the next five holes
Seventy for the day,
Three strokes behind the leader
Eighteen holes left to play.

The final round you're paired with a man
Whom everyone respects,
He hits it long and putts with touch
He is for sure the best.

The pressure mounts as the time draws near
It's no help looking back,
You can't sleep too well the night before
Because you're paired with Jack!

You start with birdie—birdie
Your friends just can't believe,
One ahead of Jack
Two strokes from the lead.

You make the turn at 33
Three under par,
You know that you can win it all
The lead isn't far.

Two ahead of you
Five up on the rest of the field,
He's making it look like a walk in the park
Could he possibly yield?

At the fifteenth you both take par
At sixteen you make a mistake,
On this tricky 5 par
Your drive goes splashing in a lake.

Jack with an easy birdie
You with a scrambling par,
Three strokes behind, two holes to play
The lead looks so far.

The seventeenth, a long par 3
Jack hits it in the sand,
You know what you must do
And you can hardly stand.

Your fairway wood on this par 3
Goes zooming at the hole
It's long enough, straight enough,
Oh, wow, it hit the pole!

It crashes, rattles, spins and rips
Electricity is in the air,
You aren't sure if the ball is in
Because of all the glare.

The people jump, hug and scream
Where will the ball finally rest?
It's in the cup, a hole in one
On this amazing quest.

You think you're dreaming
The people can't be controlled,
The thunderous applause is deafening
As you run up to the hole.

You take out the ball and give it a kiss
No doubt The Greatest Ace,
Jack bogeys, you're tied for the lead
The eighteenth hole to face.

You hit your drives on eighteen
Straight down the track,
In your hands a three wood,
A wedge in mighty Jack's.

The 3-wood stops within twelve feet
Fifteen for the pro,
If Jack misses and you make it
To the top you're sure to go.

Jack looks it over, studies, strokes it
But not too pure,
He pulls it to the left of the hole
A par he has secured.

If you could stroke it smoothly
And the ball goes in,
Publicity, fame, wealth and happiness
A new life would begin.

You can't believe it
You make the golf ball roll,
As you raise your arm to show your joy
The ball is in the hole!

You made the putt, you've won the Open
As everyone has seen,
I hope that you've enjoyed it
Every golfer's dream.

Jay Golden

The Brand New Golfer

It does look like a very good exercise. But what is the little white ball for?

Ulysses S. Grant

The first hole at the Mobile, Alabama, Municipal Golf Course was something to behold on that beautiful spring day several years ago. The tee sat atop a hill, looking down a narrow fairway, and the hole ended at a postage-stamp-sized green, surrounded at the back side by water. It was a hole that did not appear to be very forgiving to the careless or inexperienced golfer.

It was a busy Saturday morning, and my foursome was waiting to tee off, as were several others. As the golfers in front of us stepped to the tee, I noticed one man in particular. He was in his early thirties, slightly pudgy, wearing a spotless shirt, trousers, shoes and every other golfing accessory his charge card could buy. Even his golf clubs, bag and pull cart fairly sparkled with "newness."

As we watched, the other three men made decent shots, and then waited as their fourth, the new golfer, stepped forward and teed up his ball. The man looked down the fairway, then carefully addressed his ball, made his backswing and swung mightily, missing the ball completely. His face reddened somewhat, but he did not look up as he again addressed his ball. His second attempt made a noisy *whooshing* sound, but missed his ball by an even wider margin. No one made any comment, and his three embarrassed friends simply looked away and cleared their throats.

For the third time, the new golfer addressed his ball, taking great care to place his feet, position his grip and waggle his club several times. Finally, he executed a careful and extremely slow backswing, followed by a vicious downswing of his club that barely topped his ball, which fell from the tee and rolled forward about four inches. For a moment he stood perfectly still, reddened face pointed to the ground. He finally looked up at the large group of waiting golfers, and with a perfectly straight face said, "This is the toughest darn hole I ever played!"

I have never laughed so hard, nor heard so much laughter on any golf course, before or since.

Stan Reynolds

THE FAMILY CIRCUS®   By Bil Keane

"Golf's real easy. You just hit the
ball, then shake your head
and say 'Oh, no, no!'"

Reprinted by permission of Bil Keane.

Playing Through

*L*aughter *is the sensation of feeling good all over but showing it principally in one spot.*

Josh Billings

Parachuting from a helicopter over a drop zone inside Camp Dawson, West Virginia, a lieutenant colonel from the Special Forces Group Airborne found himself doing battle with a sudden twenty-two-knot wind, which forced him onto a nearby golf course. On landing, the Green Beret fumbled for the release but another gust drove the chute and its struggling captive down the fairway, catching the attention of three players about to tee off. "Can we help?" shouted the golfers.

Sliding by them, the officer clung to his sense of humor as well as his pride. "No, thanks," he called out. "I'll just play through."

Sondra Sue Ward Elder

Rub-a-Dub-Dub

Rub of the green. This idiom, in the parlance of golf, conjures the karma of the fairways, the luck of the links. A flubbed shot ricochets off a tree. Onto the green. Toward the flag. Into the hole. *Ker-plunk.* Or a flawless drive kicks into the rough. Down a slope. Toward a pond. Into the water. *Ker-plop.* Rub of the green.

I am well acquainted with the capriciousness of the gods of golf, the sudden confrontations with miracles and mortifications. My most poignant memories do not concern my exploits as a player, but rather as a caddie, and how that life came to such an astonishing end.

The scene: Acacia Country Club near Cleveland, Ohio. The time: the summer of '65. The protagonist: me, a high school kid.

Acacia divided all caddies into an A list and a B list. Caddie ranking was ruled by a ritual as intricate as the minuet: length of tenure counted. So did consistency of signing in, predawn, at the caddieshack. So did the grading cards golfers filled out at the end of a round. But a caddie's fate was also inexorably linked to the whims of the caddiemaster.

Our caddiemaster was a red-headed wise guy in his

early twenties. I had always given him a wide berth, respectful but not sycophantic. By the summer of '65, my fifth year at Acacia, I had ascended to the near pinnacle of the A list—A-5. Tote early and tote often, that was my mantra. On good days I caddied three loops. Popular with the players, I offered sage golfing advice, which was reciprocated by generous tips.

Then came my rub of the green. Early one morning, trekking up a steep hill toward the caddieshack, my head in the clouds, I heard a smash of glass, followed by a shout of profanity; I hurried to investigate, only to find shards of a whiskey bottle outside the shack. Without a tincture of savvy, I picked up some glass, finding myself face-to-face with the caddiemaster, wisps of smoke seemingly curling out his ears. Though I didn't break the bottle, I spoke incoherently. A one-minute trial took place. Guilty, I was sentenced to demotion: from the top of the A's to the tail end of the B's. Like a golf ball rolling downhill, I was ineluctably on my way to the bottom.

An abundance of free time was mine that summer as I awaited the possibility of an early evening loop. I read voraciously. Given my lingering mood of nihilism, I turned to the French existentialists. Camus. Sartre. At Acacia Country Club, I was a stranger with no exit.

Came early September and the club championships, and I received a reprieve from caddie purgatory. Mrs. Silverman insisted I tote her clubs. The caddiemaster could hardly refuse; she was outlandishly wealthy.

Mrs. Silverman, who bore a striking resemblance to Eleanor Roosevelt, was always attired in the dowdiest of golf outfits: paisley blouses, black orthopedic shoes. But she was a woman of great enthusiasms and not a half-bad golfer, either, though far from a favorite to win.

The match-play tournament of sixty-four began, and what a team we were: Eleanor Roosevelt and the club's lowliest caddie. But lo and behold, Mrs. Silverman was about to sustain the highest level of golf in her life. She was the epitome of confidence: crackerjack drives, precision iron play, uncanny putting. We soared into the final four; we pounced into the championship match.

The title match was tied after eighteen holes; we entered sudden death. On the first fairway, a brisk wind blowing over the course, I told Mrs. Silverman: "You can get home with a 6-iron. Hit it all out." She caught the shot perfectly but was short-snagged by a bunker. I cursed my misjudgment, the ill will of the loopy summer seemingly unending.

Then Mrs. Silverman bladed her sand wedge. The ball took off like a shot, struck the flagstick with a bang and careened miraculously into the hole. *Ker-plunk.* Club championship.

After the celebration, Mrs. Silverman handed me my tip: a thick stack of hundred-dollar bills. "For college," she said. I walked away from Acacia forever, that summer of '65, my existentialism jettisoned, my career as a caddie ended, my future bright as I thumbed a stack of fresh bills—a most delightful rub of the green.

Tommy Ehrbar

Slicker Sam

Giving never moves in a straight line—it always travels in circles.

Robert Schuller

Twenty years ago, a car accident claimed the life of longtime Augusta National Golf Club Manager Phil Wahl. Janice, his widow, was left with nine children. Phil's friends wanted to help.

As the club's photographer, I had gotten to know Phil pretty well. The idea of a golf tournament to raise funds for his family seemed like a good one, so I made a few phone calls and was heartened by the overwhelming response.

The one-day benefit tournament was set for West Lake, a popular Augusta country club that donated use of its course. Fee was set at one thousand dollars per player. The first obstacle was that some of Phil's friends could not afford the fee; still they wanted to show their support. While agonizing over this dilemma, I received a phone call from a member of the National who wished to remain anonymous. He offered to put up the fee for those who could not afford it. We were off and running!

Fifty-five players came out, including such notables as Jack Nicklaus, Ken Venturi, David Graham, Chris Schenkel and Ed Sneed. One of the first guys to sign up was Slicker Sam of Chicago, an internationally known golfer who regularly played for large sums of money—and usually won. Anyone who knew Slicker agreed he should be deemed a national treasure. I say this because of his reputation for charity.

At the end of play, we gathered in the dining room for tournament awards. A substantial prize—a luxurious new Cadillac donated by a local dealer—stood out from the usual closest-to-pin and longest drive awards. All eyes were riveted on the shiny new set of keys that Master of Ceremonies Ken Venturi held up. After a long, dramatic pause, Ken finally smiled, and said: "Come on up, Slicker Sam, and claim your prize!"

Silence fell over the room as Slicker Sam moved to the podium. He was quite a champion. Ken handed him the keys.

Slicker Sam had broken 70 to claim the victory, but only at that moment were we to learn why he had played with so much determination.

"I already have a car!" Sam said to Venturi, returning the keys. "Please, give this Cadillac to Phil Wahl's family!"

The room responded with a standing ovation. That was class, Slicker-style.

The following day, Slicker and Doug Sanders had arranged to play for some serious money. Doug's playing partner was singer Andy Williams. I was the fourth. We played the match in Aiken, South Carolina, about fourteen miles east of Augusta, at the Houndslake Golf Club.

As we rode down the first fairway I remembered I had been given some raffle tickets to sell on behalf of my neighbors, the Adas Yeshurun Synagogue in Augusta. The one-hundred-dollar tickets were good for a chance at a new

Cadillac. As we putted out on the first hole, I pulled out the tickets. Doug and Andy bought the first two. By the time Sam walked up to us, we were exchanging money for tickets. When he heard what the prize was, Slicker's eyes flashed and he produced a roll of bills from his pocket.

A few weeks later I attended a dinner where the raffle tickets were pulled, eliminating contenders. As the night wore on, all names were eliminated except two, and Slicker Sam remained in the race. When someone else's name was called, my heart dropped. I thought they were declaring a winner. I was wrong. Slicker Sam was the winner!

I phoned him with the good news. "I knew I was going to win that car," he responded.

I guess some things are ordained by a higher power. There's one thing I know for sure: Sam had been rewarded for his wonderful generosity. As I went to bed that night I had a vision of Phil Wahl. In his own unique way that had endeared him to so many people, Phil turned his head to speak to Slicker Sam.

"Thanks, Pard," he said.

I slept happily.

Frank Christian

4

GOLFMANSHIP

*Golfers should not fail to realize that it is
a game of great traditions, of high ideals
of sportsmanship, one in which a strict
adherence to the rules is essential.*

Francis Ouimet

Straight Down the Fairway

The game has such a hold on golfers because they compete not only against an opponent, but also against the course, against par, and most surely—against themselves.

Arnold Palmer

Alberta's Jasper Park Lodge in 1940 was a place for the rich. On my first day as a caddie, I was out with an old bird in cap and pipe, a pretty good golfer who, moreover, paid me $2.50 for eighteen holes. When I asked if I could caddie for him regularly, he agreed. I asked Vic, the young assistant pro, how long he thought my old bird would be a guest.

"All summer," Vic said. "His name is William D. Mitchell. He comes every year for the whole summer, and he plays seven days a week. He was a member of Herbert Hoover's cabinet, the attorney general, I think."

Boy oh boy, two-fifty a day, guaranteed, every day of the week for ten weeks equaled—my brain worked at high speed—$175 less, say, $25 for rainy days or the old codger being sick now and then. But he never got sick, and only the foulest weather kept him away.

I seldom caddied for anyone except Mr. Mitchell. He played deliberately and said almost nothing. He knew my first name, but didn't encourage me to impart any further information. One day when we were out on the course alone, I timidly asked about the senators from Vermont (my Quebec hometown borders on that state). "Give me the 5-iron, please, David," he said. And that was that.

Mr. Mitchell's summer was dedicated to breaking 80, and I got caught up in his silent campaign. He was easy to caddie for; he didn't hit the ball a great distance, was only rarely in the rough, and he putted well.

Once in a while he would top his drive and dribble the ball off the tee. He didn't complain and never had me retrieve the ball for another drive, even when he was playing alone. He walked the few feet to the ball in front of the tee and said. "Two-iron, please, David."

The summer wore on, and my man's score descended little by little. He was seldom worse than 85 or 86, and halfway through August he hit an 81, and then 80, twice.

One day he dropped a long birdie putt at the par-4 sixteenth, and I realized that par on the last two holes would give him a 79.

"There's a good chance, sir," I said.

"Don't say it. It's bad luck, like talking about a no-hitter in the eighth inning." But there was a gleam in his eye.

He was playing with another old bird who didn't talk much either. My man's drive on the par-4 seventeenth was straight down the center. The ball carried over a little crest and out of sight. His companion had a good tee shot too, carrying over the same ridge.

Mr. Mitchell stopped to relight his pipe, and I went ahead, saw the ball when I reached the top of the ridge, and parked the bag and myself beside it, waiting for him to select his iron. He took a 6-iron and dropped the ball on the green. Easy par, I said to myself, thinking of a huge tip.

His playing partner was also on the green in two, but away. He was close with his putt and tapped in immediately. Mr. Mitchell was a little strong, but came back nicely with a five-footer for his par 4. I went to retrieve his ball from the cup and put the flag back.

I soon realized that it wasn't his ball. It was the other guy's. I hadn't checked when I'd come over the ridge and had just assumed the first ball I saw was his. I wished the cup was a hundred feet deep and that I'd fall into it.

"I'll just wash the ball," I said, heading for the scrubber on the eighteenth tee and hoping I could switch the balls. I signaled the other caddie to come quick.

"No, David, don't wash it," Mr. Mitchell said. "That might break my string."

I handed him the ball as nonchalantly as I could, without looking at him. I prayed. But when he leaned over to tee up the ball, he saw.

"I'm afraid this isn't my ball," he said to the other golfer, looking stricken.

His companion looked at his. "You're right," he said.

"There's a two-stroke penalty for that," Mr. Mitchell said. "That gives me a 6."

"Don't be silly," his companion said. "We're just playing for fun."

"It wouldn't be right. Rules are rules." I knew he would have said the same thing even if he hadn't been attorney general of the United States.

He would have to shoot an eagle 2 on the last hole to break 80. I prayed hard he would make a bogey 5, so that, even without the disaster on the seventeenth, he still wouldn't have shot 79. He looked weary and drawn. But he shot a par 4.

"I'm sorry, sir," I said, nearly crying. "It was all my fault."

"No, David, it wasn't," he said. "I should have looked too. See you tomorrow."

He played another five rounds, but didn't do better than 82. He never mentioned the switched balls.

"Maybe next summer," he said when we parted for the last time.

"I hope so, sir."

Dave McIntosh

A Lesson I Will Never Forget

*The workshop of character is everyday life. The
uneventful and commonplace hour is where the
battle is lost or won.*

Mattie D. Babcock

Probably the most important single lesson I ever got
from Dad came shortly before we moved to St. Simons. It
taught me what golf meant to my father, and how golf is
meant to be played. It probably paved the way for everything that my dad and I did together thereafter.

I was twelve going on thirteen, and the family was
together having dinner at home, as we always did. My
father asked me how I had played that day after school.

"Uh, I shot 36 today," I said.

My father looked at me carefully and said, "Thirty-six?
Even par? That's quite a score. I don't think you've ever
shot even par for nine holes before."

I had shot 36 for eight holes. Our house was near the
eighth green of the Atlanta Country Club course and I
didn't play the ninth because I was too lazy; I didn't want
to walk all the way back from the ninth green to the house

for dinner. I had quit after eight holes and 36 strokes.

"Isn't that right, Davis?"

I didn't say anything.

The next day, he started telling the guys in the pro shop, in front of me, about how I had played nine holes in even par for the first time in my life. I felt sick. I never lied about a score again in my life. I never lied to my father again. I didn't know then what I'm sure of now: Of course Dad knew that I hadn't shot 36 for nine holes. If I had, I would have sprinted from the ninth green all the way home to tell him the news, and he knew it. I think another father might have said, "Are you telling me the truth about that score?" There's nothing wrong with that. My father's approach, though, was different. His lesson took quickly and will stay with me forever.

Davis Love III

Payback

The measure of a man's real character is what he would do if he knew he would never be found out.

Thomas Macaulay

Bob stood on the first tee taking in the sunrise, enjoying a picture-perfect June morning. As the dew glistened on the neatly groomed grass, he wondered who his playing partner for the day would be. He had decided at the last minute to head out to the course without a tee time with the hope of being worked in with another group.

As luck would have it, there was a tournament going off that day. As such, no one was allowed to tee off until after 11:00 A.M., but the club pro let Bob sneak on ahead of the tournament as long as he pledged to keep up the pace. The only other disclaimer was that he was being paired with another "walk-on."

So there was Bob standing on the tee box, and enjoying the fine day waiting for his mystery partner to appear, when up walked Steve Henderson. *OH, NO!* Bob screamed to himself.

It just so happened that Bob and Steve had gone to high school together, with "together" meaning only that they were both in the same building every day. They lived in two different worlds—Bob in that of the socially awkward types; Steve in the realm of studly athletes. The only interaction Bob had with Steve was when Steve would give him a "wedgie" after gym class or administer some type of other public humiliation on him at any random moment.

Bob had spent four years constantly in fear of the sudden and cruel attacks inflicted upon him and his friends by the athletes hanging out in the hallway at the "Jock Wall."

Now here they were ten years later in a nightmarish reunion of the predator and the prey. *Only now,* Bob thought, *we are on a more level playing field,* as Bob was a pretty decent golfer. It also soon became apparent that Steve had absolutely no recollection of Bob.

Bob, sensing a chance to deliver a dose of retribution upon his tormentor from days gone by, started out with some small talk. Then knowing Steve's inherent competitive nature from his days as a star quarterback, quickly suggested putting a little wager on the round—of, say, one hundred dollars. In a flash Steve accepted and Bob was ready to deal some long overdue payback.

However, Bob had failed to factor in the fact that Steve was also a pretty decent golfer, and they were tied up as they headed to the eighteenth tee. Bob started to panic somewhat, not having much acquaintance with competitive arenas.

I can't let this guy beat me again. I can't live my whole life without sticking it to this guy at least once! Bob reached deep within to summon all of his remaining inner strength and will to finally defeat the wretched demon from his youth—and promptly shanked the ball into the woods.

Steve, being the calm, cool and collected athlete, drilled the ball down the middle of the fairway.

That's alright, thought Bob, *as long as I'm not behind a tree I'll be fine.*

Bob, of course, was behind a tree.

As he stood looking at his ball, he thought back to the day that Steve had humiliated him in the school cafeteria. Bob had finally worked up the courage to ask Nancy Lewis to the senior prom.

Steve had thwarted his effort at romance just to amuse himself and his Cro-Magnon friends who thought it would be a great stunt to dump a plate of food on Bob's head. Nancy had looked over at the commotion and saw Bob standing there with spaghetti hanging from his ears, and she had laughed.

Now, as Bob stared at his ball hopelessly pinned behind an old cottonwood tree, reliving the anguish, he felt a burning anger rising up inside him. He was not going to let Steve win again, no matter what the cost.

Glancing quickly to make sure Steve was not looking, Bob kicked the ball out into the fairway.

"Boy, I sure got a lucky bounce," Bob yelled over, trying to sound as convincing as he could, but deep down knowing that Steve would always have his doubts about the "lucky" bounce.

As it was, Bob went on to win the hole and the match, and collected his one hundred dollars. Most of the round Bob had been dreaming of the moment that he would take The Great Tormentor's cash and how he would dance around the green and joyously rub the payback in his face. Only now that the moment was here, he didn't feel like dancing. He quietly took the money and walked away.

On his way home in the car, Bob began to cry.

He was still upset when he arrived home. He tearfully recounted the entire tale to his puzzled and concerned wife, who had never before heard of the torment her husband was carrying inside.

After a while, they both decided that no matter what had happened in the past, exacting revenge in this manner was no way to behave. So together they drove over to Steve's house to apologize and return the ill-gotten wager.

As they sat in Steve's living room confessing, a curious transformation came over Steve, who had his wife at his side. At first he was visibly angry over being cheated, but as he slowly began to recall that he had in fact known Bob in the past, his face began to soften. By the time Bob had finished, both Steve and his wife were teary-eyed.

Steve had often looked back regretfully at his youth, wishing he could take back some of the mean-spirited things he had done during a time when he simply didn't know any better. Now here was an opportunity staring him in the face.

The men apologized, and the couples cried, laughed and recounted old tales late into the night. As Bob pulled out of Steve's driveway, he thought to himself that it would make a nice ending to the story if he and Steve would now become friends, and laugh about those "crazy high school days." But he knew that wasn't going to happen. Most likely he would never talk to Steve again unless they happened to have another chance encounter on the links.

But he also knew that did not matter. He knew that they both would from this day forward walk through life with a slightly lighter step, both of them having shed some heavy demons on a gorgeous day in June.

Scott Hipp

Playing It Down

*There can be no happiness if the things we
believe in are different from the things we do.*
Freya Stark

Like the vast majority of golfers, I was ruled by the concept of fairness. My self-worth was a reflection of my golf
score. When I first began playing, I would move my ball to
improve my lie or to eliminate an obstacle from its path.

As my game improved, I felt the need to move my ball
less frequently, except on occasions when the concept of
fairness came into play. When a ball is struck cleanly, soaring directly at its selected target, we deserve to be aptly
rewarded. This ball, dead center in the fairway, merits an
appropriate lie, not in a divot or another poor setting.

Good shots SHOULD be rewarded. So we move that
ball. Fairness calls for it. I, like most other golfers—winter-
rules players—moved it.

In time, guided by the wisdom of Harvey Penick, a profound change began to free me.

Golf was not about fairness. The ball was to be played
from where it sat. There are benefits to this approach,

Mr. Penick said, and I would seek to discover them. In golf, as in life, obstacles are placed in our path. In overcoming these roadblocks, our greatest triumphs occur. By improving our lie, we are only cheating ourselves of the opportunity to achieve.

There are no good or bad lies, only what is. When we see things as they are, without judgment, we provide ourselves an opportunity to come through with our best performances. This state of mind will not ensure success, only our best effort. For me, there was a gradual change in my outlook. At first, in situations when that concept of fairness came into play, the unfairness of my lie dominated my thoughts. Weak shots tended to follow. Over time, as I began to free my mind of judgments, better results occurred. I began to look at situations and make objective determinations that would give me the maximum chance for success.

One anecdote always comes to mind. I was paired with a stranger, playing a par-5 that often proved difficult. I hit two perfect shots. One hundred yards to the pin, MY perfect distance, but in a two-inch hole. My mind lapsed to a similar situation earlier that week. That divot had seized my clubhead and, as a result, I shanked my ball into the woods. I remembered that, although the result was poor, I was proud that I did what was right. My thoughts now returned to the present situation, and as I chose my course of action, I remember thinking to myself, "I'm going to stick it and make birdie." Just before I was ready to hit, I glanced at my playing partner. His look seemed to say, "What are you doing? Take the ball out of that hole."

I stuck that ball two feet from the pin and made birdie. I smiled, inside and out. As we left the green, he asked me why I didn't move my ball. After all, I WAS in a hole in the fairway. "Because that's not golf," I replied.

Leonard Finkel

We Play 'Em All

It was a typically pleasant early spring South Carolina day as our regular group of twelve prepared on the first tee for the normal Tuesday morning match. As usual, Henry's risqué jokes created enough confusion to raise Bob's dander a little as he pulled the balls from the hat to line up the foursomes to compete for the much sought-after two-dollar Nassau. . . . Nassau? Perhaps! Bragging rights? Absolutely!

As our last group teed off, the gentle breeze at our backs helped our drives travel a little further than usual down the first fairway. It was the beginning of a good game for all of us, with Dick's short game working very well, Rich knocking the cover off the ball, Henry playing his wide slice to perfection and my putter performing well enough to allow me to do better than my 24 handicap.

After about four holes we noticed a twosome creeping up close behind us. Before we could motion them through, they fell back again, only to close the gap again on holes 8 and 9. We thought that perhaps they would go through as we stopped for a snack at the turn, but they did not, only to get close again on No. 12. Being a true advocate of golf-course courtesy, I took advantage of

Henry's slice into the woods to go back and invite them to play through.

"Sorry to hold you up . . . would you like to play through?"

"Thank you for asking but we're doing just fine. We don't get in a hurry anymore. Just being out here and enjoying our friendship, this wonderful game and God's glorious universe is quite enough for both of us. . . . You see, Joel here is ninety-one and I'm eighty-nine years old, and we have enough aches and pains that we only play the downhill holes!"

William M. Bowen

A True Gentleman

If you think it's hard to meet people, try picking up the wrong golf ball.

Jack Lemmon

Several years ago, golfer William Reynders received a Christmas gift from his family: a dozen Titleist balls with the name "Billy Reynders" imprinted on them. Shortly after, while playing a muni course in Sacramento, one of his errant drives went onto an adjoining fairway. When he arrived at his ball, he found a lady preparing to hit. He explained to her that she might be playing his ball. She then picked up the ball, looked at it and coolly stated, "No. This is mine. I always play Billy Reynders balls." Being the gentleman that he is, Reynders did not argue.

Hugh Baldwin

Play It as It Lies

An inherent part of the game is a set of virtues that mirrors all the qualities desirable in society: integrity, honor, respect, rules and discipline, to name a few.

Larry Miller

Being a believer in predestination of sorts, Bobby Jones once said that a golf tournament was all "in the book" before a shot was even hit. He tried as hard as anyone to win every event he played in (and he almost did!). If he didn't win he'd just say to himself, "I guess it wasn't my turn."

Bob had a great mental image that he once used. Back in Bob's day the marshals used megaphones to control the galleries. The megaphones would blast out, "Fore, please!" to warn the gallery to stand back while a player hit. On more than one occasion Jones would be barreling into the ball and a marshal would scream "Fore" into his megaphone, causing Jones to top his ball completely. Bob said that it made him think that, just like the angel Gabriel's trumpet telling us it's our time, the megaphone told him it wasn't his time—his turn to win.

I think it was this kind of attitude that made Bob Jones one of the greatest golfers of all time. He had a sense of peace, dignity and grace about him that was almost eerie. He was one of the most self-composed men I've ever met.

Even when his formerly athletic body was ravaged by that awful degenerative disease of the spinal cord, syringomyelia, he was a model of strength, fortitude and dignity. The last year he was at Augusta National was 1971, and I'm not sure if the story's true or not, but it's worth repeating. He was in his cabin, just to the left side of the tenth tee, when he was visited by one of his old friends, who was obviously upset by Jones's physical appearance. The man began to cry, and Jones said, "Now, now. We won't have that. We are supposed to play our ball as we find it."

Sam Snead

The Day I Cheated

Golf is like solitaire. When you cheat, you cheat only yourself.

Tony Lema

Golf has always been the game I love. The physical challenge. The mental challenge. The ability to summon a shot from the depths of my being when double bogey is staring me down. Golf is pure, and that's the way I play it. Except for that time a few years ago.

For the first time, for the only time, I cheated in a golf match. It haunts me to this day. It was against my best golfing buddy, Frank, and it changed me as a person and as a golfer. Forever.

Until that heated match one Sunday afternoon, I had never intentionally broken or even bent a single rule of golf. Never.

Like so many of our duels, our match that day was all square going into the eighteenth hole, a par-5 where anything worse than par meant losing the hole. At stake was the normal whopping three dollars. I hooked badly into the woods off the tee. Frank, aka Steady Eddie, split the middle of the fairway as usual.

After a short search alone amongst the trees, I found my ball wedged between two roots. It was quite unplayable.

Through the leaves, I could see Frank striding toward his tee shot. I dropped within two club lengths and smacked a 3-iron through an opening in the trees. Frank was applauding as I emerged from the woods, and for good reason. My ball laid 175 yards down the fairway in perfect position for my approach.

A few minutes later, Frank tapped in to match my "par."

"Nice match," he said, extending his hand. "No blood."

I shook his hand and kept my mouth shut. I don't know why. I have thought about that day often, and I have no answers.

I remember throwing cold water on my face in the club-house restroom after the round. I stared at myself in the mirror and let the water drip back into the sink.

Frank had obviously not seen me take the drop in the woods. He assumed my tap-in was for par, when I knew very well that it was for bogey. So I kept my three dollars that day.

The next morning I took a long hard look at myself. I wondered who this cheating person was and how long he would be around. It pained me to have cheated, and it pained me to have dishonored a game I consider so noble.

I can't help but think about that afternoon as each new golf season begins. I remember how badly I felt, but mostly I remind myself how good it feels to walk off a green after having ground out a par, a real par, or maybe even a hard-fought bogey, from a situation that looked like a sure double. I tell myself that the shots that feel the best—the ones you remember in the nineteenth hole and in the car on the ride home—are those you pull off from horrendous lies with a clump of mud stuck to the ball. I

remind myself that my playing partners—my friends—
should never, ever, have to question my integrity on the
course, no matter how miraculous my recovery shot.

A trip to Ireland last year emphasized to me the importance of the relationship between golf and integrity.
"Lad," said an Irishman I played a round with, "over here
we touch the ball just twice each hole: when we tee it up
and when we pluck it from the bottom of the cup."

Perhaps more than anything, it is precisely such memories of the men and women whom I have had the honor
of walking a round with over in Ireland and Scotland
that compel me to be true to myself on the course. It
seems every player over there has been somehow
imbued with the spirit of Old Tom Morris. Just as they
cannot comprehend why Americans would choose to
ride around in a "buggy" when it is abundantly clear that
golf is walking, neither can they understand why anyone would ever do something as foolish and demeaning
as cheating on the course.

In the British Isles, golf is played by the rules, and never
by "winter rules."

The majority of players in this country break the
rules—or choose to ignore them—every weekend, never
understanding that they are diminishing themselves
every time they roll it in the fairway. Is there a truer adage
than the one that says we can tell everything we need to
know about a person's character by playing a round of
golf with him or her? If your playing partners witness you
bumping your ball in the fairway, do you think this
doesn't influence their opinion of you?

I only wonder what Frank thinks of me.

John Meyers

The Clutch Putt

Pressure is part of golf. It shows up when a golfer fails
to make a shot he would normally make because he tries
too hard. A non-golfer doesn't understand this when he
watches Freddie Couples nonchalantly knock in a fifteen-
foot putt.

All golfers have experienced pressure, but what is perhaps more difficult to comprehend is the amount of additional pressure that is created when golf is played as a
team sport, rather than an individual one. The fear of let-
ting your teammates down is undoubtedly the big factor.

Whether golfers are playing in the Ryder Cup or the
Border League, they have to contend with this extra pressure. In these parts, the Border League is a group of golf
and country clubs along the New York State-Eastern
Ontario border that play an annual team competition:
eight-man teams from each club—total score to count—
medal play.

One such competition was being played at the Prescott,
Ontario, Club, a nice course overlooking the St. Lawrence
River. I was a member of the Cornwall, Ontario, team.
Most observers were saying if anybody was going to beat
the home club, it would probably be us. As the day

progressed, this analysis proved correct—Prescott and Cornwall well ahead of the other clubs. Seven of our eight players were in now, waiting and relaxing at the nine-teenth hole, as golfers sometimes do, and our eighth man was now on the eighteenth tee. Our eighth man was Reggie Evans, an 8-handicapper, a school principal by profession, a keen but occasionally erratic golfer. We, of course, were tired, but anxious about the outcome. Somebody said, "Kenny, it's your turn—go over to the scoreboard and see how we stand." A quick trip over to the board revealed that all teams now had seven players finished and the scores were listed by teams. The score-keeper, whoever he was, hadn't given us any subtotals, so I checked them out, did some quick mental additions and went back to where my teammates were sitting.

"Hey fellas, we got this thing in the bag—we are eleven shots up on Prescott and Reggie was one up on his man after nine; surely he can't blow a twelve-shot lead on the back nine."

The elation and excitement were rising; somebody suggested, "Hey, let's go over to the edge of the green and cheer Reggie in."

"Good idea."

By this time, Reggie had played his second shot onto the green—pin high about twenty feet to the right of the flag.

"Let's have some fun," I suggested. "Let's tell Reggie that he has to sink that putt."

"Wait," cautioned Alex. "Before you do that, you had better check out his lead—you wouldn't want to blow us out of first place."

"Okay."

We joined the small greenside gallery as the players approached the green. The Prescott player chipped up for what looked like a tap-in par, and the other two players had played onto the green when Reg came around to where I had strategically positioned myself.

"How are you doing, Reg?" I asked.

"Pretty good, Kenny, two putts here and I break 80."

"How is the Prescott player doing?"

"Well, let me see now, he'll get his par here and he will be one stroke ahead of me. How is the team doing?"

The stage was set and set perfectly.

"Look, Reg, listen now, we have a one-stroke lead over Prescott—you've got to sink that putt."

"A one-stroke lead?" Reg muttered, as he digested the situation. His facial muscles tightened. "That's not an easy putt."

"Give it a go, Reg. Knock it in and we win, but hell, don't three putt it."

Reg was on the green now, putter in hand, crouched behind the ball, studying the roll of the green.

"Don't be short, Reggie," chirped Joe from greenside.

"Shush, Joe, don't distract him," whispered Alex. But Reg wasn't going to be distracted; he was in full concentration like I have never seen him before. Things were working perfectly. He looked over the line from both directions, studied the surface to make sure there were no impediments, and now he was back behind the ball again.

My teammates were all watching intently, some with expectant grins on their faces. We were expecting anything, but inwardly hoping he might sink this putt.

Reggie took a couple of practice swings with his putter to ensure a smooth stroke and now took his position over the ball—pause—here it comes—the ball jumped off the putter face—bobbled a bit—lots of speed—a bit to the right of the cup—now a slowing down and breaking towards the cup.

"It's in!—way to go, Reggie—you did it! Boy!"

Loud cheers and high fives from the gang and then a

sudden shushed silence to allow the others to putt out; then handshakes all around and back to the lounge to celebrate our victory.

When Reg sank into his chair, his face reflected both relief and excitement from his achievement. About this time, Joe decided to let the cat out of the bag. "Reggie, you really didn't have to sink the putt. We won by eleven strokes—we were just putting you on."

"Aw, you guys," groaned Reg, "you don't know the pressure you put on me out there."

"We just wanted to see how good you really are," I ventured. The chatter continued, only to be interrupted by the public address system: "Ladies and gentlemen, here are the results of today's tournament.

"In first place, Cornwall, with a total of . . ."

"Yeaaaa."

"In second place, one stroke behind, Prescott with a total of . . ."

"One stroke behind?"

"One stroke behind. Hey, Kenny, where did you learn to add?" exclaimed Alex.

"Aw come on, fellas," I said, "I was only telling Reggie the truth out there. You didn't expect me to lie to him, did you?"

Ken Robertson

The Difference Between the Scots and the Americans

I'd give up golf if I didn't have so many sweaters.

Bob Hope

The Scots have a much simpler, almost reverential, approach to the game, unlike Americans who complicate the game by mimicking the things they see the pros do on television—stuff that doesn't help their games but only manages to slow down play.

Take the story of the American who showed up at St. Andrews with his huge, heavy bag, high-tech clubs and most fashionable clothes.

Upon reaching his opening drive, he reached down, clipped a bit of grass and tossed it into the air to check the wind.

"What do you think?" he asked his caddie.

The caddie responded by mimicking the player and tossing the few blades of grass into the air.

"I think the wind's come up, governor," said the caddie. "You'd best take out your sweater."

Don Wade

The Gentle Hustler

It was June 1952 when Hal Bruce was transferred to Boise, Idaho. He had no trouble finding an affordable apartment, but a golf course was a bit more difficult. When he looked in the phone book only two were listed, and because one was private, he called the municipal course to ask about a starting time Sunday morning.

"Come on down any time before nine," said a friendly voice, "before church lets out."

He showed up at 8:30 A.M. and sure enough, the place was deserted. The only soul in sight was a slight woman, maybe in her seventies, chipping balls onto the putting green. After Hal paid and made his way to the first tee, he looked over at the woman. She waved and began to walk—limp, actually—toward him.

"Well, son, no sense in us playin' alone on such a fine mornin'," she said with a peculiar, lilting accent. "How 'bout if I join you? I'm Mary O'Leary."

"Good morning. I'm Hal Bruce." They shook hands.

"Hal," she said, "what with lumbago and all, I'm only good for nine holes. By the way, what's your handicap?"

"Well, since this is my first time on the course, I don't have one here, but I normally carry about a 10."

"Fine. But seein' as you're new to the place, I'll spot you a couple of strokes to make the game more fun."

Hal couldn't take such an offer and protested. "Oh, I couldn't do that. After all, we're just here to enjoy the fresh air. No big stakes are involved."

Mary seemed disappointed. "Okay, but I always play better under a bit of pressure."

Her backswing had a little hitch and she didn't have much length, but everything was hit cleanly up the middle. Putting seemed to be her main weakness, but Mary also chipped in from the fringe a few times, which evened things out. Coming to the par-4 ninth, both players had totaled 38.

When Mary requested a short rest, they took a breather on the bench. After asking a few questions about his work and home life, she said, "You know, Hal, I don't usually gamble at golf, but this mornin' I feel lucky. I went off and left my purse on the kitchen table, but Mike let me put the greens fee on my tab. Just for the heck of it, I'll play the last hole for what's on my bill. If I lose, I'll pick up the tab for both of us another day."

Hal hated himself for taking advantage of the sweet, and now tired, old woman but he agreed. The ninth sported a frog-infested pond about 180 yards out; it was straight away, but Mary chose a 3-iron and hit her ball safely to the left, into the eighth fairway. Hal used a 3-wood, hit it fat and drowned the ball. Mary hit her second near the green, chipped close and made par, which was good enough against Hal's bogey. Just before departing, she shook his hand, "Hal, I really enjoyed this game. Can we do it again next Sunday?"

"Sure," he replied eagerly. "See you next week." Then she walked off toward the parking lot and Hal went into the modest golf shop.

Mike was behind the counter when Hal told him he was paying Mary O'Leary's bill. Mike smirked, opened a

file and said, "Well, Mary is in arrears for two greens fees
. . . balls . . . and a bag of tees. The total's $15.10. But an
even fifteen will be close enough."

On the way back to his apartment, Hal knew one thing:
He wasn't about to be skunked twice by a woman—especially one old enough to be his grandmother—so that
week he hit balls every day after work, sharpened up his
short game and even took a lesson.

On Sunday, as expected, Mary offered him a chance to
get even. "What say we play for the price of my tab from
last Sunday?" she asked on the first tee. "And I'll still spot
you two strokes."

"I'll take 'em," he said firmly.

Mary had him two down on the ninth tee, so they
played the last hole with nothing at stake. Hal thanked
her for the match and, after she left, he made his way to
the golf shop. After forking over fifteen bucks for the second straight weekend, Hal went to the bar for a beer and
sat down next to an elderly gentleman who was obviously a regular.

"Well, friend," the stranger said, "I see you played with
ol' Mary today. How much has she taken you for?"

"Only about a day's wages, but how did you know?"

He took a sip of his cocktail, re lit a cold stogie and
explained, "Mary is sort of a fixture around here. I met up
with her a couple of years ago when I moved from
California. The experience led to a little research. I found
out that she came from Ireland, was a pretty famous golfer
in Europe before she turned pro over here and now sur-
vives by waiting tables at the country club. Once or twice
a week she comes out and plays with newcomers—anyone she doesn't know. During the winter she goes to
Arizona and does the same thing. Nothing illegal, mind
you, and she keeps her tab paid up, so they tolerate her."

It was about a month later when the doorbell rang, just

as Hal was sticking dinner into the oven. Upon opening the door he saw a young woman standing in the hallway. "Are you Hal Bruce?" she asked.

"Yes. Come in."

"Thanks, but I'm in a bit of a hurry. You're the last on my list. You were a friend of Mary O'Leary's?"

"Well, I met her a couple of times."

"I'm Megan O'Leary," she explained. "Mary was my grandmother. She passed away in the County Hospital two weeks ago and wanted you to have this." She handed Hal an envelope.

He couldn't begin to understand why a woman he had met only twice would send him something, but as soon as Hal opened the envelope he realized what it was—a bill from the golf course.

"Her bill began to add up," Megan said. "Just before she passed away she wrote down the names of all those who owed her a game."

As he stood there, staring at the little slip of paper, Hal realized what Megan—or more clearly, Mary—was saying. He was to pay for the outcome of a game never played.

Megan looked at him intently. "She said if anyone became angry, to take it back." She reached out her hand.

"No . . . no," Hal insisted. "I'll take care of it." Then he laughed. "Mary was absolutely right. This would no doubt have been the outcome."

Bob Brust

The Compassionate Golfer

Down south, where snowflakes are seldom seen, there lived an elderly gentleman who was an excellent golfer. Even in his seventies, he could beat the most self-assured of the younger golfers. It wasn't uncommon for him to shoot his age, and the year he turned seventy-two, he shot eight rounds that bettered his age. Over the years he was often asked why he didn't turn pro. His reply was always the same. With a mischievous grin he'd whisper, "I'll let you in on a little secret. With my job, I get to golf as much as the pros, and I probably enjoy the game more."

Many an ardent golfer would request a game with him, to which he happily obliged. Every now and then, he would get beat by a lesser golfer. For the forty-some years that he was a member of the club, no one could figure it out. How could he beat the club pro one day and lose to a mediocre guest the next? The consensus in the clubhouse was that he didn't know how to be a tough competitor. His wife knew better, however.

Whenever her husband would come home from a day at the golf course, she greeted him with a kiss and asked, "Did the guy you played against need a self-esteem booster?" If he answered "Yes," her next question was, "How bad did you let him beat you?"

Carla Muir

Victory for the Golf Rats

There are two games called golf, but the only thing the same about them is the little white balls. One game is club golf. The other game I call "golf-rat" golf.

In club golf the players arrive when they want, and play when they want. They walk or ride and rarely wait. They never have bad lies in the perfectly raked bunkers or on the triplex-cut fairways. They never get thirsty or hungry because there is something to eat or drink around the next dogleg. And after a four-hour round, their golf shoes barely hit the lockeroom carpet before an attendant scoops them up to be polished, bagged and returned. Hot showers, steam baths and a drink at the bar end a leisurely day of club golf.

In golf-rat golf, the players stagger out of bed before dawn, drive to the local public course so they can stand in a long line, drink bad coffee from a plastic cup and pray that they can get a starting time within the next three hours. When they do play they pray that the foursome ahead gets off the green before the foursome behind beans them with their drives. They blast out of bunkers that look like the lunar landscape and hit out of fairways with divots the size of craters. They eat the cold sandwiches and melted candy bars squashed into their tattered golf bags. But mostly they wait, and wait and wait. After five and a half or six hours the golf rats stagger back to their cars, stash their wet and dirty golf shoes in their trunk and head home to families who were beginning to wonder if they had been kidnapped.

Almost all the courses we see in televised golf tournaments are the guts of club golf, but the galleries that throng to those tournaments are the guts of golf-rat golf. When we gathered at Bethpage to announce the coming of the U.S. Open to the Black Course in 2002, the golf rats were there. They were the people standing behind the fence at the back of the first tee—watching and nodding silently and waiting for that day when the best golfers in the world would play their course. They knew that the decision to give the U.S. Open to a truly public course for the first time was not just a victory for the metropolitan area, for Long Island, for politicians or the businesses nearby. They knew that this decision was the greatest victory in the history of the game for public golfers—the golf rats.

It is a victory because it is a way to honor the public spaces that offer rare and precious shelter from the ugliness of urban life to those who do not have enough money to buy private shelter in places affluent people know.

It is a victory because it is a reminder that golf was first played on unmanicured farmer's fields with ruts and valleys, weeds and, yes, even cow dung. And although there will probably be precious little manure on the fairways of the Black Course during the Open, it will still, I hope, be at least a little raw, a little wild, a little public.

Most of all, however, it is a victory because, six years from now, there will be a dad who works hard and has little in material terms to show for it, a guy like my dad, who will be able to say to his son or daughter, "Oh yeah, the U.S. Open is at the Black Course this year. I've played it."

Rabbi Marc Gellman, Ph.D.

A Practice Round for Life

The ball soared forward, arching away from its perch on the ladies tee without a trace of slice or hook, and landed with a solid *"whump."* I was too far away to see it a foot or so from the cup on the eighteenth green. Grinning from ear to ear, my father said, "You'll be back next week."

When you're a kid, it seems like your parents utter the same mantras over and over, day after day—"wash your hands, eat your peas." For my father, playing golf with me was his venue for spouting forth a barrage of maxims gleaned from a lifetime of living. Often, by the time we'd reached the eighteenth hole, I'd heard, "Never up, never in" at least four times. I was never sure if this phrase related wholly to golf, or had some deeper meaning in the overall scheme of existence. Still, I was only thirty-four and had a lot of learning yet to do.

"No way, Dad," I told him. "I hate this game."

He'd heard that one a few times, too. He ignored it, even though he knew, perhaps, it was the truth.

It was, almost. As a busy, career-minded, up-and-coming investment trader who hustled and clawed her way to the top of a demanding, frenetic field, I thought golf was a pointless, boring way to spend an afternoon. It

just happened to be my father's favorite pastime since
he'd grown a little too old to play tennis the way he was
used to as a teaching pro. So now he loved playing golf
with his coterie of cronies, but he loved playing golf with
me, just the two of us, probably more than anything else
in the world.

I was, of course, a very busy person, but I loved my dad
and squeezed a round with him into my schedule whenever possible.

I drove the cart past the palms and pines lining the fairway. It was a glorious Florida afternoon with a slight
breeze off the ocean and the songs of birds in stereo. My
father could not have been happier. His grin would just
not go away. I think this was years before the phrase
"quality time" was coined, but that's what we were
spending together. Since the time I was born, my dad
sequestered every spare minute to spend time with me in
active pursuits—tennis, of course, but also surfing, basketball, skating, building sand castles, gardening and just
hanging together. Even when we puttered around, not a
minute had been wasted, because the memories that
remained were like splashes of molten gold. At the very
least, I owed him this.

When we approached my ball, he patted me on the
back, acknowledging, "You're really good at this game."

"Yeah. What about the last seventeen holes?" I had
played dismally, but a father's love for a daughter is
beyond reason or logic. He always, without fail, looked for
the good in people and in life, and every round of golf was
a good one.

"Don't worry about the past," he'd say. "It's the hole
that lies ahead that matters." Another gem of unmitigated
common sense I ignored, but which had somehow stub-
bornly insinuated its way by osmotic repetition into the
web of my life.

Even though my ball was only inches from the cup, I missed the putt. I was thinking about the beer I would be having in the clubhouse instead of focusing on the moment. I slammed the head of my putter into the green, fully aware displays of impatient annoyance irked him, the quintessential sportsman who never showed his emotions during play.

He ignored my outburst as though it never happened. His shot from the edge of the green rolled smoothly into the hole, landing with that satisfying plunk of a golf ball coming home. We tallied our scores, and he had beaten me by a mere fifteen strokes.

I had never once bested my father in anything, much less golf. He had innate athletic ability and his concentration and ability to focus were unmatched. Part of it was about being a female, about never being quite as good. When the frustration got to me at times, he would say patiently, "Don't ever let being a woman be an excuse." When he saw that one didn't work, he would fall back on the old standby, "Things will be better tomorrow." I loved that one. Never mind that he was right.

When my dad was diagnosed with cancer and the doctors said with grim finality that he would not recover, I took a leave of absence from my job. This was many years before the Family Medical Leave Act made this an acceptable and legal avenue. I didn't know how long he had to live and didn't care that I might lose my job and all the effort it had taken to get it. All of sudden, those gems of thought, those words of wisdom I'd shoved to the hinterlands of my psyche took on a crystal clarity. I wanted to immerse myself in his wisdom, understanding, patience and all the other stable qualities he had but I had been too busy to care about, before they would be lost forever. It appeared to others as though I was making a sacrifice for him. But the truth was I needed him now, even though he had been there for me every day of my life. We played golf as much as we could, until he couldn't play anymore, and I soaked up his insights like a woman lost in the desert of life without water.

When he died, all of his golfing friends, most of whom I'd never met, came to the funeral. It made me sadly aware of how little I knew of his life outside our time together. It also became apparent, as they paid their respects in various ways, that he had bragged to them about what a great golfer I was. It was a ruse I tried to stifle, but I knew that even in death, he had used his love of golf in yet another way to profess his love and confidence in me.

I don't mean to imply my dad was perfect. He could sometimes be a bit inconsistent. Nonetheless, today, ten years later, I would give up every car, every house, every everything I have ever had for one round of golf with him, just for the simple pleasure of absorbing each link in his chain of pithy expressions: "Relax, it's just a game!" which he alternated to suit the occasion with, "Golf is much more than a game, sweetheart. It's a practice round for life!"

Debra Moss

5

GOLF LINKS A FAMILY TOGETHER

The family is one of nature's masterpieces.

George Santayana

184

The Collection Basket

My mother was my dad's grand passion in life. One of my fondest childhood memories was watching my father flip on the radio each morning before he left for work, then whirl my mother around the kitchen floor in a joyous dance.

But second only to my mother in the love department was my father's adoration of golf. My dad, a Michigan dentist named Cy Collins, cherished the game. He was a deft player, regularly shooting in the low seventies for eighteen holes. He played whenever he could, at home and on vacation in Hawaii, Scotland, and other locales. Golf was truly his nectar of the gods.

In the early 1980s, we began noticing the early signs of the Alzheimer's disease that eventually took his life. Dad became confused and forgetful. Though he had paid the family bills for decades, numbers now mystified him. Once he took the family car out for a drive and became lost, stopping only when he ran out of gas many miles from home. But Dad's love of golf lived on. He couldn't remember many things, but he remembered perfectly how to play the game. His drives and his putts were as good as ever.

And this is the part of the story where Dad's love of golf and generosity of spirit converged in the most touching way. A few years before he died in the small northern Michigan town where they had a summer home, Mom and Dad went to Sunday Mass as usual. Dad smiled and shook hands with friends and neighbors, then listened attentively to the priest's sermon. And when the collection basket was passed down his pew, Dad very deliberately reached into his pocket and placed in the basket the most precious gift he could imagine: three golf balls.

Jan K. Collins

Remember When

"You know, Mom, a person's true character always comes out on the golf course. Since you never played golf, you really didn't know Dad—Pat Gardner, the golfer— now did you?" This was one of the toughest things I'd ever said to my mother. It was a calculated risk I had to take.

My eighty-five-year-old mother glared at me, slowly shaking her head, her stern look signaling me to stop. She wanted no part of this. We—my mother Goldie, sisters Evelyn and Marge, brother Don, and my daughter Jill— were sitting in the Schmitt Funeral Home in WaKeeney, Kansas, putting the final touches on my Dad's funeral, scheduled for the next day. Dad, who had suddenly died of a heart attack, was lying in an open casket about fifteen feet from us.

Because two other funerals were scheduled that weekend, the atmosphere was morbid to say the least. So I decided to lighten things up a bit.

I began telling a story about my dad's crazy antics on our golf course. He had taken up golf late in his life and never quite got the hang of it, playing to a 30-something handicap. "One day, Mom, when we were teenagers," I said, "Dad actually hit a drive in the fairway—it was the first one I'd ever seen. Huh, Don?" Don nodded, grinning, knowing what was coming.

"When we got to where his ball was supposed to be, we couldn't find it, which got Dad all riled up."

"Okay, where is it? I hit it right here!" he barked. Then he stopped dead in his tracks. He had spied his ball about two feet down a ten-inch-wide gopher hole, sitting on a dirt ledge. 'Shut up, you two, and don't move,' he scolded.

"Heck, Mom, we weren't talking or moving. Right, Don?"

"That's right, Mom," said Don, mischievousness dancing in his eyes. Mom narrowed her eyes, still glaring at me.

"Then, Dad got down on his knees and carefully reached for the ball with his 5-iron. Hope soared within him as he hooked the ball with the club face. Holding his breath, he gently lifted the ball upward, hand over hand, delicately holding the club by his thumbs and fingertips. Sweat beads appeared on his forehead. His hands were really shaking now, and he winced each time the ball nearly slipped off the club. It was painstaking work.

"'Keep quiet, you two,' he whispered. 'I've just about got it.' After what seemed like an eternity, he finally pinned the ball near the top of the hole and ever so tenderly reached down with his left hand to retrieve it. Just as his fingers approached the ball, two more balls fell out of his upper shirt pocket and slammed into the first ball, causing all three balls to disappear down the gopher hole, lost forever. Dad flew into a rage. He jumped up, kicked the hole a few times, then beat the hole half to death with his club. Don and I were dying laughing on the ground."

As Mom gave me that dreaded old schoolmarm look that she had perfected in one-room schoolhouses out on the prairie where she had taught for forty years, the family exploded into laughter. My plan was working, the gloom lifting.

Dad had demonstrated a great sense of humor all his life and loved a good belly laugh. I was banking on Mom understanding this, and I was looking for some help from the rest of the family. Just then, Don chimed in.

"Remember the time, Bud, when we were sitting on the bench behind the raised tee box on the third hole, and Dad was getting ready to hit his driver? Now, Mom, I'm not trying to degrade Dad in any way. You know he was a great baseball player, who played a mean first base and hit cleanup for the WaKeeney town team and even played against the great Satchel Paige once. Remember?"

Mom, warming up a bit, nodded at Don.

"Well," continued Don, "standing over his ball that day, he told us he really felt like clobbering a drive. Bud and I glanced at each other but kept quiet as Dad addressed the ball. Then he swung with all his might. He stared down the fairway, yelling at us. 'Did you guys see it? Where in the devil did it go?'

"The truth is, Mom, he had swung so hard he overshot the ball and just nicked it with the heel of his club, causing it to trickle between his feet and slowly meander off the tee box and down the hill behind him. Don and I couldn't hold back. We laughed so hard we fell off the bench into an anthill.

"Seeing our predicament, Dad bellowed, 'Serves you right, you galoots! Now where's my ball?' When he saw it still trickling down the hill, he realized how silly this all was and cracked up, too."

The whole family roared at that one, which brought a brief smile to Mom's face. She quickly regained her serious composure, but we were on a roll and couldn't stop now.

"Another time, Mom," I recalled, "Dad, Don and I played in an out-of-town golf tournament. When Dad's foursome was called to the first tee, Dad pulled the head cover off his wood driver and threw the club to the ground in disgust.

"'What's the matter, Pat?' asked one of his playing partners.

"'Would you look at that?' snapped Dad. 'See all those white marks on the top of my driver. Darn it, my kids have been using my clubs again.'

"His buddies all sympathized as he addressed the ball. Dad made a ferocious swing at the ball—which he had teed up way too high—and whipped the club head right under the ball, sending it straight up into the air. Then things got real serious as everybody scattered when the ball came crashing down in the middle of the tee box, leaving no doubt who had been putting the white marks on that driver."

The twinkle in Mom's eye told me I was doing the right thing. She had finally realized I was just trying my level best to help us cope with the loss of Dad. We then told a few more golf jokes about Dad, which seemed to lift the spirit of our family at this mournful time. A few minutes later, Don asked Jill and me to accompany him over to Dad's casket. Dad was dressed in his best gray suit with a matching tie. "Bud, take a close look at Dad's tie," urged Don. I couldn't believe it. It matched all right, but the words on it caught my eye. It had "Happy Anniversary," scrawled repeatedly on a diagonal its entire length.

"And watch this," said Don, as he reached for the tie. He pressed a small button on the back of the tie and out jumped a classic song. I couldn't believe it.

"Who chose this tie?" I asked when the last note had faded away.

"Mom did," said Don. "I gave Dad that tie as a joke years ago for one of their anniversaries. I guess Mom was too numb over Dad's passing to know what she had done."

Knowing my dad had a great sense of humor, I believe he would have gotten a big chuckle out of watching this scene unfold. Just then, I heard Mom laughing at something my sisters had said. It was music to my ears.

The next day during Dad's funeral, I was extremely nervous. I had agreed to do Dad's eulogy on behalf of the family. I had done only one other eulogy for a dear friend, which I had mishandled badly. I had lost control and cried throughout my entire presentation. So, I wasn't sure I could pull this one off; after all, it was my Dad's final hour. The family was counting on me. The funeral home was crowded with about seventy-five family members and friends. I was so shook up, I asked my daughter, Jill, to accompany me to the lectern—and to finish reading my prepared statement if I began to cry and lose control. She agreed.

Then it was time. The minister nodded, and Jill and I moved to the pulpit. I thanked everyone for being with us to honor Dad's life and then began to read my statement. About a third of the way through, my voice cracked and tears began streaming down my face. I paused, then started reading again. I choked up again as tears spilled onto my papers. I was about ready to have Jill continue for me when she slipped something into my left hand. I felt an old familiar friend—a golf ball. At that instant, an overwhelming wave of relief washed over me, followed by a serene peace. Just then I understood the depth of Jill's unconditional love for me. I was thankful she had made the long trip from California to Kansas to be with me. That ball—a symbol of joy and love—and Jill's reassuring smile gave me the courage to finish one of my greatest challenges.

Bud Gardner

Being There

*Regard the small as important;
make much of the little.*

Lao-tzu

The ninth hole at Caledonia Golf Course is a par-3 nestled in the mountains of south-central Pennsylvania. The tee is perched about seventy-five feet above a tiny green that is surrounded by a raised berm, with trees leaving only the narrowest of openings to the flagstick below: a donut in the middle of a forest clearing, 140 yards away, daring visitors to bite. I remember it well.

The last time I saw this hole was the first time I played golf with my father. I was fourteen. He swung a 9-iron, sailing the ball onto the rear edge of the green. The ball went into reverse and backed itself to within inches of the cup.

I stood amazed at the skill and power of my dad, hoping beyond hope that I could be just like him.

He handed me a 5-wood and said, "Okay, Don, just like that. Keep your head down and take a nice easy swing."

I obeyed his command but the ball did not obey mine.

It flew with a wicked hook into the woods. Dad didn't say a word and tossed me another ball. Then another, and another and . . . six Wilsons later, I finally managed to dribble the ball down the hill and bounced it next to the mounded barrier protecting the green.

We walked down the mountain together and all I could do was stare at the man for whom I had found yet another reason to worship. He was the best golfer I had ever seen. Better than Palmer or even that new guy on the tour, Jack Something-or-other.

I can't tell you how many strokes it took to finally sink that ball on No. 9 at Caledonia. I do remember, however, what my father said when it was finally over: "You're getting there, son, keep up the good work." He gave me assurance, not ridicule, and I loved him even more.

That was thirty years ago. Dad died six years later. We played many rounds of golf together in those six years, but I could never achieve his greatness. My mind was too occupied with girls, war protests, school dramas and more girls. Dad, though, was a patient and willing teacher who allowed my dalliance and led me to the links and through the passages of adolescence.

It was that hole at Caledonia, though, that burned a vision in my soul. I have often described that particular par-3 to others, without regard to a reciprocated interest. It was not only the memory of a perfect golf hole I described, but a perfect day, a perfect shot and a perfect dad.

Today, the first time in thirty years, I stood at that same tee box on the same mountain. Not much had changed. It was the same trees, the same hill, the same green below, but a different me. I thought not about people, politics or work. I thought only of Dad and how a hole-in-one would sanctify and honor his memory. I reached into my bag and withdrew the 9-iron.

His mentoring filled my ears as it had not done in many

years. Head down . . . feet shoulder-length apart . . . slow backswing . . . eye on the ball . . . follow through . . . !

With his instructions I teed the ball up and prayed for redemption. My life has not turned out the equal of my, or most likely his, expectations. The trees, the hazards, the traps along the way got the better of me so many times. I have survived though, and I'm happy to report that my life has found the fairway again. But with this shot, with this ball, with his memory, I could atone for my sins.

I drew the club back slowly and reached for the heavens above, begging salvation and guidance. Head down, eye on the ball, follow-through. The club struck squarely and the ball soared into the crisp mountain air. I could swear there was a halo around it.

"You da man!" my partner screamed as the ball headed for the flag that was waving down below. I smiled and kept my eyes peeled on the tiny white dot as it moved away into the distance.

The mountain breezes and early morning mists play tricks, not only with the flight of golf balls, but on the eyes as well. What had looked to be a perfect shot suddenly turned bad. I screamed, "Go baby! Go! Turn! Get there!" The ball, which was out of earshot, did not heed my pleas. It landed short and plugged itself in the right-hand berm. It never had a chance.

Instead of agonizing over a shot of improbable proportions, I laughed at myself as I recalled Dad's most important lesson. "It's the little things in life that matter the most, Son."

Just being there was enough. I didn't need a hole-in-one or even to land the ball on the dance floor to obtain the peace and redemption I sought. He already gave that to me. He gave me the fortitude, the perseverance and the will to overcome difficulties many years ago. When I needed him most he was always there. He still is.

Thanks, Dad.

Don Didio

Way Above Par

One afternoon I had the chance to meet a couple of friends on the course for a quick nine. We were paired together for a scramble at our church the next weekend and we admittedly needed the practice. As I was driving to meet them, I started reflecting on my marriage. After seven years, we had become too predictable. No itches mind you, but more than enough rashes and hives from the children. With the kids, the mortgage, the bills and, of course, the job to pay for all of the above, we had landed in a sandtrap.

In college, it seemed like everything enjoyable in life centered around our time together. People always said that we were the ones that lit the fires, but it seemed like we had forgotten the matches.

Golf was an escape for us. I'd chase that stupid white ball around a deep green golf course and would never get any better. My wife drove the electric golf cart, always wearing a shorts-and-tank-top set, dark sunglasses, and a white golf visor. For ten yards in either direction, you could smell the unmistakable scent of cocoa butter. The only reason she went was to get a suntan.

If the truth were known, the only reason I went was to watch *her*.

One afternoon, she studied my golf swing more intently than ever before. Finally, on the seventeenth hole, she came out with her notion.

"Let me try to hit one."

At first, I thought *what a novel idea*. Then I changed my mind. Golf was a man's sport, or so I thought. "You? You can't hit a golf ball. You're a girl."

"Thanks for noticing. Just the same, I think I can lose golf balls as well as you can."

A very true observation.

I handed over my 3-wood and dug the tee into the hard clay at the tee box. Without even a practice swing, she promptly knocked the ball straight down the middle of the fairway. When we got to our balls, her drive was five yards further than mine. From that day on, she started playing golf.

Some of the best times we shared early in our marriage were on the golf course. We'd go in the mid-morning before the temperature would climb. The time we spent together laughing and teasing under the sun cemented our relationship. As I pulled into the parking lot outside the clubhouse, I realized how much I missed seeing her on a golf course.

All the guys at church looked forward to playing our annual tournament. Mike and Danny, a couple of fellow church members, were going to play on my team along with a mystery partner. Hopefully someone who could drive and putt, our collective shortcomings.

Every team invited someone outside our church to play. Sort of a community involvement thing. What I always found amazing was how all these strangers could hit the cover off the ball and always straight down the middle! Let's face it, there are more ringers in a church golf tournament than in the children's bell choir.

When I got to the practice green, I saw Danny and his

wife, Beth, pulling out Danny's clubs. A second golf bag was resting on the side.

"Whose clubs are those, Danny?" I asked, expecting him to say that next week's mystery golfer was already inside the clubhouse, paying for our tickets.

"Why, they're mine," said Beth as she threw them across her shoulder.

"Yeah, she's my secret weapon today. She tees off from the women's tee box, you know. With her drives, we are guaranteed at least a good one."

I snickered at the thought of a woman playing golf, then I caught a whiff of cocoa butter.

The three of us spent the afternoon chasing balls, hitting horrible iron shots and missing almost every putt. Danny and Beth didn't care. They enjoyed playing golf together in a way that I suddenly recalled.

It's not the winning but the losing together that matters most.

As we were starting to leave, the conversation came to the tournament. Danny asked, "Well, do you think you can find a fourth player by Saturday?"

"Yeah. Playing this afternoon reminded me of the perfect partner."

I came home to find my wife in the kitchen. She smiled and asked, "Did you play well?"

"Nope. Just as hopeless as usual."

"How did the others play?"

"Hopeless as well. We need a fourth player for the tournament and I think I found one."

She looked up at me with those bright eyes and asked, "Really, who?"

"You."

Surprise grew across her face. "Me? I haven't played golf in years. I can't help you win."

"Can't help us lose either. But it sure would be nice to see you out there again."

That next Saturday, the four of us played golf on perhaps the most beautiful spring day that I can recall. We laughed and teased all over the course as shot after shot missed the mark. On the last hole, we finished with a score of 79, seven shots above par, buried deep in last place.

Afterward, the awards were handed out and we got the prize for having the roughest day, a kind way to say we lost. Each of us received a sleeve of shiny pink golf balls for our hard day's work. On our way back to our table, I put my arm around her shoulder and whispered, "These guys just haven't figured out who really won!"

Harrison Kelly

Divorce, of Course

We took a mulligan.

Cheryl Kratzert

As most public-course golfers know, it is not uncommon for a weekend round to take five or six hours, if you can even get a starting time on your favorite local course. The volume of people who cannot play mid-week, coupled with those looking for a respite from yard work or the spouse, causes a flood of players filling every available tee time. Slow play is inevitable because of the varying capability of weekend golfers. As a result, you will hear complaining, more-than-occasional cries of "Fore" and frustrated players waiting on every tee.

Marching into this fray one weekend, I joined a threesome following a group of older women. My playing companions were male, somewhat grayer than I, and seemed unusually anxious about playing behind the women. They muttered while the women teed off, they muttered while waiting for the fairway to clear and they muttered continuously until they reached the green. I could only make out a few words here and there, mostly about slow play.

After several holes, which seemed to take forever, one of the men asked me if I was married (I am), and if my wife played golf (she does not). I returned the conversation by asking the same questions.

The first gentleman waived a disdaining hand and said, "No more, and thank God." I was not certain which question he was answering.

The second man smiled and said, "Divorced, and she does." I just smiled back.

The third man looked intently down the fairway at the women ahead of us and then turned and spoke. "I was married to the woman in the blue pants, up there in the fairway. George was married to the woman in yellow, and Dave to the one in white. My wife hit the ball farther than I could, and she putted better. Asked her for a divorce last year, after thirty-seven years of marriage."

"Is it just a coincidence that they are in the group ahead?" I asked.

"No," the third man (I can't recall his name) replied, "we've been doing this every weekend for two years."

"You mean you arrange this, even though you are divorced because of golf? But why, if it frustrates you?"

"Frustrates us? What do you mean?" George asked.

"Well, you're muttering on every hole, complaining about how slow the round is. Why would you want to play behind them?"

They smiled at each other, then looked back to me. "Son," George started, "we're not frustrated. We've got new clubs, good health for our age and a regular game every Saturday."

"You see," the third man continued, "our playing golf left them home alone. So, after George's wife divorced him three years ago, and then Dave's, the women took up the game with my ex. They enjoyed it so much, it changed their attitude. In fact, they became like girls again, and

George and Dave have been dating them ever since."

"But you said you were divorced last year."

"Sure. It improved George and Dave's sex life, so I con-vinced my wife to divorce so we could have the same thing. And it worked. Couldn't be happier."

"But the complaining I hear, what's that?"

George and Dave smiled again. "Slow play!" Dave said. "The sooner we get done with this round, the sooner we get to date night."

Gordon W. Youngs

"When your car was stolen you said your golf clubs were in the trunk. You failed to mention your wife was in the front seat."

Reprinted by permission of David W. Harbaugh. Originally appeared in Golf Digest.

The Ace Man

I consider myself an incredibly lucky man, possessed of a wonderful, interesting and eclectic life. I have a remarkable wife and life partner, Ewa, a fantastic and truly unique stepdaughter, Nikki, a wonderful twin and mother, and, thanks to a truly mystical golfing adventure, a magical dog that enhances all of our lives.

The Charlotte Golf Links is an expertly crafted layout carved out of the rolling farmland outside of Charlotte, North Carolina. It has often been the scene of peaceful late afternoon walks, one of the few courses where you can still walk nine holes at dusk. That, as well as its obvious ties to the traditional roots of the game, has made it a place where we sometimes can feel a connection to the deeper, more spiritual side of things. We were, however, unprepared for what was to happen one eventful morning.

On a clear, beautiful Thursday, Ewa (who shares most everything in my life, including a passion for golf) and I had an early tee time. I felt completely at ease warming up, and had, surprisingly, become aware of and was able to repeat a simple swing thought that was allowing me to hit the ball better than I had in quite a while. I hoped the thought would stay with me.

The course was serenely uncrowded, rare nowadays,

especially on such a gorgeous golfing day. We began the round in a relaxed and unhurried mood, both grateful, as we often are, for the kind of lives that allow us to be out on the course together.

I was +1 after six holes (not bad for a 10 handicap), and Ewa and I were laughing as we went to the seventh hole, a long, uphill par-3 whose tee is surrounded by tall, heather-like grasses, waving in the breeze. As we turned to approach the tee, we cleared the tall grass, and there, standing at the tee, was a small dog staring straight at us. We all seemed to pause for a second, and then, being unabashed dog lovers, Ewa and I said our hellos to this funny, playful, reddish-coated pup. A mixture of long-haired dachshund and something resembling a fox (with no tail), he rolled around on the tee, licked us a few times and stood watching as we hit away.

We said, "See ya later," and proceeded up to the green. Before we got there, our little friend ran up to the green and picked up my ball in his mouth, looking child like and full of mischief. After we stopped laughing, Ewa and I bogeyed the hole, but before we could leave the green, there he was again, this time with his head entirely in the cup, looking, no doubt, for the deeper meaning of the game.

We proceeded to the next tee, followed of course by you-know-who, who jumped into our cart (sadly you must ride early in the day) and climbed into Ewa's lap. The eighth is a dogleg left (of course) par-5, and I snap-hooked my drive into the trees lining the fairway left, feeling my score slipping away a bit. I heard no contact with wood, so I presumed my drive was out of bounds. I re-teed and hit a provisional ball, trying not to think too much about losing a good round's score. On returning to the cart, I found our new friend asleep in my wife's lap, and chuckled at this strange new golfing partner.

After Ewa hit her tee shot, we drove out to the fairway, and lo and behold, about two hundred yards out, dead in the middle, was my first tee ball. *Incredible,* I thought, and turned to Ewa and said, "It has to be the pup. He's lucky. That ball never touched a tree." I proceeded to hit a flush 3-wood, then a really crisp 8-iron to about three feet, and made the putt for birdie. Back to +1, and really laughing now.

The ninth hole is an uphill par-3 that was playing 167 yards that day. I took a look at the still-asleep, gentle face of my good-luck charm and suddenly was reminded of the swing key I had used earlier in the round. I hit a pure 5-iron at the flag, the bottom of which was hidden by the elevated green. I watched the ball in flight, and, as we are wont to do after a feel-good strike on a par-3, yelled "Go in the hole," or some such brilliantly worded phrase. As I walked back to the cart, Ewa remarked on the seeming ease of my play that day, and we both looked again at the dog. I said, "If the ball is in the hole, we're keeping the dog."

Ewa hit her tee shot, and as we approached the green, there was only one ball visible. Still in a playful mood, I asked Ewa to go pick my ball out of the hole, and I sat with a now wide-awake, furry-faced pooch staring at me. I looked up in time to see Ewa jumping up and down, a beaming smile on her face, saying, "Yes, yes, yes. . . ." I ran up to the green, followed by, you-guessed-it, and, some-what in shock, picked the ball out of the hole, the first time in eighteen years I ever had that privilege.

It wasn't much of a choice after that. His name is, natu-rally, Ace, and along with our other two, Stella and Raquette, he is now an integral part of our home and lives, and is, I think, a symbol of all the reasons that golf is the greatest game—he gives us joy and constant surprise. Although he is often frustrating and difficult, when we pay attention and allow him to teach us, he rewards us with unending gifts.

Mitch Laurance

Early Retirement

My fiancée, Lauren, and I were in her hometown of Philadelphia, where her aunt was hosting Lauren's bridal shower. The plans for the day largely entailed my staying out of everyone's way until the end of the shower, when I would then be introduced to several of her parents' friends and family.

My prospective father-in-law, Milt, who had only recently taken up golf, naturally thought the best form of introduction would be a golf outing involving me, him and a family friend whose wife would be attending the shower.

Now I hadn't picked up a club in months, but not wanting to disappoint Milt (and not wanting to play a larger role in the bridal shower than absolutely necessary), I agreed.

As it turned out, we were running a little late in making our tee time and I didn't have any opportunity to warm up with a bucket of balls before the round, as I had hoped. There was also a slight backup on the first tee. To make room for the influx of golfers, Milt had pulled our cart a little further forward than safety would normally dictate. I thought about saying something to him but as he was to the left of the tee box, and I normally hit the ball so far right that golfers in the next fairway are occasionally sent ducking for cover, I assumed he would be in no danger. I was wrong.

I caught the ball off the heel of my driver, sending it directly into my future father-in-law's right hand. Now, my relationship with Milt had always been friendly, but formal. At this point, not only was I confident that was going to change, but I wasn't certain Milt was going to lend his blessing to my marrying his youngest daughter.

I was also convinced that I had, with that one blow, sent my future father-in-law heading toward an early retirement. Milt is an ear-nose-and-throat doctor and is required to perform certain types of surgery in order to continue his practice.

Horrified at what I had just done, I began to shake so badly that I couldn't even think about finishing out the hole. So I picked up my ball, got an ice pack for Milt, and took the wheel of the cart while Milt bravely attempted to continue playing. By the time we got to the second hole, Milt somehow had me laughing about the whole incident.

"Todd, you didn't hit me hard enough," he told me. He explained that if I'd done more significant damage, he'd have been able to retire (something it turned out he'd been contemplating anyway), while collecting on a nice insurance policy he'd taken out just in case of golfing accidents involving future sons-in-law.

I chuckled, then replied, "Well, we've got seventeen more holes. I'll see what I can do."

It was the first time I'd felt completely at ease with my future father-in-law, and perhaps more than anything else that took place during Lauren's and my engagement period, his gentle, good nature during the incident made me feel like a part of her family. After all, who else but a family member could have forgiven such an act?

Milt finished the round and made it to the bridal shower

before heading to the emergency room. It was determined
that I had, indeed, broken a bone in his hand—a fact he
kept hidden from me until well after the wedding as he
didn't want me to feel any worse than I already did.

But now that I know, I feel even better.

Todd Behrendt

Mom Hits the Links

*A*ge *is not important unless you're a cheese.*

Helen Hayes

I talked to my mother on the phone one night. She had just returned from her first golf school, which also happened to be her first golf game.

"I sure do love this game," she gushed.

You see, my brother and sister and girlfriend and myself had purchased a starter set of clubs for Mom last Christmas. She runs her own business, in the sports insurance and benefits arena, and over the years her travels to meetings had taken her to places like Doral and Pebble Beach. But she was the only member of the family that didn't play golf. So the rest of us would hear: "Well, I could have played a round there if I played golf. But I did enjoy riding around the course in a cart. You know how I love the sound of the ocean."

Naturally, there was only so much of this we muni hacks in the family could take. So we took a chance and surprised her with the clubs. We figured she'd be decent because we'd seen her take a few swings one time at a driving range. Although she's a southpaw she seemed comfortable swinging right-handed, and she had whacked the heck out of the ball. Plus, it seemed like a good mode of exercise for her as she moved into a different phase of her life.

She was very excited, but knew so little about the game and how to play it that she feared embarrassment.

"Just go to the range for a while, Mom. Then you can try playing a few holes, and gradually work your way up to a full round," I counseled.

Those first few months, she went to the range just a couple of times. But it was exciting to buy the clothes.

"I got myself a new golf outfit today. And I now have golf shoes."

"How about your swing—have you hit any balls lately?"

"No, but I'm going to be all ready when it's time for golf camp!"

We siblings conferred and separately advised her to start some simple stretching and exercises a few weeks before going to Pine Needles. Then we sat back and waited.

I didn't hear from her the entire week. The day I knew the school ended I called her not long after she arrived home.

"Oh, we had so much fun," she said again. "And you know what? Yesterday I played my first round."

"Wow, a full eighteen?"

"Well, it was a nine-hole round. And my team won! It was what they call 'best ball.' And on one hole I drove it all the way to the green and we used my ball."

"What do you mean—was it a par-3 or a par-4?"

"Oh, I don't know."

"I love that kind of attitude, Mom." I really did.

"All I know to do is try and get the ball into the hole in as few strokes as possible," she continued succinctly. "The other ladies' shots were back a ways, and one of them said, 'Oh my gosh, Sally's ball is on the green.'"

I could tell that this was one of those watershed conversations, the kind you only have once.

"So I played another nine holes later, and guess what? I shot a 46."

"Holy cow," I said, stunned, "you must have even had a par in there somewhere."

"Oh yes, I had a couple of those, and also did one of the holes under par."

"A birdie?" I said, sitting down. "That's incredible! What was it, a par-5?"

"I don't remember. When I told the bartender what I had shot, he was surprised, and said, 'Sally, do you realize that if you doubled that score for a full eighteen, you'd break 100? That's fantastic.' But I thought it wasn't that great, since it was over par."

I paused to let that settle in.

"Thank you again for the clubs, Adam. Oh, you know what? I need to find out where you got them, so I can get a sand wedge and pitching wedge."

"Oh yeah," I said sheepishly, "we only got you the starter set. I suppose you'll need some even-numbered clubs too."

"Oh, heavens no. Not yet. But I did learn about what to hit what distances. Of course, I'll probably fall back some now, but I sure love this game!"

It was a wry turning of the tables, as I, the son, pondered the wonderful, fleeting innocence of my mother's introduction to golf. There she was, discovering the pleasures of the game, apparently still whacking the heck out of the ball and enjoying the very act. The experiment had succeeded, and she was launched on a late-blooming golf career. Perhaps she will never pay attention to the score . . . until she reaches par that is.

For me, and anybody else who is unlearning the techniques and visualizations and just learning to hit the darned ball, it is a lesson in rediscovery. Chances are we sure do love this game too. And I, for the thousandth and not the final time, get to say . . . thanks, Mom.

Adam Bruns

Silent Swing

If it is a part of you, golf can heal. Without it, I couldn't withstand the challenge my life has become. It is God's plan, I guess, that my little girl live in a world of near silence. I just wish she could live with me.

Despite normal intelligence, at age seven Angela could read one word: her name. Boarding school was her best shot—perhaps her only shot—at a future.

So a few weeks after Angela's seventh birthday, I found myself printing her initials on socks, a dozen pairs of Pocahontas panties and the derrieres of her Barbies. Tying her bike to the station-wagon roof we drove her to a school for the deaf—a place I swore she'd never go.

Angela is adopted. So no matter how much I love her, she may someday wonder why her mother gave her up. When she came to us, I swore she would never be given up again. Yet, by sending her away to school, that's exactly what I felt I was doing.

I knew it was her best shot—perhaps her only shot—at a future. But as the reality of her leaving sank in, I ran from it. I had learned, while fending off cancer, that when you're doing all that can be done, and the rest is out of your control, denial can be a good thing. I knew only one place to escape the pain: the golf course. Golf is so much a part of me, it's hard to tell where it leaves off and I begin. It was a gift from my father. It brought me together (on a blind date) with my husband. And it provides a home for the part of me that needs to fight—and win.

When I faced the possibility of losing my own life, I practiced chipping and putting, with plastic tubes hanging out of my left armpit (a capital violation of the dress code). So it was natural that when it came to losing my daughter, I found myself at the golf course that wraps around our weather-beaten Kansas house like a mother's arms.

In a primal way, golf is my earth mother. It held me all that summer, many times past dusk.

It also held Angela. I hadn't expected my baby to be like me. Then one day when she was barely two, I walked into the playroom and found her plumb bobbing a plastic putter a friend had given me as a gag. My heart soared. That summer before she left, we spent hours together at the driving range and chipping greens. On her own, Angela would quietly tote her little bag to the front lawn, where she taught herself to smash a ball seventy-five yards into the woods. Golf spoke to her, in her silent world.

With all of that devotion came the gift of improvement. In July a woman friend and I won my club's member-guest tournament. I even won a longest-drive contest. Then, one steamy August day I did the unthinkable:

I broke 90.

This was golf as I'd only dreamed it. Surely it would sustain me through the darkest hours looming ahead. Three weeks later, Angela left, and so did my game. It was a full face-down collapse. I couldn't drive. I couldn't putt. I couldn't do anything. My scores skyrocketed back to where they had been ten years before.

Maybe I could have withstood the cruel, below-zero Kansas winter missing my daughter, if I could have looked forward to the golf season. But even that promised only the humiliation of revealing the flailing nincompoop I'd turned into. I cursed God for piling it on. There was no place for me to go. Then, finally one day it dawned on me: golf school. The school would restore my game. The game would restore my spirit. Then, before I'd know it, golf season would begin in April. Soon Angela would be home for the summer.

Many times during that monstrous winter I worried that Angela, born brave, would cope by gradually disconnecting from me. During an early visit home, she headed outside to play, layered and looking like a balloon in the Thanksgiving Day Parade. When I looked out the window to check on her, I couldn't believe what I saw. She was standing out front, hitting snowballs with her sawed-off 8-wood.

A revelation rushed through me: Angela has it, too. The love that won't die. The spiritual link. I felt as if I were looking at myself, and I knew we would survive intact.

Betty Cuniberti

One at a Time

My introduction to the game of golf came as a teenage caddie at an exclusive country club near our home. The $3.50 I was paid for eighteen holes of carrying singles and $5.75 for doubles was a welcome wage for my first job outside our home. My blue-collar family could never afford to belong to a club like this, so my duties were also my entry inside the gates that we so frequently passed. Every Monday was "caddie day," which meant we could play the course for free.

I had always been an above-average athlete. I expected I would do as well with golf. Never having taken even basic lessons, my transition from a baseball bat to a 5-iron was not pretty. My ability to deal with this fact was uglier still. My frequent shots hit out of bounds, whiffed at or drubbed thirty feet up the fairway generally led to a loud, blue stream of cursing. More than one golf club was left to decorate some elm tree, having been thrown and caught up too high to retrieve. At eighteen, even I was mature enough to realize that I needed to either get serious about my golf or give it up. Shortly thereafter, college pursuits gave me little time to play, and a new job meant I would have to pay real greens fees. The "pleasure" I derived from playing made not playing an easy decision.

   At the age of thirty-five, I found myself the father of two boys—eight and ten years old. Their friends in our Iowa neighborhood all played golf. So one summer, our boys took group lessons at a public course near our home. They were both quickly hooked. The lessons they took and a "kids play all day for five dollars" program at a short course in town made for a great summer. About this time, my new job was requiring some very long hours, and my wife suggested that I take up golf as a way to spend time with the boys. I quickly confessed my "dark past" with golf and that I didn't think I would enjoy it any more now than I did then. In the end, her motherly instincts and wifely persuasion won out. "Free Lessons with Every Purchase of a New Set of Clubs" caught my eye, and armed with my credit card I trekked down to the discount golf store.

   Much to my surprise, it was different this time. Same basic instruction . . . the grip . . . the setup and stance . . . backswing and follow through . . . all helped me focus more on the process than necessarily just the result. After many hours on the driving range, I was still not breaking 100 but I enjoyed the experience of learning something new. It propelled me out of the office and into the fresh air of the Iowa heartland. And it did give me more time with my boys. It was interesting, though, to see how their own impatience and lack of maturity caused problems on the course. The ebb and flow of good moods and bad determined what kind of an outing we had. Both boys had inherited my competitiveness. After each hole, they would argue about the accuracy of the score reported by the other sibling. While I was older and more patient than when I first took up the game, I still did my share of carping about lost balls and their slow play as other foursomes waited behind us. Back at home, I was usually greeted by my wife's insightful, "Well, how did it go this time?"

It bothered me that our time together on the course was not creating the father-son bonding experience that my wife and I had envisioned. In my earlier years, I might have become discouraged and vowed not to take the boys out anymore. But giving up is seldom the answer, and some of my favorite memories were of my own dad's love of sports and the way he taught me to play by playing with me. At times like this, if we can only discard discouragement and replace it with a search for new possibilities, we can often rekindle an earlier dream.

I decided to take the boys out one at a time. I also decided to relax and let them play their game at their pace without regard for the result. If they lose a ball, we'll buy another. When they say their score, I'll just write it down. After all, it is their score not mine. I would also take half-days away from the office so we could play during slow times and maintain our own pace. But above all, I remembered, be encouraging, no carping and no criticism. The time we spend together will be our goal and our reward. And it worked! I have great memories now of times on the course with the boys. My best Father's Day gift was when my oldest son took me for a free round of golf at a course where he worked.

I am forty-seven now. My scores are not much lower than they were in the past. But I can play all day and not care. So what has changed since my first set of clubs and the frustration of those early years? Golf has taught me much about life, even as life has taught me much about golf:

1. Relax—the easier you swing, the farther the ball will go. A white-knuckle grip and a harder swing will probably only increase the tension and reduce the joy—with poor results to follow.
2. Get some basic instruction from the experts . . . better

yet, find a mentor and vow to have a listening, teachable spirit.

3. Focus on people. Choose to play with people you enjoy, people who you've found that lift your spirit. Head out to the course on your own sometime and practice showing interest in whomever fate may place you with that day. Look for ways to be an encouraging and uplifting gift to their day.

4. Refresh yourself by learning something new. New experiences will help to keep you young, will rekindle your interest, your vitality and your love for life. Find a partner who shares your interest in learning and in experiencing new things.

5. Look for the positive possibilities in every challenging situation. Very seldom will you have no shot at all. Even when you do, you may be able to take your drop and scramble back into play. Go for it.

6. Realize that life, like golf, has its ups and downs . . . its bunkers and fairways. Ride it out. Beyond each bunker is a well-groomed fairway or green. It only takes one shot to put it back in play.

7. Sharpen up your "inner game." A smooth, relaxed swing—like a smooth, relaxed life—begins in your mind and heart. Learn to stir and rekindle the human spirit by stopping to "smell the roses" along the way. Take a deep breath. Look around at the beauty of the course and get the most from the experience.

8. Tempo is important. Get in touch with your feelings. A good swing has a distinct and gratifying feel. Developing a feel for the game is as important as the mechanics.

9. Above all, have fun—enjoy the journey and the process and let the results take care of themselves.

Larry R. Pearson

The Substitute Caddie

An unusual experience occurred at the L.A. Open, where I came out of retirement from my previous job to caddie. My husband Tom Lehman's longtime caddie, Andrew Martinez, was injured the night before the tournament, and Tom asked me to fill in. I agreed under the condition that I did not have to carry Tom's Taylor Made tour bag, which is huge. We struck a deal, and they got me a much smaller bag.

My first duty as caddie was to meet Tom on the driving range so he could warm up before his round. Other players and caddies were stunned to see me. I proceeded with my job like any other caddie—marking balls, cleaning his clubs and getting the towel wet.

Things went smoothly, and Tom played okay, but the whispers and comments from the gallery as I passed by were amusing. The only rather tense moment came on Sunday on the sixteenth hole. Tom had been having a very, let's say, trying day as far as golf. But I was proud of him because his temper was under control.

When Tom three-putted for bogey, I noticed his putter

in mid-air, sailing into the middle of the pond. The crowd gasped and looked at me for my reaction. I just smiled and walked with Tom to the next tee.

As we walked, I whispered to him, "That's fine. At least you didn't swear. But now I get to pick which club you'll be putting with on the last two holes."

Tom went along with it.

The seventeenth hole started with a drive down the middle, and his second shot landed just over the green. He proceeded to hit a sand wedge and left the ball six inches from the cup. I told him to putt out with the same club, and the crowd loved it. Especially when he made it.

The eighteenth hole, a par-5, started with Tom's driver straight down the middle, and his second shot got him in position for an easy approach. I handed him the wedge that had just served as his putter. He almost holed it (that would have eliminated the putting problems), the ball rolling to six feet.

Just for effect, I handed him his driver. After the crowd figured out that he didn't have a putter anymore, they were all eagerly awaiting a birdie with the driver. He missed it. But ending on two pars was not such a difficult lesson to learn.

Melissa Lehman

"All you'll need is your sand wedge."

Reprinted by permission of David W. Harbaugh. Originally appeared in Golf Digest.

Angel's Flight

"Fore!"

Instinctively I ducked, covering my head with my arms. A golf ball sizzled past me and landed no more than twenty feet from my quaking body. It careened off a hillock, rolled down a nearby cart path and, then, as if to punctuate its passing, neatly *plopped* into the water hazard beyond the green.

"What the . . .?" I turned slowly, nostrils flaring, my eyes fixing upon the culprit. Marching up the fairway and smiling radiantly was a creature of such incredible beauty I have yet to recover. Her hair, blowing back from her temples, was fiery red. Her prancing gait ran a shock through my senses. It was the kind of shock any man would love to receive.

"Oh, I am sorry," she said, glancing at me and then peering beyond to the murky pond. Her enormous green eyes returned to me and she said, "Did I frighten you?"

I began to stammer my response. I was frightened, but more as a result of being intimidated by her ravishing beauty. She stood patiently, alternating her gaze between me and the pond. I finally emitted something audible.

"No, no, certainly it's a part of the game. Nothing

special about having a ball fly by."

She looked again at the pond and then said, "Well, I must say, I never will trust the yardage on this scorecard. I was sure I had at least a hundred yards to the pin." She frowned and then again looked directly into my eyes.

"Ah, well, this is a short hole," I offered. "The seventh has something of a reputation for being deceptive that way."

"The seventh?! Oh, I feel so foolish." She paused, and then began fumbling through the pockets of her neatly tailored windbreaker. Then, after examining a wrinkled scorecard, she said, "I thought I was playing the sixth."

She smiled and looked at me sheepishly, perhaps expecting me to be amused by her mistake. But I stood silently, my face expressionless. Finally, after a moment, she extended her hand.

"I'm so sorry. I have neglected to introduce myself."

Her soft hand, warm for so brisk an autumn morning, fell across my palm as gently as a feather. Her voice betrayed a Southern gentility. This beauty had so soundly smitten me, I was nearly catatonic.

"I'm Clarice McGraw," she said.

Fumbling with my golf bag, and feeling as if my cardigan sweater was starting to unravel, I mimicked her polite gestures and sputtered, "Ah yes, ah well . . . I'm Jimmy Olden."

As I shook her hand and looked into her eyes, I imagined I saw a growing discernment of my condition. *She must encounter fools like me often*, I thought. But in a comfortable way she gave my hand one last shake, surprisingly firm for so soft a hand, and released it. Somehow, I felt assured that I would not be so quickly dismissed.

I gradually loosened up, and we had something of a conversation. Since we were both playing alone we finished the front nine together. She had an appointment, so

I continued on alone, enjoying the back nine. But before we parted I did learn that she was new to the area, had opened up a ladies' dress shop along the boardwalk in town and liked to play golf in the early morning. I told her a little about myself and expressed the hope I would see her again soon. She smiled warmly.

That night I couldn't sleep, and it was still dark when I pulled my car into the club. As I rolled down the long sloping drive to the parking lot I could hear sprinklers clacking faintly somewhere in the distance. I parked and turned off my headlights. A lone light shone over the door of the golf shop.

I sat quietly, clutching a cup of decaffeinated coffee. As the rays of morning sun began to filter through the stand of eucalyptus at the edge of the course, I started wondering if I was doing the right thing. *What if we did hit it off? What if my dreams came true? Could I take all the pressure of being at my best every moment of the day? How could I survive with this beauty?*

The sunlight strengthened, and the warming glow of a new day filled my car. I stretched my arms out across the rim of the steering wheel, and cracked my neck with a sudden twist. After a while the assistant pro opened the shop and turned on the lights. Soon he would be brewing his own coffee, dark and strong, and setting up for the morning business. His name was Ted, and we called him "Go Ball." He was a young, strong man who could drive the ball prodigiously. When he really laid the wood on he'd shout out, "Go ball!" He had such exuberance—it was more natural than anything.

There it was. It struck me that I had the perfect medium through which I could speak to Clarice. It was the game of golf. There is nothing more natural or easy than the bond that grows between players enjoying a round. All I had to do was to play a round of golf with her. I thought of the many times I had teed off with three strangers who soon became three friends. In fact I had met many of my oldest and dearest friends playing golf.

Clarice drove her Volvo into the parking lot and pulled in right alongside my old Fiat Spider. I just happened to have arrived there a mere hour before, and so I casually dismounted my rusting steed.

"Oh, hello," I said in my best Gary Cooper voice.

"Oh, Jimmy, so nice to see you again."

"Are you about to go play?" she asked, looking at me with those beautiful eyes.

I was slightly dumbstruck but finally said, "Yeah sure, you bet. Would you like to join me?"

She smiled broadly and laughed. "I suppose you think it might be safer to play with me instead of ahead of me."

I had to laugh.

We teed off and walked down the fairway, speaking of the things golfers do.

By the time we had completed the front nine we knew each other well enough to say we were friends. We laughed and commiserated over errant shots and generously conceded putts. I was encouraged when she asked if I would play the back nine with her. By the time we came up the eighteenth fairway we each in our own way began to hatch plans. I asked if she would have dinner with me.

She feigned a moment of concentration, as if to envision her cluttered social calendar. Then, smiling impishly, she invited me to her house for meatloaf and mashed potatoes.

Our friendship was born, and we met regularly to play during the remaining fall days. We found new passion in the winter months as a snowy shroud covered the greens. She gave me a driver for Christmas. I gave her a putter. We became more than friends and traveled to a warmer climate to try them out. By spring, I had asked her for her hand.

We were married at the church on the road behind the tenth green, and as we walked out the front door a band of our golfing friends saluted us with golf clubs held high, splashing us with grass seed. At first, the game did all the talking, but soon our hearts were filled with love. It all was so natural and relaxed. And I grew to like being at my best all the time for Clarice.

In sharing our new life together we spent what time we could on the links. We vacationed by traveling across the country and playing all the finest courses.

One year I cheered as Clarice nearly won the ladies' championship at the club. I bought a bottle of champagne with which we celebrated her third-place finish and drowned her disappointment. Our heads clouded with the bubbles, I told her she had easily won the championship of my heart. She was my champion of all champions. She was the winner of the Angel's flight.

For twelve years the game gave us joy, and made it possible for us to see each other in ways that were otherwise probably impossible. Our lives together were filled with many rich experiences. The people and places and our love for the game that brought us together were all so interwoven. It was like a warm quilt, and my memories of it will never tarnish with time.

But one day my Clarice came home from a checkup with her doctor and told me that she had been diagnosed with breast cancer. We sat for an eternity, looking into each other's eyes, neither wanting to show weakness in the face of so daunting an ordeal. Her last days in the hospital came just after Christmas. At home for the last time, we had exchanged gifts beneath the tree. She gave me a new driver, one picked out by our head pro, Ted. I gave her a red sweater with a pattern of falling leaves. It reminded me of the day we met.

My Clarice passed away the first Tuesday of January.

I took a long trip, but I left my clubs at home. When I returned in early spring my first impulse was to go out to the club. When I arrived I was greeted by all our dear friends. I decided to go to the range and see if I could loosen my spine. After a while I found I was hitting the ball pretty good. I decided to go out and play a few holes alone. As I set my bag down aside the first tee, I realized that this would be my first opportunity to see how my new driver felt. It was a beauty. I laced a good drive straight up the fairway. From the golf shop window I heard Ted yell out, "Go ball!" I smiled and waved to him.

Of course, my mind was on Clarice. The first buds of spring were just beginning to open and the grass was a deep lush green. We always reveled in the beauty of springtime. I was playing well for so long a layoff; I hit a nice shot toward the seventh green. My ball lay at the edge of the green, so I used my surefire 7-iron and chipped it to the very lip of the cup.

As I walked toward the hole a gentle breeze gave my ball just a nudge and in it went. A warmth filled my senses as I looked skyward and whispered, "Are you with me, my Angel?"

As I collected my ball from the cup, I heard a distant voice. It spoke to me with urgency, and sounded almost like . . .

"Fore!"

A golf ball landed with a thud no more than twenty feet away. I raised one arm belatedly to protect my head. Then I turned and looked up the fairway. There, in half-gallop, was a young redheaded lad with a bag nearly equal his size draped over his back.

"Sorry, mister, I didn't think I could reach this green."

As he stood before me I smiled, thinking back to someone else who didn't think she could reach this green. I looked into this young boy's green eyes and said, "It's all right, boy. It's part of the game. Nothing special about having a ball fly by."

We walked in together and talked of the things golfers do.

That evening I sat near our fireplace in the company of a glass of red wine. As the embers cast an orange glow about the room, I looked back over the years and thought about how the game of golf had enriched my life. I thought of Clarice and how golf had introduced us, nurturing first our friendship and then our love. Somehow, I knew that every day I spent on the course Clarice would be with me, and perhaps occasionally, with the gentle breeze of her wing, would give my ball a nudge into the hole.

J. G. Nursall

The Law of Maximum Irritation

I had a big golf game planned for the following day. The forecast was lousy, so all afternoon I kept my TV tuned to The Weather Channel. Every time the radar map came on, I dropped what I was doing and stared. It is sometimes possible to create a localized high-pressure system by exerting fierce mental and optical energy on the screen. On rare occasions, I have succeeded in diverting full-blown tropical depressions.

The following morning, I read only the sports section of the newspaper and never turned on the TV. Checking the forecast on the day of a golf game greatly increases the likelihood of rain, because rain clouds, like wild animals, can smell fear. As I left the house for the course, at eleven o'clock, my wife asked if I would be home for dinner. "I'll probably be back before lunch," I said. "It's supposed to rain hard all afternoon. Why don't we plan on taking the kids to a movie?"

That was a desperate move on my part. The sky looked so dark at that moment that I had felt compelled to invoke the Law of Maximum Irritation. The law states that the likelihood of completing a given round of golf increases in direct proportion to the amount of trouble the golfer will get into when it is over. By virtually promising my wife that I would be available for a wholesome family activity in the afternoon, I came close to guaranteeing that the storm would hold off until *Titanic* was sold out.

As I drove to the course, the morning's sprinkles became real rain, but I never turned the wipers above intermittent speed. Running the wipers at full force encourages a storm and may promote lightning. I also opened my window a few inches and put on my sunglasses.

Alas, those bold measures didn't work. In fact, the rain became more intense as I pulled into the parking lot. So, in a final heroic attempt to appease the golf gods, I threw a maiden into the volcano. I sacrificed the back nine.

"Just give me nine holes!" I cried, while smacking the dashboard with my (gloved) left fist. "Rain all you want! Just hold the thunder until 2:30!"

And that, finally, was enough. The clouds began to break up just before we teed off, and the rain stopped altogether before we made the turn. Of course, I was in big trouble when I finally got home, at seven o'clock. But I didn't care. To tell you the truth, I almost always get in trouble when I play golf.

David Owen

"Walt? Her pains are ten minutes apart.
I may have to quit after nine."

Father and Son

Golf is the "only-est" sport. You're completely alone with every conceivable opportunity to defeat yourself. Golf brings out your assets and liabilities as a person. The longer you play, the more certain you are that a man's performance is the outward manifestation of who, in his heart, he really thinks he is.

Hale Irwin

Writing, painting or music can often capture the splendor of the best of life, but occasionally life mirrors art. An experience occurred recently that brought this home to me: Our student son Mark and I enjoyed a round of seaside golf near the Giant's Causeway in Northern Ireland—one of the most beautiful coastlines in the world.

I write not as a good golfer in the technical sense, but hopefully as a "good" player who enjoys a round in the company of family or friends, who tries hard to win but who doesn't mind losing to the better golfer. Sadly, "good golfers" in that sense are becoming harder to find in a competitive world.

Mark and I were intent on enjoying a day out together, one of those rare occasions where a father and son can share each other's company totally without interruption. Mark had just returned from a vacation job in Germany, where he had been shoveling curry powder in a spice factory. He was about to return to the University of Manchester in England, and I was due to go back to my busy desk at Queen's University in Belfast the next morning. So we settled for a sharing of seaside golf.

Those people who do not understand golf should still read on. I'm not sure that I understand golf myself, or why grown men and women spend so much time, money and energy—and suffer so much anguish—in trying to knock a small white ball into a tiny hole in the ground using a long awkward-looking stick, and trying to do so in as few strokes as possible. It is more than a game: It is a lesson in life. I have seen mature men pale at the prospect of knocking in a final three-foot putt to win a match. Even worse, I know men who have found it hard to lose gracefully to their close friends, or to their own sons. Sometimes such winners are really the losers.

Despite all such angst, there is a totally irrational surge of satisfaction—sometimes peaking into joy—when the golf swing works well and that little white ball zooms down the fairway as if Jack Nicklaus himself had hit it. It was one of those great days of unexpected golfing successes when Mark and I strode along the fairways, bounded on one side by the picturesque River Bush. I had played this course for more than twenty years, but on this particular morning I realized that Mark was coming of age and was beating his father for the first time, fair and square.

As we walked and talked, my mind lingered on the theme of life imitating art, and particularly the art of that great and much-loved English poet Sir John Betjeman, who captured the magic of "Seaside Golf":

How straight it flew, how long it flew,
It cleared the rutty track,
And soaring, disappeared from view
Beyond the bunker's back —
A glorious, sailing, bounding drive
That made me glad I was alive.

As our game progressed through the regulation eighteen holes, it was obvious that Dad, playing quite well by his standards, was hanging on for dear life. And at the very last hole, Mark, a gentle giant of a young man, strode forward none-too-confidently to try to sink a short putt that would win the match. As he stood there concentrating, I wanted him to sink the putt and win, but I was equally prepared to play on to a "sudden death" if necessary. Agonizingly he hit it, and the ball rolled gently—into the cup! A beam of joy lit up his face, and I felt deep in my heart: "That's my boy." I thought, too, of the lines of Betjeman:

It lay content
Two paces from the pin:
A steady putt and then it went
Oh, most securely in.
The very turf rejoiced to see
That quite unprecedented three.

Afterwards, in the clubhouse, we had a simple but splendid lunch overlooking the very green where Mark had clinched his memorable victory. We replayed every stroke, we talked about sport and we philosophized about life. I even pointed out, for the umpteenth time, the sparkling white hotel across the headlands where his mother and I had held our wedding reception a quarter century earlier, and I told him, yet again, of my early and troubled attempts to learn to play golf on this very same course. One day I became so frustrated that I put the ball in my pocket and walked on with my partner, rather than try to play a few holes. Later, my editor, when reading of this in my Belfast newspaper column, wrote the following headline: "The Day I Played Four Holes in None!"

Mark, for his part, listened intently and appreciatively to this family history. He too has an eye for beauty and an ear for poetry. He is (I'll say it) a treasured son, a partner and confidant in his own right, and his triumph on the golf course had underlined his maturity and growing sense of independence. With such a son I, technically the loser, knew that I was, happily, a long-term winner in a much deeper way.

That night, I read to Mark the last stanza of the Betjeman poem that recaptured so beautifully our feelings of privilege and joy.

> Ah! seaweed smells from sandy caves
> And thyme and mist in whiffs,
> In-coming tide, Atlantic waves
> Slapping the sunny cliffs,
> Lark song and sea sounds in the air,
> And splendor, splendor everywhere.

Indeed. There had been enough splendor on that fine day to warm the hearts of a father and a son for a lifetime.

Alf McCreary

DENNIS THE MENACE

"YOU SHOULDA SEEN IT, MOM! DAD GOT TO HIT THE BALL MORE THAN ANYBODY!"

Return to Inwood

What a beautiful place a golf course is. From the meanest country pasture to the Pebble Beaches and St. Andrews of the world, a golf course is to me a holy ground. I feel God in the trees and grass and flowers, in the rabbits and the birds and the squirrels, in the sky and the water. I feel that I am home.

Harvey Penick

We used to drive past a beautiful-looking golf course on the way to Rockaway Beach, touring about in our '57 Studebaker, and then after that, a '63 Dodge Dart. As we passed by, I would crane my neck and look out the back window. It turned out to be Inwood Country Club.

I had never seen a piece of land as beautiful. A wrought-iron fence surrounded the grounds, setting it off from a series of dilapidated single-family houses. Traffic breezed by, making the stately parkland site all the more intriguing. So one summer morning, I would guess when I was nine years old, I headed off on my bicycle and an hour later found myself at its gates.

It was something out of a movie, or better yet, the cover of one of those Hardy Boys books I had at home, with me standing there, looking up at this massive stone entrance-way, and deep inside the grounds was this spooky, old-fashioned clubhouse. Beneath the metal plate announcing "Inwood Country Club" was a warning about "Private: Members Only." All of this was too inviting for me to turn back now. My sole act of deference was to get off my bike and to walk it up the private road.

Various groups of people stood around in the dis-tance—golfers, accompanied by caddies. Dense shades of green were everywhere, all of it framed by graceful trees and some lovely shrubbery and flower beds. It all seemed in such contrast to the world I had passed through to get here. I thought it best to avoid the clubhouse because there was no way I was going to be able to explain away my visit if any member confronted me. Just as the path climbed up to the clubhouse, I veered off to the right and headed down behind the parking lot. There I found a spot behind some bushes and left my bicycle unlocked.

On one side stretched the swamps of Jamaica Bay, and across the water were the main runways of Idlewild (later John F. Kennedy) Airport. To my right was a row of hedges, and just beyond it unfolded this huge expanse of lawn and trees. We had a black-and-white TV set at home, and the only other time I remember being overwhelmed like this was when I first watched a baseball game on a neighbor's color set. It wasn't just the size of the yard here, it was also the intensity of the green color and all the shades and varieties, and the way the branches draped so lovingly over everything. I walked down by a putting sur-face, headed across a little stone bridge that carried me over a lily pond, and then walked along one side of a fair-way back toward a group of golfers.

Way in the distance, I saw someone swing. The metal

shaft glinted, the ball rose against the blue sky, and then I heard a kind of "click" sound as the ball headed right at me, except that it gently climbed, then leveled off and floated, seemingly forever. By the time the ball butter-flied down to earth in front of me, I had fallen in love with the game.

More than twenty-five years later I returned to Inwood CC, this time with our eleven-year-old daughter, Cory, in hand, to show her the spot where my fascination with golf had started. Like my father, she had done a good job of playing along with my interest, at one point even tak-ing up the game as a way of spending time with me. She could even watch it on TV with me and began to register a certain familiarity with players. So I thought it a good idea one morning while we visited my parents to conjure yet another reason for an early morning escape.

She was always quick to join a conspiracy, and so we set off together in my '90 Toyota Tercel.

The ride didn't seem nearly as long this time. Strange, how age shrinks distance. The buildings along the way all looked a little smaller than they had been when I was growing up. The roads were more packed with chintzy businesses, neon signs and the general sense of nowhere that has become typical of strip-mall culture. But then I made the right turn off Sheridan Boulevard and it all came back to me just as it had been, replete with the empty sandlot in front of the country club and the sign remind-ing me that I didn't belong.

This time, though, there was nothing to hide. One key to American society, I have learned, is that if you act as if you belong, people will play along. It's just a matter of knowing how to look like you're part of what's going on. This time I parked close to the clubhouse, waved a friendly greeting to the doorman, and then headed off with Cory to the pro shop, where we introduced ourselves to the resident professional. Tommy Thomas, his name was, and I had known him tangentially from my caddie days on the PGA Tour several summers earlier. He had been one of the many journeyman golfers who tries his hand at the big life and then finds out for all sorts of reasons that he just can't quite compete or that life on the road is too demanding. In any case, I remembered him not for any success he enjoyed—on the contrary—but for his trademark use of a certain suspect golf ball: "the Molitor man," he had been called, and now, some twelve years later, he smiled when I recalled this nickname. There is no escaping a nickname on the Tour.

In brief compass, we divested ourselves of our limited supply of shared Tour memories. "Would it be okay if we headed off to the eighteenth hole? I want to show Cory where I . . . well, where I first discovered golf." "Sure," he said, "just make sure you stay out of the way of any play. We have a few early birds; they went off the back nine and may be finishing already."

This time, the grounds took on a meaning that had not been available to me in my youth. Inwood Country Club, after all, had been the site of two major golf championships, the 1921 PGA and the 1923 U.S. Open. That stone bridge fronting the green was copied from the famous original on the eighteenth hole at the Old Course at St. Andrews. I recounted this to Cory as we walked down the right side of the eighteenth fairway.

It was a lovely day, the air warming up, the sky clear, and none of those noisy airplanes disturbing the morning calm. And as we walked over and stood on the exact spot where so many years ago I had begun my affair with the game, I turned around and saw a historic marker that, I later found out, had only recently been placed there in the ground. "In 1923, Bobby Jones clinched the first of his four U.S. Open titles by hitting a two-iron from this spot to within six feet of the hole during a playoff with Bobby Cruickshank."

Cory read the marker aloud without really understanding it. She did, however, understand what the moment meant to me. This eleven-year-old, who usually talked for hours without coming up for air, stood quietly by my side for a few minutes while I relived all the emotions of my first visit.

Then she looked up at me, and with utter seriousness in her gray eyes, said, "Cool."

Bradley S. Klein

A Measure of Love

It was the afternoon of Christmas Eve, and I had just finished wrapping the last gift for my family when Greg, my sixteen-year-old son, came into the bedroom after returning from shopping with his dad.

"Mom, you are not going to believe what Dad got you for Christmas!" he announced. "It's a gift that shows how much he loves you."

My mind immediately envisioned a diamond ring or gorgeous tennis bracelet. Without giving away my idea of a "love" gift, I responded with the question, "Do you think I got Dad enough for Christmas?"

After a few moments of thoughtful consideration, Greg answered, "Gosh, Mom, I don't know. You might want to run down to the hardware store and buy him that tool chest he's been wanting. It's going to be hard to match what he got you though."

With a teaser like that, I found it as difficult to sleep on Christmas Eve as I had when I was a kid. Visions of rings and bracelets danced in my head and I was the first one up in the morning. I eagerly gathered Greg, my other son Jeff, and my husband Randy for the ritual of opening gifts. As each one took his turn opening, we oohed and aahed over the selections each had made to show our love. I opted to open my gifts last, saving the moment when I would see the gift that would be the measure of my husband's love.

Finally, it was my turn. The first gift I opened was a blender. Next, I opened a set of pots and pans. I took each one out of the box and carefully looked inside them, on the handles, and even in the packing for anything that resembled a piece of jewelry. My next gift was some cologne, my favorite kind. Still, I didn't see any evidence of the spectacular gift for which I had been preparing myself to be surprised and overwhelmed. My last gift from my husband was a pretty gold nightgown and robe (in the wrong size).

Hiding my disappointment, I good-naturedly thanked Randy for the gifts and planted a big kiss on his lips. Mentally, I was trying to determine which gift in a sixteen-year-old's mind had deserved the assessment that it showed how much he loved me. I decided probably the pots and pans!

We started to clean up the mountain of wrapping paper, bows and boxes. Randy came up behind me as I was stuffing them into the trash bag, put his arms around my waist and navigated me into the living room where we had another Christmas tree. My deflated spirits took wing, and I fully expected to find the ring or bracelet decorating one of the branches. Instead, he took me over to the tree and pointed behind it, where I saw a golf bag filled with shiny, new clubs.

My face fell as I tried to figure out how a new set of golf clubs for Randy was going to show how much he loved me. I already knew how much he loved golf, so he certainly didn't need to convince me on that point.

My boys said in unison, "She doesn't like them, Dad."

Randy, so secure in his choice, calmly reassured the boys, "Don't worry, guys. I knew she'd react like this. It's just going to take some time for her to learn the game and enjoy it like I do!"

"They're not yours?" I dumbly questioned. "They're for me?" I was now becoming indignant. "I can't believe that you think I would want to play golf alone!" Randy, an excellent golfer who consistently shoots in the 70s and always attracts a gallery of spectators even on the driving range, had often expressed his frustrations with women golfers who slowed the play down because they weren't very good. I, a woman with no athletic ability, had only swung a club once or twice. With a giant stretch of the imagination, I would not even fit into the category of "not very good."

Randy, undaunted by my less-than-enthusiastic reaction, said, "I thought this would be something we could do together. When the boys and I go out, we could have a foursome, and I know you'll grow to love the game like we do."

"You're serious, aren't you?" I asked incredulously. Things were starting to make sense. To take me on the golf course was a true measure of love to Randy. To allow me, a woman who was totally incompetent at golf, to play with him really was a sign of how much he loved me. And in the months that followed, his patience and perseverance in . taking me to the driving range and enrolling me in lessons had proved that his gift was a gift of love and not a mere whimsy or desperate last-minute purchase for Christmas.

Because we are both teachers, we spend our summers at the beach in San Clemente, California, camping and now going to the golf course. With our sons grown and busy with their own lives, we have something that we can share as a couple that will keep us active and young. Randy still loves to play competitive golf and he is awesome, but he takes the time and patience to help and encourage me and keep me motivated to participate in what I have found to be a very challenging and alluring activity.

Greg, the sixteen-year-old who prepared me for the gift of love seven years ago on Christmas Eve, married recently. I gave him a little womanly advice on gift giving to take with him into his marriage. I looked him in the eyes and said, "Son, when you want to show Sarah how much you love her, go for the bracelet or the diamond ring in the first five years. Save the golf clubs for later when she can fully appreciate how much love that kind of a gift shows."

Judy Walker

"How's a frozen dinner sound?"

Reprinted by permission of David W. Harbaugh. Originally appeared in Golf Digest.

Dad's Magic Clubs

My father died last month. He was eighty-six, in poor health, and his passing was not unexpected. His funeral was marked by an outpouring of affection and accolades. If novenas, Masses and prayers mean anything, then Dad is already a consultant to St. Peter. Ironically, this outpouring of adoration was not fully appreciated by his children.

My father was a medical doctor, and by all accounts, a good one. His specialty was bringing babies into the world, and he loved it. He came from a generation that believed that the doctor an expectant mother saw throughout her pregnancy was the one who should be there at the birth. Many a seashore excursion, vacation or special occasion was delayed, curtailed or postponed because Mrs. So-and-so's baby was due at any moment.

I was always amazed at how many parents named their sons Joseph, after my father. Patients loved him. He had a way of making each individual feel like the most important person in the world. He was also a man of the people outside the office and hospital. His Irish heritage, of which he was immensely proud, his love of poetry and his sense of humor made him a sought-after speaker for public and private affairs. In short, he was a charming man. Unfortunately, his children believed that wherever he parked his car each night was the same place he parked his charm.

Dad was a strict and demanding parent. He was the oldest of five in hard economic times, and his childhood was purposeful, tough and short. In turn, he expected his children to think and act like adults. Our dinner table was not always a happy place.

Having said that, it was my father who introduced me to golf. In the late 1940s and early 1950s, sports to a young male teen meant baseball, football and basketball. I did not know another teenager who played golf. My friend Frank Costello and I were recruited to caddie for Dad and his friends. The bags were heavy, the pay pitiful, and we were expected to find balls in places where no golf ball— much less human—should go. Frank and I soon discovered it was good sense to have something else planned for Wednesdays and Saturdays.

As a caddie, I learned about the quality of golf scores. I knew that anybody who could regularly break 100 was a good golfer. And if they could score in the 80s, they were great golfers. It never dawned on me that an amateur could shoot in the 70s.

Then my father joined a golf club—Upper Montclair Country Club, a quality 27-hole layout a dozen miles west of New York City. We had a family membership, and I was encouraged to play. I did so only as an activity of last resort. I usually played by myself and only nine holes. I rarely broke 50 and only did so with the help of mulligans, generous gimmes and a few should-have-beens.

Playing with my father made Latin seem easy. From him, I learned almost nothing about how to play golf, but everything about the game of golf. My first lesson was in the proper pace of golf. Slow play was sinful. To this day,

I am uncomfortable when groups behind us have to wait, even when we are not at fault.

A golfer never steps to the tee without at least two balls in his pocket. If you need to hit a second ball, it is bad manners to make everyone wait while you return to your bag. Dad was a stickler for preparation. Have enough tees and know where your ball marker is. He would be appalled at the condition of my sons' golf shoes. His were always clean and shining. I suspect, at age sixty-three, I am one of the few left who regularly take polish and brush to their golf shoes.

He disdained practice swings, and his view on winter rules was simple: They are for cheats. Through the years I have played with generals, admirals and politicians, many of whom can give great speeches on honor, duty and country but think nothing of moving the ball all over the course.

Dad was scrupulous about the accuracy of his scores. In later years, when he knew his memory was failing, he would ask his fellow golfers to help him keep track. To Dad, the difference between a seven and an eight was important. I learned that some of the most boring people in the world are those who have to relive every shot after the round. Dad said, "What was done was done, and since most golfers dwell on their bad shots, who cares?"

Dad always had a bet, if only a modest one, but to him competition and survival were synonymous. All of this I learned about golf long before I could play it.

After graduating from college, I went off to a career in the Air Force. Early on, I caught the golf bug, and thanks to Uncle Sam, I had the opportunity to play around the world and throughout the United States. Thanks to Dad, there was never a doubt about how to play the game. As my handicap drifted in the low teens, I put into practice every one of my father's rules of golf. During those years,

I rarely played with Dad. Until my last assignment, we were never closer than one thousand miles, and often our trips home to New Jersey were not compatible with golf weather.

At thirty-eight I gave up golf for nine years. My wife and I were blessed with seven healthy, active children, and their many activities left little room for golf. When, on his own, my oldest son Michael took up the game, I was lured to golf again. This time the bug hit hard. In 1984, I bought my first semi-custom-fit clubs—Ping woods and Ping Eye Two irons, the blue dot model. New clubs, a back operation and the resultant compact swing brought new vigor to my game and handicap. It also brought a return to playing golf with my father.

Residing in Virginia, I was able to make regular trips north to New Jersey. Dad was now in his mid-seventies and his golf game weak. In his prime, he was thrilled to break 100 and broke 90 only once in his life. But his zest for the game never diminished. We always played for a bet, but his 36 handicap drew a surplus of strokes and he always won. And despite the quality of my handicap, by now a 5, I never played Upper Montclair at my best. Losing to my father I accepted, but Upper Montclair was something else. No matter how well I played, I could not break 80. Shooting 80 or 81 was easy, but I could not get through the barrier.

In late summer of 1991, I headed north to play what turned out to be my last rounds at UMCC. On that glorious weekend I shot 76 and 74. I was pleased beyond measure, but what surprised me the most was the great pleasure my father took in my accomplishment. At age eighty, he made more of a to-do about it than I ever could.

For me, that weekend was the culmination of a forty-year golf odyssey—from a disinterested teenager to a competent amateur golfer. Shortly thereafter, my father

fully retired from his medical practice and moved to
Hilton Head, South Carolina. We played a number of
times at his Moss Creek course, but because of his declin-
ing health, we could never relive the magic of that day at
Upper Montclair. Through the years, I have come to realize that my father had an appreciation and love for golf
that few ever realize.

To him, golf was not just playing eighteen holes; it was
the whole experience: the preparation, the wager, the
good holes and the bad, the occasional par, the traditional
cold potato soup and beer afterward, the discussion of
world events, the hot shower and clean clothes. All were
integral parts of a golf day, with each segment to be
enjoyed to its fullest. The score was important, but only
briefly and a small part of the picture.

After that weekend in 1991, my game continued to
improve. By late 1992, I was taking myself seriously.
Modest success in several one-day senior events led me to
believe my golden years would be spent collecting golf
prizes.

And then I got greedy. Deciding that my 5 handicap
needed to be further lowered, I fell prey to modern technology. Never mind that with my trusty Pings I was playing the best golf of my fifty-eight years. I needed to do
better. I gave my clubs to my son John, who is now playing the best golf of his life.

Technology has done wonders for me. Five years and
five sets of clubs left me with a 14 handicap and a
mechanical hack of a swing.

And then my father died. After the funeral, I remained
in Hilton Head for a few days to help Dad's wife settle his
affairs. Our mother had died suddenly many years ago,
and we had come to love Dad's second wife, Louise,
dearly. She offered the love and care that few men receive
once in a lifetime, much less twice.

One of my tasks was to do something with Dad's golf equipment. He had a garage full of odds and ends, unopened catalog-company packages containing "magic" putters and wedges. At age eighty-five, Dad was still looking for that par-saving club. All of those were given to junior golf, with one exception: Dad's final and little-used set of irons were Ping Eye Twos, the blue dot model.

I took them back to Virginia, having no idea what I would do with them. Shortly after my return, I participated in a local three-day tournament. My play was indifferent, and I failed to make the third-day cut.

During the ensuing week, discouraged with golf, I played with my father's clubs. What happened was mystical. In an eleven-day period I shot 76, 75, 73, 75, 74 and 75. Conventional wisdom says there is no way an honest 14 handicap can play that kind of golf. The next few rounds were not as impressive, but there is no doubt my game has taken an amazing turn. My handicap is plunging, and my swing is easier and more fluid than it has been in years.

Golf is fun again. Why? I only have a clue. For his entire life, my father was considered the consummate charmer. In his lifetime, I received little of that charm. In his clubs, he gave me my share.

John Keating

Her Mother's Presence

Friday, March 20, 1998, was a bright, sunny day in Phoenix, Arizona. I was preparing for my afternoon tee time at the Standard Register Ping LPGA Championship. My sister lived in nearby Scottsdale and my parents were in town. I was looking forward to having them there to follow and enjoy the day.

My mother especially enjoyed spending time in Phoenix with both of her daughters. However, what we didn't know was that this trip to Arizona would be her last. It also was going to be the final golf tournament she would watch me play.

Mom was one of my biggest supporters and loved being out on tour to watch and cheer me on. She never missed a shot; she saw everything from the first tee shot to the last putt. She was known for her high-pitched screams that followed every birdie I made. I always enjoyed looking into the crowd and seeing her beaming smile. Mom took advantage of any chance she had to spend time with me.

In September 1997 our entire family life changed drastically. Mom experienced a small stroke and the doctors found multiple brain tumors. Two brain surgeries followed, and the final diagnosis was cancer. Six months later, as the disease was destroying her body, Mom was confined to a scooter to navigate the golf course. Instead of her smile and high-pitched screams, I saw a weary, defeated, blank face. Only the hum of the motor came from her direction.

God blessed me with a fantastic round on that Friday in March. I shot a 64, one of my lowest scores of the year. The golf was enjoyable and the results great, but I felt more joy knowing Mom was able to watch me play. Throughout the day I found my attention focused not only on my golf, but on her as well. It seemed as though she had to concentrate hard on maneuvering the scooter so as not to hit anything. I wanted to understand how she felt having to rely on a machine to get from one point to another, but I couldn't. My heart was breaking as I saw how the deadly disease was consuming her body and her mind.

It was a day of overwhelming emotions. Joy, laughter, sadness and tears seemed to flood my heart all at the same time. This was a reality check for me on the perspective of life. Shooting a 64, having a chance to win a golf tournament and making a career out of walking a green fairway is not what life is all about. Remembering Mom as a part of my gallery is a much greater treasure than shooting a 64. God's word says to store up treasures in heaven—things that cannot be destroyed by the hands of humans, for "where your treasure is, there will your heart be also." Life is about enjoying time with family and friends. Life is about love—loving God and loving those around us!

Mom died from cancer on May 31, 1998, just two months later.

I will never forget that Tour stop, the last tournament Mom watched. Under the hum of that scooter, I knew in my heart she was screaming at each birdie. Mom is gone now and I miss her very much. But what gives me comfort is the fact that she is in heaven and I will see her again. As I continue through my life—both in and out of golf—Mom's presence will always be with me. I can still hear her sweet voice cheering me on.

Tracy Hanson

A Sudden End to a Love Story

All love stories should include a moment when the heroine sends out her 2-iron for repairs. This one does.

Renay White's 2-iron shots flew on a line not much higher than a wallaby's belly. So the Australian teenager decided the stick needed a new shaft. Her coach delivered it to another young player, Stuart Appleby, a country boy off an outback dairy farm who made ends meet by doing the odd club repair.

As it happens, Appleby earlier had admired a small, strong, smiling woman striding with wonderful cockiness through his field of vision. He asked, "Who's that?"

"Renay White," said Ross Herbert, her coach.

"Does she have a boyfriend?"

"No."

So in the summer of 1992, Appleby came to know White as smart, funny, cute—and altogether too much the flirt. She returned the favor by declaring him drop-dead gorgeous with those blue eyes—and what a snob.

Ah, young love, sweet love. She was nineteen, he was twenty-one, they were confused.

He knew certainly that he wanted to put his hands on her 2-iron. Within minutes, Appleby gave the club back to the coach, who later said, "Stuart was very keen to do a good job on it. Even then he and Renay were using golf to communicate."

Words had failed when they mistook voice for character. She was loud, laughing and sassy. He was quiet, reserved and serious.

But soon enough they understood each other. No flirt, she had been born vivacious. No snob, he came to work focused. They filled in the gaps of each other's personality. On the Australians' tour of U.S. college teams that fall, it was only natural Renay and Stuart were mixed-twosome partners.

And from then on they were always partners, first friends and lovers, then husband and wife who lived by one of life's coolest rules: *Dance as if no one's watching, love as if it's never going to hurt.*

The story really begins on a beach.

After the American matches, Appleby knew he wanted golf and Renay. He had the one but not the other. Then she asked, "Why don't you come visit my place?"

It's a five-hour drive from his home to hers on Australia's southeast coast.

Appleby made it in, oh, five minutes. They spent a day together before he went home. His mother soon said, "Stuart, you're moping, you're useless. Go back to Renay's."

This time around, Stuart and Renay swam, took the sun and sat on the beach, where by the end of a week he said words that came so easily they seemed inevitable.

He said, "I've always wanted to meet someone like you. I want to spend the rest of my life with you." She said, "I want to be with you." And she thought, *Oh, my God, this is it.*

She told her sister, Duean, she had met this guy, she adored him, they spoke each other's thoughts, he made her laugh and he laughed with her.

Renay had been a promising golfer since age twelve, a contemporary of Karrie Webb, who became a sensation on the American tour. But, however talented Renay might have been, she no longer cared. She knew her passion for golf ran a distant second to her passion for Stuart.

She would rather be with him than put in the work demanded of a Webb or an Appleby. She sat for hours on practice ranges from Melbourne to Orlando, watching her guy, waiting, talking, sometimes even curling up to sleep on the night's-coming grass. She often caddied for him.

They had great dreams together, and there came a day when he said, "These dreams were fulfilled to a very high extent right up to the time she left us."

From the road, she wrote letters to her parents. She carried a laptop computer and filled cyberspace with laughing emails. Any happenings, any new jokes, any sudden realizations would put her on the phone to Duean, determined to keep her sister within five seconds of all the news.

When Stuart drove to the golf course, Renay told him where to turn.

When he dawdled, she said, "Stuey, move your rear," and he did, laughing all the way, a two-hour tiff for some couples, for them two seconds.

When he groused, "I'm putting so bad," she brought light to his eyes by saying, "Bad? Bad? You're putting bloody *terrible!* And, by the way, I love you."

When Stuart played, she walked along by the gallery ropes, wearing a schoolgirl's shorts, T-shirt, sneakers, a funny little cap and a backpack.

When he missed seven cuts in nine tournaments early in 1998, she wrote an email to his coach, Steve Bann, saying, "Stuart's playing so very well. He's about to win." And he won the Kemper Open.

He had become a star at age twenty-seven. Through

two-and-a-half seasons on the PGA Tour, he had won twice and earned about $2 million. He and Renay bought a house in Isleworth, the Orlando development that is home to Tiger Woods, Mark O'Meara and tennis pro Todd Woodbridge, whose wife Natasha had become Renay's best friend.

Renay won Tash with laughter. Such a happy woman. Todd Woodbridge thought to teach the golfer tennis and heard Renay shout, "Why is it the ball's NOT STILL?"

One evening Tash needed a glass for red wine.

"The crystal," Renay said.

"But we're going out in the boat."

"So?"

So crystal stemware awarded to the winner of the 1997 Honda Classic found itself in use at a backyard picnic.

This June, Renay sat on her veranda. She had played golf with the Australian pro Jody Adams. Renay's first round in months, a 75, had been so remarkable Adams encouraged her to try the tour.

"No need, Jody," Renay said. "I couldn't possibly be happier with my life."

She and Stuart painted bedrooms, finished a television room and installed a twelve-seat dining-room table made of Australian wood. They hung aboriginal art and set out bowls carved from Australian trees. In the kitchen, after workmen cracked a kitchen countertop, Renay re-ordered it. She loved its look, loved to move her hand across its face. It is black Italian marble. They wanted children. "She'd have been an amazing mother, so loving, so patient," Stuart said. Tash Woodbridge once whispered to Renay, "I might be pregnant," and Renay punched her arm. "No, no, you can't be. We're getting pregnant at the same time!" When the pregnancy test came back negative, Tash said, "We jumped around together like two-year-olds," so happy were they to still have a chance at simultaneous maternity.

The last time they spoke, Tash heard happiness. Renay and Stuart were on a second honeymoon. From London they would take the next day's train to Paris. So Renay called to ask about Paris. Where to eat, which churches, which museums.

They spoke across the Atlantic for forty-five minutes. Then Tash's husband said the girls should get off the phone. He said they could talk another day.

The next day, she died. Struck by a car backing up as she waited with Stuart to leave their taxi at London's hectic Waterloo train station, Renay Appleby died before reaching a hospital. The watch she wore that day, Stuart carries in his pocket today, still on London time.

She wore a chain around her neck with her name on it. He wears it now. On his golf visor is her PGA Tour wife's badge. He touches her pajamas. He looks at the train tickets, London to Paris, and says, "They're the end of the story. Full stop."

The light of joy disappears, emptiness rushes in with its darkness. Stuart Appleby, empty, came to the PGA Championship four days after last taking flowers to Renay's grave. He asked to do a press conference. He came to the dais a haunted man, unshaven, stricken, weeping and brave as hell.

He called Renay "first prize of a raffle in life." He talked about her laughter, her friends. He'll mention her name, he'll talk about the memories.

One day when he needs her, she'll be there, a force of belief working for him.

It's the little things you miss, a kiss goodnight, orange juice in the morning, a half-hour's conversation. "They make up someone's life," he said.

Stuart asked that Renay's headstone be carved from the black Italian marble she loved in her kitchen. Her

family and Stuart agreed on an epitaph, leaving the last
lines to him . . .

> *In Happiest, Loving Memory of Renay Appleby*
> *We can only hope to pass on your qualities to*
> *those we meet*
> *We are blessed to have had you in our lives*
> *The memories you have given us will all remain*
> *Adored wife of Stuart*
> *"My best friend forever."*

Dave Kindred

$\overline{6}$

OUT OF
THE ROUGH

It is the constant and undying hope for improvement that makes golf so exquisitely worth playing.

Bernard Darwin

Just One More Time

Perhaps it comes to all men, or perhaps just to middle-aged former athletes. I'm talking about the Just One More Time Syndrome: Score one more touchdown, ride one more bull, hit one more home run. But when you're forty-five and your waist measurement has just passed your expanded chest measurement, then Just One More Times aren't easy to find.

I live in the little Texas town of Mason (population 2,153) and because we have no golf course, I play on the course in Brady, twenty-eight miles north. One day I was in Bill O'Banion's drugstore when he said, "The hospital fund drive is coming up soon."

"By all means put me down for a contribution."

"Had this idea that might raise a little extra money for the hospital. I thought we'd alternate our shots and hit a golf ball from the Mason courthouse to the hole on the ninth green of the Brady course. We'd get somebody to establish par, and then we'd get folks to contribute per stroke, as to how many strokes we'd finish under par."

"When y'all planning on doing this?"

Bill looked at me and said, "The date is June 11. And there ain't no *y'all* to it. It's *we*, as in you and me."

"Sorry, partner, I can't do it. Ain't no motels between here and Brady."

"We're not going to walk. Nobody would expect that. We'll figure out some kind of golf cart to ride."

"That aside," I said, "when I shoot my average 90 I'm exhausted. I'll be hitting the ball at least three hundred times before we make our way to Brady and *all* of them will be hard-swinging shots."

"It'll be all right. Just don't worry."

"Bill, we're talking about high weeds along the right of way. We're talking about pastures with cows and bulls. We're talking hills that go up and down."

That was in May when it was still cool, so finally I agreed. It looked as if I'd found my Just One More Time.

Then the local papers started running stories, and the Brady radio station wanted to follow us tee to green. Sure I wanted my Just One More Time, but not in front of a packed house.

June 11 and summer arrived at the same time. We were to tee off from the courthouse square at 10 A.M. By 9:30 the temperature was eighty-five degrees. Par had been determined at 688 strokes. Don't ask me how.

Bill got us past the Commercial Bank's window with his first swing, a beautiful 7-iron shot. Now it was my turn, and I hit a dribbler into a yard full of old farm machinery.

I left Bill a lie under a horse-drawn hayrack. From there he put it into the service bay of the Chevron station. It took us six strokes to get out.

From then on, things got worse.

Bill put one across the street and under a truck at Eckert Equipment. I got down on my belly to try to swipe the ball out so we wouldn't have to take a penalty shot. Half the people of Mason were following us, and I was lying there thinking that none of them knew that I once had held the interscholastic record for the hurdles or that

I had made my living riding bulls on the circuit for a year. I turned the putter on its side and swiped the ball fifteen yards.

Bill's next shot got us out of plate-glass territory at last, and we were approaching the edge of town when I knocked a 4-iron into the cemetery. By the time we got the ball headed back in the direction of Brady, we were at the foot of Mason Mountain and six strokes over the pace I felt we should have maintained coming out of town.

We call it Mason Mountain, though it actually rises no more than one thousand feet. But try hitting a golf ball up it.

Bill, using a 5-iron, made a shot straight up the middle that hit the pavement and bounced up and then rolled and rolled until it came to a stop. After that it started rolling backward until it was one hundred yards behind the spot where Bill had hit it. Now we had no choice but to keep the ball high in the grass beside the highway. So we hacked our way up that mountain, sometimes getting one hundred yards out of a shot, more often having to settle for less. When we finally got to the top, I estimated that we were twenty-six strokes over par.

Then it began to rain.

We had an extensive entourage in addition to the spectators who were following us. We had an ambulance with Dr. Jim Pettit in attendance; we had Mason policeman Jack Boring, who'd been empowered by the state to hold traffic; we had fore and aft trucks with signs warning that a "golfathon" was in progress. Most important, we had Brock Grosse, our caddie master. He had rigged up a trailer behind his three-wheeled motorcycle with a couch for Bill and me to ride in between shots.

It rained for almost an hour. Our gloves got wet as did the grips of our clubs. It was difficult enough to keep the club head square to the ball as we hit out of the grass. It was quite another matter with the club turning in your hand. Once I hit a shot that went right at a little better than a ninety-degree angle. I wouldn't have thought this was possible.

Our rules were that anything between the barbed-wire fences on either side of the road was fairway. Over the fence was considered the rough, and the ball had to be played as it lay, with the exception that we could take a drop and a one-stroke penalty. Thus we found ourselves in the rough when we hit one into a herd of cows.

We climbed over the fence and there they came, crowding around, shoving up against us, bawling and mooing and stepping on the golf ball.

Finally, our policeman jumped the fence and fired his revolver in the air. The cattle departed. But they'd buried the ball in the ground to the point where it was barely visible. Mayor Willard Aubrey of Mason, our course judge, calmly gave us a ruling: "This is rough. Play it as it is or take a stroke penalty."

Bill said, "Whaaat? Where in the PGA rules does it talk about cows stepping on a golf ball?"

The mayor was unmoved, and we took the one-stroke penalty.

By now we were gaining on par, but time was becoming a problem. To get to the Brady course we'd have to go directly through town, turn left at the courthouse and go another three miles out Highway 87. I had arranged with the Brady police to hold traffic up as we hit through. Otherwise we would be reduced to rolling 20- and 30-foot putts along the side of the road and there would go our chance to break par and make money for the hospital. I'd naively told the police we would reach the outskirts of Brady by 3 P.M., and they said they would meet us at the town limits.

At 3 P.M. we were fifteen miles from Brady. Seriously

tired, I went stumbling down the bank toward the spot where one of our caddies indicated the ball was. I suddenly heard a dry whir. I immediately executed a 180-degree turn and quit the area. There are several things I am more afraid of than a rattlesnake, but I forget what they are. After Jack Boring and a woman went down and trapped the snake, Bill took the next shot.

By the time we were five miles out of Brady I figured we were fifty strokes under; but we were so late, that so far as I knew, the cops had all gone to supper.

We went forward, but I was just going through the motions, hacking at the ball, hoping to move it forward a few yards so that Bill could then take us a couple of hundred yards farther. Dr. Pettit came over and said, "Rest in the ambulance. Let Bill hit it for a while."

I said, "After one or two more shots."

But I didn't rest, and soon we were at the outskirts of Brady. The police were still there to help us get through. Now we were seventy strokes under par.

A strange thing began to happen. The streets weren't exactly lined, but people were waiting for us. Folks who had been following our progress over the radio were driving to meet us, blowing their horns.

I don't know whether it was adrenaline or pride or some strange hormone, but my tiredness seemed to melt away. All of a sudden I realized that this was truly my Just One More Time.

We were using Bill's "chipper," a heavy weighted club faced like a 5-iron. And disregarding the plate-glass factor, I was hitting the best shots I'd hit all day, straight down the street, carrying one hundred yards and then rolling fifty more.

We got to the courthouse square in five shots and then took that left turn toward the golf course. We were within 150 yards of the ninth hole when Bill lifted a beautiful

9-iron shot that settled about ten feet off the green.

The green was ringed with maybe two hundred onlookers. I had never hit a golf ball in front of that many people. My chip up to the green was miserable. I left Bill a forty-foot putt. He lagged and left the ball three feet from the cup.

A knee-knocker. As I walked across the green I said to myself, "For once, don't choke." I knocked the ball dead in the center of the cup. Then I stepped across and shook hands with Bill.

They tell me there was a celebration. They tell me we went to dinner. I don't know. It became a blur after that putt went in. All I knew were three things:

We'd come in 108 strokes under par.

We'd raised fifty-five hundred dollars for the hospital.

And I'd accomplished my Just One More Time.

Giles Tippette

The Drive of a Champion

Having already accumulated a host of trophies since starting to play competitive golf at the age of ten, Larry Alford, at sixteen, had developed into one of the best young golf prospects in the country. Already shooting in the 70s, he was elected the most valuable player of the McCullough High School team during both his sophomore and junior years. Following his junior year, Alford matched against seventy-four of the nation's best junior golfers at the Mission Hills Desert Junior Tournament in Rancho Mirage, California. He was tied for the lead going into the final round after firing a 72 and a 71, but he dipped to a 78 in the final round, which tied him for second place, five strokes behind the winner—Tiger Woods.

Alford's performance drew the interest of coaches from some of the best college golf teams in the country, including Arizona, Arizona State, Stanford and Oklahoma State. Wanting to stay close to home, he accepted a scholarship at the University of Houston. "Just think, everything will be taken care of, and I'll be close to home, and it won't cost you anything while I'm going to college," Alford said to his mother, Missy, "and I'll be playing for one of the best college teams in the country."

Fighting back tears, Missy Alford hugged her son tightly, knowing that he had worked so hard to earn a scholarship to make it easier for her. "That's wonderful, Larry," she said. "I'm so happy for you."

That summer, Alford worked harder than ever on his golf game, hitting hundreds of balls daily while working at the golf cart barn at The Woodlands Country Club. At night, he and one of his best friends, Brendan, waded into water hazards at nearby golf courses to retrieve golf balls. Salvaging as many as 2,000 a night, they sold them for eighteen cents apiece, which enabled Larry to play more golf that summer. His paychecks from his golfing job went to his mother, an art teacher who also made and sold decorative wreaths and did wallpapering. "That's Larry," his father, Larry Alford Sr., said. "Finishing second in the biggest junior golf tournament of the year and then wading into water hazards to fish out golf balls. In no way was success going to change him."

Late that summer, a golf teammate asked if Larry could do him a favor and drive the teammate's father's Corvette to a relative's house. The teammate in turn would follow in his car and then drive Larry home. Larry said fine and off they went. Shortly after 6 P.M., while it was still broad daylight, Larry lost control of the Corvette on Interstate 45. The car flipped over three times, catapulting Alford through the open sun roof and onto the highway. Alford's friend braked his car to a halt and saw his teammate lying motionless and bleeding badly from the head, face and left arm.

In the emergency room at Hermann Hospital in Houston, a doctor emerged from behind a curtain and asked Larry's parents to come in. *Oh my God!* Mrs. Alford screamed to herself on seeing her son, who was the color of gray ice with a head as big as a basketball. Out of the corner of one eye, she saw what she perceived to be a look of horror on the face of one doctor.

"I got the feeling that they wanted us to see Larry once more, maybe for the last time," Missy recalled. Then, as she and Larry Sr. were led out, she pleaded to herself, *Dear God, please save him.*

From the moment Larry Alford arrived at Hermann Hospital, Dr. James "Red" Duke, the hospital's chief trauma surgeon, knew that his severed left arm could not be saved. Far more important was a life-threatening head injury. Then there were the lesser injuries: a fractured eye orbital bone that had jarred Larry's eye partially out of its socket, a broken jaw, ankle and shoulder blade, a collapsed lung and a badly injured right arm. "I'm sorry, but we had to amputate your son's arm below the elbow," Dr. John Burns, an orthopedic surgeon, told Larry's parents.

"Is he going to be all right?" Missy Alford asked.

"We don't know," Dr. Burns answered.

Standing alongside Missy was Jay Hall, a friend of hers who could not help but wonder about Larry's reaction to the loss of his left arm if he were indeed going to survive. *How would Larry ever get along without golf?* Hall thought to himself. But then, catching himself in mid-thought, Hall also realized there was a far more pressing matter than a golf career at stake. *They've got to save Larry's life,* he said to himself. *That's all that matters right now.*

For almost ninety days Larry Alford remained unconscious and in critical condition. Then, gradually, his condition improved and he was no longer in danger. But his parents knew that difficult days lay ahead. For one thing, he would eventually learn that he had lost his left hand.

One night Larry awakened and suddenly realized that his left hand was missing. He cried out for a nurse. One hurried into his room and said softly, "I'm sorry, Larry, but they had to amputate your hand." Meanwhile, his father, alerted, raced to the hospital.

"Dad, how am I ever going to play golf?" he asked.

"Don't worry, Larry," his father replied. "You'll play again, and you'll do fine."

Young Alford did not remain depressed for long. "Mom, I did it to myself," he said one day to his mother, "so I'm to blame. And God saved my life, so I'm lucky."

A few weeks later, while talking about golf, Larry turned to his father and asked, "Dad, do you have my clubs with you?"

"Yeah, I've got them in the trunk of the car, Larry."

"Good," Larry said excitedly. "Can you get my pitching wedge? Maybe we can chip some balls outside."

Within minutes Larry and his father were on the lawn outside the Del Oro Institute in Houston where Larry was recuperating. Although he had lost forty pounds and was weak, young Larry began to chip with his right arm. Ball after ball went soaring in beautiful arcs as both father and son looked on in delight.

"Dad, will you look at those shots," Larry said, ecstatic at swinging a golf club again.

"You're doing great, Son, just great," his father, replied heartened by Larry's joy.

A week later, at young Larry's suggestion, he and his father went out to play a round of golf at one of the four courses at The Woodlands Country Club. Understandably, Larry's father was both happy and apprehensive.

God, I hope he does all right, Mr. Alford said to himself. *Don't let him be upset.*

Larry Alford Sr. needn't have worried. Though still weak and lacking in stamina, his son hit his shots cleanly and accurately during his first outing as a one-handed golfer. His chipping and putting in particular were superb. "Boy, Dad this is great," he said at one point as he and his father walked down a fairway.

At the end of eighteen holes, Larry had shot an 86,

about ten strokes above his average before his accident, but an extraordinary score for a one-handed golfer. As they headed for the clubhouse, Larry, obviously elated at how he had played, turned to his father and said, "Dad, do you think that I can still make the PGA Tour?"

Larry Sr. was prepared for the question. "Yes, I do," he replied. "But I think we're going to have to take this one day at a time."

After that, and unbeknownst to Larry, Jay Hall began calling prosthetic manufacturers to find out if there was such a thing as an artificial golf hand on the market that would enable Larry to play competitive golf. Finding none, Hall decided that he, himself, would try to design a golf hand for Larry on his own. "First, I had to ask myself just what does the left hand do on a golf swing for a right-handed golfer," said Hall, a professional psychologist and a good golfer himself. "And the answer is quite simple. It holds the club with three fingers and it hinges or cocks the club. Essentially, it provides those two functions, and that's about all."

Of paramount importance, Hall knew, was that the hand had to grip the club firmly enough so that the handle wouldn't be twisted by the force of the swing. To ensure that, Hall designed the palm of the hand with pumped-up air cells. For the wrist, he came up with a ball and socket mechanism which, Hall felt, could perform the function of a human joint.

Hall then took his design to Ted Muilenburg, the owner of a prosthetics company in Houston. "Jay knew nothing about prosthetics, and I knew nothing about golf," Muilenburg said.

"But I must say I was impressed with his design—so much so that we went ahead and made 'The Halford Grip,'" as it came to be known, blending Larry and Jay's last names. Muilenburg used an aluminum child's knee prosthesis for the wrist and some air cells, which when inflated, fit tightly around the grip on the golfing hand like human fingers. Then a silicone suction sleeve, which slides over the elbow to hold the hand in place, was attached.

Seeing the mold the first time, Missy's eyes brimmed with tears, as she envisioned her son's reaction to the hand, which she was going to give to him on Christmas morning. "It'll work," Hall said, after looking over what Muilenburg had wrought. "I know it's going to work."

Unwrapping the last Christmas gift of the day, Larry peeked inside the box and, a look of amazement on his face, cried out. "It's a hand—my golf hand."

"It was Jay's idea," Missy said to her son. "He even designed it."

Overwhelmed with emotion, Larry threw his arms around Jay. "Thanks so much."

The Halford Grip has been a rousing success, although a number of adjustments have been made over the years. "Some golfers, seeing how well my golf hand works, have said they'd like to trade arms with me, but I tell them, 'No way.'"

Since receiving his golf hand, Alford has shot his lowest score ever—a 69. He also recorded his first hole-in-one and played three years of varsity golf at Sam Houston University. Since his graduation in 1997, Alford has worked as an assistant golf pro at his home course, The Woodlands Country Club, and has helped raise money for a number of charities by challenging golfers to try to get closer to the pin than he has on par-3 holes. "Not many people have," said Alford, who shoots in the 70s and booms his tee-shots more than 250 yards.

"My accident has been a blessing for me," said Alford who delivers inspirational talks to young people in schools and churches in the Houston area. "It happened for a reason. I thank God for saving my life, for giving me such a positive attitude and then giving me a second chance as a golfer. As for having to play with only one real arm, I tell people that golf is hard enough with two hands, so it can't be that much harder with one."

Jack Cavanaugh

On His Own Two Feet

One of the most fascinating things about golf is how it reflects the cycle of life. No matter what you shoot, the next day you have to go back to the first tee and begin all over again and make yourself into something.

Peter Jacobsen

Bob Hullender is telling the story of his life when he suddenly can't continue. The emotions flooding from the memories of what he went through, twice, are too traumatic. His voice breaks and his eyes well up, and a man who flew 221 combat missions in an F-4 Phantom jet over Vietnam as an Air Force general asks to be excused.

Like almost everything else about golf, senior amateur competition in America is thriving. Given the time, energy, dollars and sufficient game, golfers fifty-five and up can play a tournament a week, as Hullender almost does, most of them requiring gross scores of par or better to win. The memberships of the elite seniors' associations that operate the bulk of these highly formalized 54- and 72-hole events are full to bursting. Entries for the U.S.

Senior Amateur Championship have grown from a few hundred at its inception to more than two thousand— and rising. And perhaps twenty times that many gray-beards possess a good enough game to compete beyond the club level.

Hullender is at the top of this flourishing world. How he got there is a story of will over adversity.

Born in Ringgold, Georgia, in March 1937, Hullender grew up on a dairy farm loving any sport involving a ball. After high school he attended Georgia Tech as a coopera-tive student, alternating three months of classes with three working for the Tennessee Valley Authority. There wasn't much ball time then.

In 1959, about to be drafted, Hullender began an Air Force career through the Aviation Cadet Program, start-ing as a second lieutenant and ending as a general. Except for a thirteen-month tour of duty in Vietnam, ball time was sufficient for him to become a champion fast-pitch softball pitcher capable of under-arming at 105 miles an hour, close to the world record. He played some winter golf then, to a low handicap, but it remained secondary to his summer sport.

That changed as he got older, and since 1987, when he turned fifty, Hullender has played in three Senior Opens, making the cut twice. He's also qualified for every Senior Amateur since becoming eligible at age fifty-five, with a runner-up finish in 1994. His contemporaries swear it's only a matter of time before he wins the title. That's partly because of the astonishing distances he hits a golf ball, but mostly because of what getting to become the player he is says about his desire, determination and plain, unadulter-ated grit.

You see, both of his hips are artificial.

Newcomers to the senior-am fraternity don't learn this from the general himself because he never volunteers the information. But it's invariably the first thing they learn about him from his peers. Most of those who compete with and against Hullender still cannot believe a golfer so doctored can play the game so much, so powerfully and so successfully.

His hips began degenerating with osteoarthritis in his late forties. As they did, sport after sport became impossible, including his beloved softball, when pain and reduced mobility prevented him from taking the steps necessary to throw. The right hip went first, then the left.

Hip-joint replacement was pretty new in the early 1980s, but eventually Hullender found an orthopedic surgeon expert in what's known as the porous-coated procedure. This is done without cement, as the bone adheres to the porous coating of the prosthesis after it's press-fitted into the hip and leg bones.

He had the right hip replaced in 1986. Then came a wonderful surprise. Because of the way he swung the club—mostly with the hands and arms—as rehabilitation progressed, he discovered that the new hip wasn't a handicap to golf. That inspired him to work hard enough at the game to be shooting around par within a year.

By the fall of 1992, the left hip had degenerated to the extent that pain and impaired mobility prevented him even from tying his shoelaces. He went back on the operating table.

"Because I'd learned how to rehabilitate, that second time wasn't as traumatic as the first. And getting through it produced a big change in attitude. You know, when something's as bad as those hips were, getting worse every day, the hopelessness seems to increase. . . ." And here his eyes well up and he asks to be excused. This is tough to talk about.

"The rehab is the critical part. It's hard at first, but you have to do it religiously, no skimping. They get you up and moving the leg around isometrically the day after surgery. Then it's six weeks of progressively more strenuous flexibility and strengthening exercises, first in water, then in the gym. You walk on crutches until everything is fully weight-bearing, and they want you to walk as much as you can. I did miles and miles around my neighborhood and still do, every morning.

"The motivation is, if you do the work on your body you know it will steadily get better, stronger. Pretty soon after the second operation, I was exercising eight hours a day, for the hip and leg, but also, with golf in mind, on my hands and arms and upper body. The knowledge that I was going to play again inspired me. I wanted to make it the best playing I was capable of."

Back to swinging all his clubs to their full value in twelve weeks, a year later Hullender was one of America's top-ten senior amateurs. His first official number-one ranking came in 1995, followed by second in 1996, and top again in 1997. And he figures to get better yet, continuing to work at his game.

"But you know when they're wheeling you down to that operating room, you're not worrying about golf. What you're worrying about is whether you'll ever be able to put one foot in front of the other again, whether you'll be able to get around under your own steam. So, play well or poorly, win or lose, I'm a very happy guy just to be out there."

Ken Bowden

Close to Home

The kindness we extend to others in their hour of weakness will return to us at the time we most need.

Harriet Johns

For six years, Bob and Nancy Mills celebrated their favorite week of the year—the week of the FedEx St. Jude Classic—with a house full of friends and clients. Over-looking the Tournament Players Club at Southwind's eighteenth hole, the Mills's home was a hotbed of activity for this family of golf-lovers who'd participated in the tournament for fifteen years.

But a week after the 1997 Classic, Nancy Mills walked out her back door not to join a party but to capture a quiet moment alone as she grappled with a parent's worst nightmare. Doctors had told the Millses earlier that day that their five-year-old daughter, Ali, had can-cer. Incredulous, Nancy stared at the tournament's scoreboard across the lake that now read "The St. Jude Kids Say Thanks" and realized that Ali was now one of those children. The tournament the Millses had loved and been involved in for years was now to affect their lives in a larger way than they ever imagined—by ben-efiting their Ali.

During the tournament the week before, Ali's leg had begun to ache, and she lost her appetite and grew very pale. Nancy instinctively knew something was amiss, and she was right: Ali's bloodwork looked wrong and the doctor could feel something in her abdomen. She was sent to St. Jude, and by that afternoon the Mills family knew they were dealing with cancer. A grueling series of tests the next day confirmed Ali had a very rare and potentially deadly solid tumor called neuroblastoma. The tumor stretched from her abdomen to her neck, and had already spread to her bone marrow, the most advanced stage of the disease. The Mills were completely shocked.

"I thought, 'How did I miss this?'" Nancy says. "We were just numb. We couldn't think. You know there are bad things that can happen to your children, but I never thought of cancer. There's no history of cancer in our fam-ily at all. For the first week, I couldn't even say the word 'cancer.'"

St. Jude doctors moved fast to begin treating Ali because her condition was so serious. She began chemotherapy treatments the same night as her battery of tests and the diagnosis. Groggy from sedation to get her through the tests, Ali awoke the morning of July 4 in the hospital and learned she had cancer.

"She was very quiet—which isn't like Ali," Nancy says. "We told her she had a tumor and were very up front with her. She took it all very well. Even though she had just gotten her hair long, she was okay when it started falling out from the chemo. On her second treatment, she pulled it out and saved it in a plastic bag to give to the birds to use in their nests."

The Millses lived through tough days as Ali's doctors at St. Jude Hospital attempted to put her cancer into remission so she could have a bone marrow transplant—

her only hope for a cure. Despite a year of various high-powered chemotherapy treatments and a surgery to remove the primary tumor, however, the cancer remained in Ali's bone marrow. At last, though, the Mills family received the wonderful news that for the first time Ali's bone marrow was free from cancer.

Ali had her bone marrow harvested the week of the FedEx St. Jude Classic.

"It's so hard to watch your child go through this, to know it's life-threatening," Nancy says. "You don't want to see them suffer, miss out on things, be stared at. We try to keep life normal."

Bravely soldiering through her treatments, Ali emerged from them with few outer signs of illness other than her bald head. A popular, bubbly presence at St. Jude, she entertains her nurses and doctors with songs and pranks. "She hasn't let her trials get her down," Nancy says.

In March, Ali went to see "The Lion King" on Broadway in New York. Her chemotherapy-induced baldness attracted the attention of another child in front of her. She heard the little girl say, "He doesn't have any hair!" Ali tapped her and told her, "A) I'm a SHE, B) it's called cancer, and C) it's the drugs." Then she leaned her smooth head toward the girl and said kindly, "Do you want to feel it?"

This is Ali's true spirit. She is known for bringing the St. Jude staff to tears with her favorite song, which says, "God doesn't see the same way people see. People see the outside of a person, but God looks at the heart."

It's Ali's beautiful, courageous heart that gives significance to the FedEx St. Jude Classic. This isn't lost on the Mills family, whose devotion to the tournament is ironically helping save their daughter's life.

Bob Phillips
Submitted by Phil Cannon

A New Perspective

For today and its blessings, I owe the world an attitude of gratitude.

Clarence E. Hodges

The ball hooked right again. A loud cracking noise ripped through the air like a gunshot, then a mesquite branch fell and shattered on the fairway. My son beat the ground with his driver and shouted, "That's why I hate golf!"

For weeks Trey, a left-handed golfer, had been knocking the limbs off trees on courses across three counties. Now, just days away from the last high school tournament before the district championship, he still hadn't figured out what he was doing wrong.

I sat cross-armed in the cart, regretting the unguarded moment when I'd offered to bring my son to this course for a practice round. I resented his self-centered attitude. Mentally, I tallied all the vacation days my husband and I had used to drive him to out-of-town tournaments. All the money we'd spent on custom clubs and private lessons. All the efforts I'd made to time the delivery of "first-come, first-served" applications to prestigious qualifying events.

I was beginning to hate golf myself. But I said nothing, afraid of what I might say.

Trey, a freshman on the varsity golf team, struggled to fit in with four seniors who shared a world in common. Unlike his teammates, my son had no driver's license, no girlfriend and no confidence that he could hit the ball as far from the blue tees as he had from the white ones. He'd gotten used to scoring in the 70s off the white tees, but since joining the team, his stroke average had jumped to 83.

My son was suffering his first slump.

Maybe, I thought, his snarly ways had everything to do with this misery. I tried to comfort him. I cast a bright light on his dark doubts. I promised an end to these desperate days.

But my son continued to wallow in his misgivings . . . until he overheard a comment at his next tournament.

The big world of boys' and girls' competitive golf is really a small community of players and parents who soon recognize each other at all the tournaments. So Trey knew immediately that the woman following his foursome was the mother of a player who had died a few months ago in a wreck on the way to practice. A teammate had lost control of the car on a steep, rain-slick hill. Everyone survived, except her child. This woman, despite her own crushing grief, worried about how devastated the team was, and came out to encourage her son's friends.

The mother didn't reserve her inspiring words just for that team, but offered them also to a competitor who complained that he was having a lousy round. "You're a talented golfer," Trey heard her tell him. "Be happy to play any golf."

Four days later, at the district championship, my son shot two great rounds in the 70s. The team won first place and Trey was named to First Team All-District. His coach told the newspaper reporter: "The kid really came through."

My son and I both know what really came through
were the words of a grieving mother who is grateful for
the time she had with her son and who now takes nothing for granted.

Melissa Russell

Taking a Swing at Stress

The most wasted of all days is the one during which you have not laughed.

Nicolas Chamfort

In the world of business, golf is touted as a game that relieves the stress of the job. It's where big deals are made and friendships are won.

In a world exploding with information and change, trying to keep from being wired and tired is a major chore. For far too many people, the stresses of life have zapped their ability to do their best, be their best and enjoy their daily activities.

Consider this for a moment: One million Americans have heart attacks each year. Around thirteen billion doses of tranquilizers, barbiturates and amphetamines are prescribed yearly. Well over eight million Americans have stomach ulcers. There are an estimated fifty thousand stress-related suicides each year. This is only the tip of the iceberg. In fact, reports indicate that 80 percent of the illnesses treated in this country are emotionally induced illnesses.

I went golfing not long ago with some business friends who really like to have fun. We affectionately refer to our group as "the Golfing Angels" because we take ourselves lightly. One of the men has dubbed our particular brand of the game "flog" (golf backwards), and we've added some rules to the traditional game. One of the first rules is that everyone must laugh when something is funny. When somebody misses the ball while teeing off, laughter is mandatory. No offense is taken. In our game of flog, the only failure is the failure to have fun. One of the doctors on the flog team figured that if you live to be seventy years of age, you will spend 613,200 hours wandering the planet. That is far too much time to be stressed and not to have fun. Fun is a diversion from the norm that gets us out of the "dullness" rut that the stresses of life tend to create.

Another rule of the game is to never keep score. We've found that most people cheated anyway. If you do keep score, you must write it on the scorecard before you leave the cart to tee off. If you get close enough to the green, you can just throw the ball if you wish. The rule I like best is that you can tee the ball up regardless of where you are on the fairway. One flog angel loves to find someone's ball on the fairway and tee it up for them. He then hides in the trees to see their reaction. People look around in disbelief. Most just shrug it off and hit it off the tee. When we let people play through, everyone claps for them. Our group of hackers just has fun.

One day when we were just about ready to tee off, a foursome drove up behind us. We knew that they were serious about this game as we noticed they had their own golf carts with names boldly printed on the sides. This bunch had no smiles but lots of Zantac. Hole after hole, we could hear them yelling at each other and their putters. Sand flew and divots were dug. At the last hole, which was surrounded by water, one particularly intense fellow blew his final putt by inches. He grabbed his golf bag with all the clubs in it. He was so frustrated that he took the bag and tossed it as far into the water as he could and headed for his car. There he felt in his pocket for the keys. He threw his hat to the ground in disgust as he remembered where he had left his keys. He headed back to the water's edge and waded out to his sinking bag. He opened the zipper and grabbed his keys and threw the bag further into the abyss. By this time, we were laughing so hard that we just threw our golf balls onto the green. The team does get a lot of strange looks on the golfing fairways, but we sure have a good time.

One day late in the spring, someone complained to the course pro about the team's unorthodox conduct. The pro looked at the man, smiled and said, "Don't worry, they're on a hospital release program."

Steve Densley
Submitted by Pam Jones

Reprinted with permission by Johnny Hart and Creators Syndicate, Inc.

An Embrace in the Bittersweet Middle

I first thought to write all this down so I wouldn't forget. As I look back, I realize there's no way I could forget. It was a handful of time . . . an experience out of plain sight. I was witness to a moment or two I don't know if I can adequately describe.

Mark O'Meara and I had just sat down for what has become a ritual since Paul Azinger won the PGA in 1993: SportsCenter's "Sunday Conversation" with the winner of a major golf tournament. As the cameramen were making the final lighting adjustments, the door flew open and in walked Ian Baker-Finch.

Baker-Finch had been something of a story himself during the tournament week. He had won the British Open when it was last played at Royal Birkdale in 1991 with weekend rounds of 64 and 66. He had seized that Sunday as if by birthright. A few years later though, his game mysteriously began to disappear. He went through a two-year period where he didn't make a single cut, routinely shooting in the 80s. He said at one point that his driving was so erratic he would stand on the tee with no idea where his ball was going to go. In the first round of the Open at Troon last summer, he shot 92 and withdrew. He had decided it was time to take a break and sort things out. He retired from competitive golf.

Baker-Finch had returned to Royal Birkdale as a commentator for ABC and ESPN.

I don't know if I could have done it if I were in his shoes. His trip back to the scene of his greatest triumph was not only a reminder of how skilled he had once been, but of how much it had all slipped away. Here were his colleagues, his peers, his mates having a go at a tournament and a course he once ruled. There he was, at age thirty-seven, holding a microphone instead of a golf club.

And now there he was, standing in the doorway. He had earlier asked me to convey his congratulations to O'Meara and his wife Alicia. When Baker-Finch won at Royal Birkdale in 1991, he had been paired the final Sunday with O'Meara. They both lived in Orlando and had become friends.

Now, before anybody could say a word, there were these two men, locked in a silent embrace. The room was full of officials and producers and technicians and family, yet these two men shamelessly hugged each other and cried, sharing a meaningful, wordless moment as if they were alone. One player was at the top of his game, filled with confidence and accomplishment, the other at the bottom of his, consumed by bewilderment and resignation. They met in the bittersweet middle, where the line between joy and sadness was impossible to find.

Later, Baker-Finch and I walked back to the SportsCenter set for our final segment of the night. As we made our way across the now-deserted eighteenth green, he stopped and looked at the empty stands, as the sun sank into the Irish Sea.

"Where was the cup?" I asked, not exactly recalling the details of 1991, but knowing he would.

"There," he said softly, pointing to a flat area on the back right of the putting surface.

"Where was the last putt?" I said, already knowing the answer.

He said nothing, but walked to the spot and pantomimed the winning stroke. Suddenly, the stands were full, the crowd was cheering and Baker-Finch was once again "the champion golfer for the year," as the R&A Secretary annually proclaims at the awards ceremony.

He smiled for a moment, but then his face turned blank. He said nothing, but it was clear what he saw: The vast distance between where he had once been and where he stood now. He looked frightened.

"I've held it in all week. Stuffed it, and I just can't do it anymore," he said. His eyes were now red, and the tears were streaming down his cheeks.

I stammered something about how they could never take that great tournament away from him, but I knew it was lame. We walked down the fairway in silence for a moment before I offered that maybe he might like to spend a moment alone.

As I walked away, I looked back. There was a once-great champion taking one long, last taste, drinking in how good it had all once been, before turning and walking into his new life.

Jimmy Roberts

Lightning Strikes Twice

"Impossible" only describes the degree of difficulty.

David Phillips

During a round with friends on March 18, 1990, seventy-four-year-old Margaret Waidron of Jacksonville, Florida, approached the par-3 seventh hole.

Legally blind, Waldron had lost her vision ten years earlier to an eye disease. Instead of giving up sports, though, she continued to be an active golfer, relying on her husband, Pete, to line her up and to describe the hole, distance and playing conditions.

Pete handed Margaret a 7-iron and pointed her toward the flag on Long Point's eighty-seven-yard seventh hole. "I hit the ball solidly," Margaret recalled. "One of my friends said, 'Good hit, Margaret . . . Wow! It's going for the green! It's going toward the hole!'"

"Another friend shouted, 'You've got a hole-in-one!' We all hugged and I felt a great sense of fulfillment. That night, Pete and I celebrated."

When Margaret arrived at the same hole the next day, she took the same 7-iron and once again hit the eighty-seven-yard shot perfectly. The ball rolled into the cup for another ace. "When we went back to the clubhouse, I was so proud," Margaret said. "I don't consider myself handicapped. I am challenged to do the best I can with what I have. What else should I do? Sit home and knit? Not me!"

Experts have computed the odds against an amateur scoring a hole-in-one at twelve thousand to one, and no one yet has attempted to establish the likelihood of a blind golfer recording an ace. "To do it twice on the same hole, two days in a row, using the same club and the same ball, makes the odds beyond comprehension," said Long Point golf pro Ed Tucker.

Bruce Nash and Allan Zullo
with George White

A Wing Grew Back

So much has been given me, I have no time to ponder over that which has been denied.

Helen Keller

At any golf course, it's usually respectfully quiet around the first tee.

But when Bob Cox prepares for his opening drive, he can hear the whispers and low-voiced comments from the onlookers.

"Look, that guy's got only one arm."

And after Cox cracks a long shot straight down the middle of the fairway, he'll often hear, "Wow, I can't hit it that far with two arms."

Cox, who lost his left arm in a motorcycle accident twenty-two years ago, has a remarkable golf game. In a sport where the majority of fully able-bodied players can't break 90 for eighteen holes, he can do it.

"I'm very competitive," said Cox during a recent round. "I actually like the challenge of hitting the ball while people are watching."

In his weekly men's golf league, played at the Winchendon

Country Club in Winchendon, Massachusetts, he'll consistently shoot a 45 or less for nine holes.

His record for eighteen holes is an 88 (44-44) at the par-71 Gardner Municipal Golf Course.

"It's fun going out to play with friends and actually beating them," Cox said. "I love this game."

Cox, forty-one, wasn't always an avid golfer. When he was a teen, hockey was his game. That was, of course, before the accident.

In one fateful instant on June 9, 1976, around noontime, Bob Cox's life changed forever.

While riding his Suzuki 250 motorcycle on Elm Street in Gardner, he collided with a car. In the accident, Cox's left arm, from just inches below his shoulder, was completely severed. Cox and his motorcycle crashed to the road, while his entire left arm lay on the street twenty yards from his body.

"They told me later that there wasn't a lot of blood," Cox said. "I really don't remember anything. I was in a state of shock."

Rushed to a local hospital and then quickly transferred to Boston, Cox remembers waking up in Massachusetts General and asking the doctors how badly his arm was broken.

Just eighteen years old, Cox was given the terrible news. A reattachment operation would not have been successful.

Readjusting his life with only one arm took patience and acceptance. Said Cox, "It was the little things that were tough, like putting toothpaste on your toothbrush, tying a necktie or tying your shoes. And hockey, that's the one thing I really miss. I just couldn't shoot the puck anymore."

But there was never a sense of self-pity or "Why me?" attitude in Bob Cox. "It doesn't do any good," he said.

"Obviously I wish it had never happened, but you just have to go on."

So Cox, never looking back for too long, went on, staying active in sports by playing golf.

He's even quick to joke about his situation.

When asked by a playing partner, "What's your handicap?" Cox will often let the question float in the air for a few seconds. When asked why he doesn't wear a golf glove, he responds, "How will I put it on?"

Cox, who had played golf occasionally before the accident, decided to take the game seriously in his early twenties.

A few teaching pros advised him to swing from the left side, or backhanded, using his right arm to pull through the ball.

"I just couldn't hit from that side," Cox recalled. "I didn't have enough power."

Still, Cox developed a solid swing from the right side, a swing he could rely on.

He sets up with the ball in the middle of his stance, grips down almost to the metal part of the shaft with his muscular right arm and concentrates on hitting down on the ball.

"The hardest thing to learn was to keep my head still," Cox explained.

"I probably hit my irons better than my woods," Cox added. "I take big divots."

The best part of his game occurs on the greens where he displays a smooth putting stroke, keeping the club on line with an accurate follow-through stroke.

In years of practice, Cox has crafted a solid game using his right arm to draw back the club. He then shifts his weight and moves into a powerful downswing at the ball.

For twenty-one years Cox has worked as a customer service representative for Bell Atlantic. And he's very

active in the Bell Atlantic Pioneers, a volunteer organization in which he has served as president.

Cox works closely in the administration and organization of the Special Olympics of Massachusetts.

During weekends and vacations, Cox and his wife,
Becky, enjoy their thirty-six-foot boat on Lake
Winnipesaukee, their summer haven.

In the winter Cox loves to ride his snowmobile.

When June 9 rolls around every year, Cox pauses and
thinks about the accident.

"When it comes up on the calendar, I look at the date
and remember," he said. "I think about the time of day
when it happened. It sticks in my mind."

But most of the time Bob Cox looks ahead, to days of
helping people during his job or his volunteer efforts with
the Bell Atlantic Pioneers or to the time spent relaxing at
the lake or golfing with friends.

His life brings to mind a poem by Nina Cassian, a writer
from Romania. In her poem, "A Man," she writes about a
soldier who lost an arm while fighting for his country.
After a brief period of grief, the soldier moves on in life
with an outlook of hope.

Cassian ends her poem with the following:

"From that moment on, he set himself to do everything
with twice as much enthusiasm.

And where the arm had been torn away a wing grew."

Jay Gearan

The Healer

When someone asks you, "What's your handicap?" you probably respond with a variety of numbers, depending on if you are trying to impress or win a bet.

"I'm a nine," you might say to a new business associate, or "On a good day? Fourteen," to your weekend $5 Nassau buddies. For most golfers, "handicap" is a measure of how much the game of golf has gotten the better of them.

For Gus Bernardoni, a PGA Teaching Professional from Deerfield, Illinois, "handicap" is an expression of how much in golf—and life—can be overcome. In 1944, serving as a paratrooper with the 101st Airborne, Gus Bernardoni jumped out of a plane over Holland. His chute did not open properly, causing him to fall 300 feet onto a hostile bit of the Netherlands. Plummeting toward earth, he had what he describes as "a talk with God," during which time he asked him to bless all the friends and loved ones he would never see again.

Instantaneously, Bernardoni's body went limp as wet newsprint. He lived—and, understandably, became a life-long Christian. But for seventy-eight days on the front line, trapped under heavy fire, Bernardoni went without proper medical treatment, leaving his spine twisted and his right leg paralyzed.

After corrective spinal surgery, which restored movement to the young paratrooper's lower body, doctors at the Mayo Clinic suggested Gus swing golf clubs as part of his recuperative therapy. Employing all the tenets of a "correct" stroke—stiff left arm, keep the head down, rotate the hips, etc.—Bernardoni suffered excruciating pain.

But he didn't quit. He adapted.

"I found a way to hit the golf ball within my physical limits," Bernardoni explains, introducing himself to a small group of golfers at a Moline, Illinois driving range. "You can, too," he says.

The golfers at this instructional clinic, sponsored by United Cerebral Palsy, are not looking to shave strokes off their score. They're not trying to cure a troublesome slice. They don't want to play golf better—they just want to play golf.

And Gus Bernardoni wants to help them. "I know therapy can be difficult. I know the fear of working toward health and not being sure you'll ever get better," Gus says, pacing before the group, limping slightly. "But I also know there's somebody out there in worse shape than you. So you better start counting your blessings."

Telling someone like Mark De Vrieze, a parapalegic, or Don Smith, who lost the use of his left side to a stroke, to count their blessings might seem insensitive to some. Not Gus. "Let's not pretend we can do everything exactly like other people can. You may be 'less abled.' Maybe you can't walk or run too well. And maybe certain activities are hard for you. But you manage. So I don't want to hear about 'disabled,'" he tells the group of nascent golfers. "'Disabled' is someone who quits."

Gus tells the group he could have laid in a V.A. hospital and collected a pension, or convalesced at home. Or done nothing. Instead, he taught himself to play golf— not traditionally, but well. In 1974, still enduring chronic back pain thirty years after his parachuting mishap, Gus Bernardoni won the Illinois PGA Senior Championship. In 1978 he wrote a book, *Golf God's Way*, outlining his peculiarly effective methods. In 1993, he was inducted into the Illinois PGA Hall of Fame.

Bernardoni is a staff consultant to the Tommy Armour Golf company, whose eponym, coincidentally, also overcame a host of physical ailments en route to golfing greatness. Now seventy-four, Gus still plays out of the Pine Meadows Golf Club in Mundelein, Illinois, and coaches several Senior PGA Tour players, including the remarkable Joe Jiminez, who regularly shoots his age. But much of Bernardoni's life is devoted to work with the Special Olympics and hospitals around the country, coaching people with debilitating illnesses like multiple sclerosis, muscular dystrophy, and arthritis, to develop self-esteem, confidence and willpower through a game that normally inspires none of those qualities in its practitioners.

Today, on an autumn morning in the heartland, Gus Bernardoni is teaching this group of "less abled" athletes that, despite their various infirmities, they, too, can hit a golf ball. "If you can do that, you can do just about anything. Just ask anyone with the use of all their arms and legs, they'll tell you the same thing," he jokes, flashing the kind of smile you tend to see on those who really like their work.

Gus tells his audience that golf is really a lot simpler than most people think. "You've got to get balanced, you have to swing the club, and you have to hit the ball: That's it," he says, shrugging. Most of the game is mental, he explains, so someone's coordination, or lack thereof, is hardly an impediment to making contact with the ball. "There's no such thing as 'mechanical positioning,' no individual can copy anyone else successfully," Bernardoni says, growing impassioned. "Would you tell a blind man he 'looked up'? Would you tell a man with one leg he needs to 'shift-and-pivot' his weight on the backswing?"

To demonstrate, Gus hits golf balls from one foot, on his knees and facing backwards. And when I say "hit" I don't mean "makes contact with," I mean powders. "You've only got one hand to work with? You can't see? Can't use your legs?" Gus laughs. "You've got this," he says, pointing to his head. Bernardoni calls up John Irwin, who, since a massive stroke, can only move his left side. Gus has Irwin tuck his right hand into a pocket. "Get that thing out of the way," he says. Then he adjusts Irwin's left hand grip, turning all his knuckles on top of the club. Shifting Irwin's torso closed to the target line to "redefine his center of gravity," Bernardoni asks his student to pick up the club and chop at the ball while exclaiming "Pow!" at impact. "Pow. . ." Irwin whispers, as the ball dribbles off the tee. Gus stands with his hands on hips, in mock disbelief.

"Not pow," Gus says weakly. "POW!!"

His student laughs. But now he's all business. After a few emphatic practice swings, John Irwin addresses his ball, makes a mighty wallop and says "POW!" The ball sails into the distance.

Everyone applauds heartily. But John Irwin doesn't notice. Holding his golf club out like a sword, he's too busy savoring every wondrous yard of the ball's flight, a journey that he, a massive stroke victim, authored. When the ball finally comes to rest many glorious yards from where it started, Irwin shuffles, six inches per step, over to his chair. For the remainder of the morning, that golf club never leaves his hand.

The next time you are playing badly and want to throw a club or let loose a string of curses or behave with any-thing but dignified grace, imagine trying to play golf from a chair. Or with one arm. Or without sight. And then be profoundly thankful you have the limbs and faculties and ability to hit a golf ball, no matter how wretchedly.

Eric Black, eleven, has spina bifida. From his chest down he has no sensation, and must be strapped into a chair. His pal Mark DeDecker, twelve, has cerebral palsy, epilepsy and is deaf in one ear. Like most young boys these two love to watch sports on television, especially Mark, whose mom says he is crazy-nuts for golf. Mark dreams, as we all do, of one day making slam dunks like Michael Jordan or hitting home runs like Ken Griffey Jr. or blasting drives like Phil Mickelson. But unlike other eager boys his age, they are dreams that will come true only in his imagination.

Mark DeDecker and Eric Black can only watch the Masters broadcast every year. They will never play golf at Augusta National. They will never know the thrill of making par on a championship golf course.

That is why, after a dozen earnest whiffs and much cajoling and coaching and encouragement from Gus Bernardoni, when Mark DeDecker makes a bold one-handed swing with his 9-iron and sends his ball airborne, flying free and clear from all his earthly despairs, I am not the only one watching who has a tear in his eye. With a shot of maybe forty-five yards, Mark DeDecker has just eagled the Amen Corner of his dreams.

Michael Konik

Happy

I remember golf when it was played B.C. (before carts). Caddying was a great way to earn money. It also taught me a lesson or two about human nature, and how an act of kindness can change a man's life.

I was caddiemaster at a busy club. One morning, a gentleman asked me if I could use another caddie. He said he had a nineteen-year-old mentally retarded son who was strong and healthy. "The boy knows nothing about golf," the gentleman said, "but I'm sure he can be taught how to caddie."

The man's son, named Happy, had never been to school nor had any training. (Back then, there were no special education programs.) Despite a speech impediment, he could communicate fairly well. He quickly learned the fundamentals. The other caddies readily accepted him.

Happy was well-named, with a pleasant disposition. From time to time, though, I observed him sitting by himself in the caddieshack, with a pensive look. It almost seemed as though he were contemplating his condition and wondering why he was not like other people.

As expected, some people did not want Happy to

caddie for them. Many days, he could not get out. I explained this to his father as tactfully as possible, but his dad was just grateful that Happy could be part of a normal activity and make a few dollars each week. Still, I did not want to give up on him.

Then, a group of ladies who played regularly invited a newcomer as their guest. Mrs. Wentworth was her name. She appeared to be in her forties and was an excellent golfer.

Because it was a busy day, only four caddies were left, including Happy. He was assigned to Mrs. Wentworth. When the ladies finished their round, the newcomer reported that she had been very pleased with Happy. His manner was pleasant. He kept his eye on the ball, kept his mouth shut and generally did what a good caddie should do. She added that she planned to play more often and requested that I reserve Happy for her.

When I explained this to Happy, he was more than happy!

Every day he would wait in the caddie yard next to the parking lot. He eagerly watched as each car arrived at the club. When he would recognize Mrs. Wentworth's car, he became as excited as a child. "Here comes my lady!" he would proudly tell the other caddies.

As long as I was caddiemaster there, only Happy caddied for Mrs. Wentworth. She routinely tipped him twenty-five cents, a hefty sum in those days.

I often wondered why Mrs. Wentworth so wholeheartedly accepted this young man. She made him feel that he was important; he could do as fine a job as the other caddies. I think she saw something in him that so many others had missed.

I went into the service in mid-summer, losing touch with Happy, Mrs. Wentworth and others at the club. After four years in the Army, I returned to my hometown and visited the club. The pro was still there. When I inquired about Happy, he said that the young man had continued to caddie for Mrs. Wentworth regularly, never losing his enthusiasm. "But," he said sadly, "there is something I have to tell you."

Happy did not live to reach twenty-one. He died of a respiratory illness. His particular form of retardation carried genetic risks, untreatable at that time.

The pro told me that Happy was not only mourned by his father; his absence left a void in the lives of Mrs. Wentworth and others at the club.

The pro added that although Mrs. Wentworth continued to play golf, she often remarked that there would never be another Happy.

Though it was a long time ago, I'll always remember Happy and his lady. I think about how he put his heart and soul into that job. Perhaps Mrs. Wentworth was just being kind. Or maybe she saw in him that part of the human spirit that cannot help but soar, when given the chance.

David Field

The Benefits of Being King

King Hassan II of Morocco loved the game of golf and had his own private course built. The 9-hole course had forty-three bunkers, and the king could never seem to avoid landing in most of them. He called in golf pros who were experts at sand play to help him improve his game. After this failed, he did what any king would do. He ordered the course changed and all forty-three bunkers filled in with sod, proving once again, it's good to be the king.

Rich Mintzer and Peter Grossman

A Humble Beginning

I played in my first golf tournament—the Minneapolis Ladies Championship—in 1933. I was fifteen and had qualified for the tenth and very last flight with a score of 122, which for me at the time wasn't too bad, my usual score being about 140. My opponent in the first round of the tournament was an older woman who had qualified with a score of 121, so obviously the course record was in no danger of being equaled or surpassed by either one of us. Even so, my opponent beat me like the proverbial drum; I lost every hole and lost the match 10-and-8.

When I got home my father asked how I'd made out, and I said, "Not very good. I got beat 10-and-8.

"Oh," he said, "you played thirty-six holes."

"No," I had to admit, "just eighteen."

"You really weren't very good, then, were you?" he said. "Did you do anything right?"

"Yes," I replied, "I paid the caddie."

That defeat, humiliating at the time, made me determined to work—and work hard—on my game, the result being that the very next year I qualified in the championship flight and won the tournament.

Patty Berg

7

THE NINETEENTH
HOLE

*After all, as every golfer in every land will
attest after a good round, it may well be
the best game ever invented.*

Putter Devotion

When I was working for General Electric in Ithaca, New York in the early 1950s, I began to notice an interesting phenomenon on Mondays and Fridays during fair weather. Several of my fellow engineers seemed to be in high spirits those days. When I listened in on their conversations, I figured out why. Fridays they were planning their weekend golf outings; Mondays they were ribbing one another about what went on in them. It all seemed such a good time that I asked if I could join in.

I was forty-two years old and had never so much as picked up a golf club. "How hard can it be?" I asked myself. That Saturday, after borrowing some clubs and meeting up with my friends, I found out: harder than I could ever have imagined.

On the first tee, I watched my friends and took a few practice swings, imitating them as closely as I could. It felt pretty good. Then it was my turn. I teed up a ball, waggled the driver as my friends had and took a good cut. Whoosh! A clean miss. Then another. "Take it easy," my companions said. "Just keep your eye on the ball and swing evenly."

I did, and caught a huge clod of dirt, but not the ball. Soon dirt and grass were flying everywhere, but my ball just sat.

I was still swinging away when my friends gave up and told me to catch up to them on the second tee. Grimly, I hacked my way to the first green, only to discover that putting was even more frustrating. As an engineer I was confident that I could figure the slope of the green and anticipate the correct trajectory for my ball. Not so. I couldn't get my putter to send the ball where I wanted it to go. *There's no reason putting should be this hard,* I thought.

My score for the round would have been a good one if I'd been bowling. I was frustrated, but I liked spending Saturdays outdoors. Being with the fellows was fun too, so I kept practicing. I was determined to find out why a seemingly simple game was so difficult.

After playing several times more, I felt confident I could make some improvements in the clubs, and I shared my ideas with my wife, Louise.

"It seems to me that if a fellow can putt well he can certainly improve his game," I said. "And I've got some ideas about this putter. . . ."

"I was wondering when you would get around to the nuts and bolts of it!" she said with a laugh.

"Well," I said, showing her my borrowed club, "it's no wonder I have a hard time putting, the way this thing is made."

She nodded and smiled knowingly. "No doubt you'll have it fixed up to your liking soon."

She was right about that. In time I bought my own clubs and began working on the improvements I had in mind. I loved working with my hands, fixing things. It's something I had discovered back in my dad's cobbler shop, where he taught me the basics of shoemaking. Before I was out of grammar school I was helping him resole shoes. It was a good place for a curious and handy kid to get his start.

Later, I started college with high hopes of becoming an

engineer, but the Depression put an end to that after only one year. So I ran one of my father's two shoe-repair shops. Soon after, I met Louise, just out of high school, at church, and I asked her father's permission to marry her. He said no. Louise and I were disappointed, but I told her I was sure our marriage was meant to be and God would direct our path to it if we could be patient and trust him. When her father saw how determined we were to marry, he accepted it.

I resumed my engineering studies, but soon World War II intervened. I went to work in the defense industry, designing radar and missile systems, then moved to GE, where I worked on improving existing products and developed a new portable television set with an attachable rabbit ears antenna.

It was all this engineering experience that I put to work fashioning a new putter. I made myself a simple blade putter by shaping a block of aluminum and inserting weights in the heel and toe. The effect was to keep the putter from twisting in my hands. Finally the putting motion began to feel right to me.

I started haunting the practice green at our local golf club, and my handicap began going down. Even some of the pros were asking me to play with them.

One afternoon a club pro stopped me as I was coming off the practice green. "You really putt well," he said.

I laughed. "Thanks, but you should have seen me before I made this."

"You made the putter?" he asked. "Well you should make more and sell them, because it sure does work."

That afternoon I determined to make my putter even better. I took my design to a nearby toolmaker, who soon returned to me a putter head. I took it home and inserted a shaft, then struck a ball. *Ping!* So that's what I called my putters, PINGs, and I began trying to sell one at local golf shops. That's exactly what I did. I sold one—in six months of trying.

I started traveling to golf tournaments and asking pros to try my club and give me their opinions. I took their suggestions back to my garage workshop and made improvements. My youngest son, John, then in junior high, helped me with a jerry-rigged drill press to bore out the club heads; then I heated the heads on the kitchen stove to insert the shafts.

That may sound funny, but back in the beginning I had to make the best use of the equipment I had. Besides, some people say I've always had a mad scientist side. Like the time I was working on a more aerodynamic wood club head, only to be stymied by how to test my different models. Riding along in a car one day, I got an idea. I persuaded my son Allan to take me to a deserted secondary highway in our 1959 Citroen. When there were no cars in sight I told him to step on it, then I held each of my dirvers out the window at different angles to test their wind resistance. We had a good laugh over that, but the test worked and I got the answer I was looking for.

Still, none of my improvements made my PING putters any better looking. One pro told me, "That thing looks like a hot dog on a stick." I didn't care much about its appearance, just its performance.

I was having so much fun with my fledgling enterprise that I wanted more than anything to devote full-time to it. But the advice of the first pro-shop owner to stock my club haunted me. "These putters of yours are great, but whatever you do, don't give up your job. This is a fickle business." Even so, sales began to pick up when a few professionals started using the PING putter on tour. Then a well-known professional, Julius Boros, used one in winning the 1967 Phoenix Open.

But by then Louise and I were mulling over a big decision.

The previous fall my boss had told me that General Electric wanted to transfer me to a plant in Oklahoma City. I was torn. My job was solid and safe, and more than anything, I wanted my family to be secure. Yet we had invested a lot of time and money in my putter business, and my latest one was selling so fast we couldn't keep up with the orders.

"What do you think?" I asked Louise one morning at breakfast.

"I think back to that confident young man who courted me," she said. "Remember what you told me? You said, 'God will direct our path. He will lead us where he wants us to go.' Besides," she said, her brown eyes twinkling, "I'm keeping the books. I know we can make it."

So in early 1967 I retired from GE, and we began manufacturing clubs full-time in a small building we had bought in northwest Phoenix. More and more golf professionals were winning with PING putters, so I turned my attention to building a better iron, then to woods and other golf products. Karsten Manufacturing Corporation, as we've called it since 1967, became a storybook success.

It's hard to believe a golf outing more than forty years ago, when I couldn't sink a putt no matter how hard I tried, has resulted in a company that ships clubs to seventy countries worldwide and employs fifteen hundred people. Yet in a way I'm not surprised. As Louise and I learned so long ago, if you trust completely in God's goodness and follow where he leads, things have a way of turning out nicely.

Now I'm proud to say that our son John is president of our company. These days I'm taking it a little easier. But who knows, one day I might even figure a way to make that putter of ours a little prettier. Meantime, even I can sink a putt with it.

Karsten Solheim
As told to Gina Bridgeman

"Someone stole your putter?
Well, that solves one of your problems."

Reprinted by permission of David W. Harbaugh. Originally appeared in Golf Digest.

Maybe I Need a Crystal Ball

Until I started playing golf, I thought that wine tasting had to be the most confusing thing I'd ever done. People with names like Higgins rambling on about residual sugar and tannin, describing each quarter-ounce sample in terms like "full-bodied, yet unpretentious." And I could never remember whether I was supposed to age it, chill it or drink it with fresh fish during a full moon. Just when I thought I was a genius for knowing the difference between a cabernet and cabaret, I went to the pro shop for golf balls.

"What kind?" the pro asked.

"I dunno, white, I guess."

He rubbed his hands together as he scanned the tri-level ball display. "Do you want a two-piece ball?"

I though this was a joke, of course. "No," I said. "I like to start off with them whole. They'll break when I wallop them with my driver."

"Oh," he said without as much as a smile. "A big hitter. Then you want distance."

He handed me a shiny box with gold lettering. The price tag on the end was more than I'd paid for dinner for my wife and I the previous evening.

"These have computer-generated dimple patterns and use a complex two-piece injection molding system. They offer blistering distance."

"Perfect," I said. "Course I'll probably overshoot the green now on any hole less than four hundred yards."

He still didn't laugh. He just removed the box of balls from my hand and said, "Aahhh . . . stopping power."

He slid another brightly colored box across the counter, looked me in the eye and said, "Lithium Surlyn."

I offered my hand. "Ernie Witham," I said.

"No," he said. "The cover. It's made of Lithium Surlyn. You know what that means."

"It's radioactive?"

"It's soft. And it's been reformulated for more feel. Plus the aerodynamics have been modified for lower trajectory. . . . Did you want lower trajectory?"

"Well, sure. I guess. If that means it'll go straighter."

"Oh, oh. Accuracy problem, huh? Slice? Hook?"

"Yes. Yes."

He walked down to the end of the ball display and came back with yet another package.

"These offer less sidespin. Plus they're 2 percent larger than a regular ball."

"Wow. Two percent. Guess I'll need a bigger bag." I looked at my watch. "Oh, oh. Tee-time."

He apparently didn't hear me. He grabbed more boxes from the shelf. "How about a balata ball? This one spins at more than eleven thousand RPMs and maintains consistent compressions. This other balata carries 266 yards and is an evolutionary achievement in balata ball performance."

"I—aahhh—"

"Don't want a balata? This brand precisely blends five different dimple depths for raw length and pinpoint control. Or one designed for swing speeds in excess of ninety-five miles per hour."

"I—aahhh—"

"And here we have one that rockets off the club face, with an earlier peak and shallow descent. . . . This one penetrates the wind. . . . This one rolls longer. . . . This one has Trilyn. . . . This one has Zylin. . . . This one . . ."

"I—aahhh . . . I think I'll just take a few of these." I picked two yellow balls and one orange one from the used ball jar and threw a five-dollar bill on the counter. I felt bad, but my foursome had already finished the first hole.

He sighed, took a deep breath and started putting all the bright shiny boxes away. Then the little bell above the door jingled.

"I need some golf balls," the young woman said. "But I'm not sure what kind. Do you have any suggestions?"

"Do you want a two-piece ball?" I heard him ask, as I ran for the second tee.

Ernie Witham

Riders

Preparing to tee off at our municipal golf course, I over-heard two women discussing their games. "I had eight riders!" one woman exclaimed happily.

"That's wonderful!" her friend said.

Never having heard of a "rider," I interrupted to ask what it was. The women looked at me in surprise.

"It's when you hit the ball a long distance," one finally said. "Instead of walking that far for your next shot, you ride in the golf cart."

Arthur Berk

The Man Whose Secret Was a Secret

He was born in a small cow town that didn't have a golf course.

His parents didn't play golf and discouraged him from playing.

He was so small the other kids made fun of him, and the only club he had was left-handed even though he played right-handed.

At age nine, his father killed himself with a .38 revolver.

He never finished high school and never won a single amateur tournament.

He turned pro at seventeen and joined the tour, but ran out of money and had to return home a failure.

At twenty-three, he played in his first U.S. Open and missed the cut.

At twenty-six, he was down to his last $8 when a thief stole all four tires off his car and left him stranded on the road.

Through his first four U.S. Open attempts, his best was a tie for 62nd.

Through almost nine years as a pro, he didn't win a single tournament.

At thirty, when most golfers are in their prime, he was drafted into the service.

At thirty-six, he fractured his pelvis and broke his collarbone in a car accident and the doctors told him he'd never play golf again.

He never became a television commentator or played the senior tour or wore a logo on his hat. He never had a teacher, a manager or a sports psychologist. And his total career earnings amounted to less than $210,000.

Despite all these failures, by the time he retired, Ben Hogan had won sixty-four tournaments and established a reputation for pure ball striking unapproached by anyone before or since.

He wrote a series of articles for *Life* magazine in 1954 that purported to explain "The Secret." Ever since, there have been rumors that Hogan had held back a key element of The Secret, which he allegedly intimated to various friends and acquaintances over the years. Several professionals have claimed to know it, but they say Hogan put them under a seal of silence. A visitor was once pulled into a kitchen at Shady Oaks Country Club in Fort Worth by Hogan, who started to whisper that the secret was in the "weight transfer" until a busboy came by with a tray of dirty dishes and the moment was gone.

Shortly before his death in 1997, the former president of the Hogan Company arranged for this writer to meet with Hogan himself, because himself said he was finally ready to reveal The Real Secret. But within hours of the appointed meeting Hogan abruptly canceled.

Tom Kite, who wore Hogan's name on his visor, says he doesn't think Hogan ever held back any secret, or at least he had never revealed any secret to Tom.

"He had nothing to gain," said Kite. "He's not trying to beat anybody now."

Kite thought that Hogan's secret was simply that he

never stopped learning and improving.

"Mr. Hogan felt a constant desire to gain information, knowing that whatever he found would be improved upon by the players who came after him, who are constantly finding a better way to do it," said Kite. "He was always willing to admit that today's golfers are better than they were twenty years ago.

"His whole life was devoted to learning about golf. While winning tournaments is what everybody tries to do, it was the learning that he sought. He believed the journey was better than getting there."

The lesson of Hogan's success is a rare but familiar one in sports. Duffy Daugherty, the old Michigan State football coach may have put it best. In trying to explain what it took to be successful, Daugherty said you needed only three bones: A wish bone, to dream on; a back bone, for strength and courage to get through the tough times; and a funny bone, to laugh at silly things that happen along the way.

No one ever doubted Hogan's ability to dream, and certainly no one ever questioned his strength and courage.

As for a sense of humor, that was always his secret.

Jerry Tarde

Brush, Brush

I like golf because you can be really terrible at it and still not look much dorkier than anybody else.

Dave Barry

Seven years ago, at the age of forty-three, I was a novice golfer in a vendor-sponsored best-ball tournament. A friend had signed me up a month earlier, and I had spent that month getting lessons from a local pro. The vendor had brought in Johnny Miller as their celebrity photo-op for the attendees, and as I approached the par-3 where Mr. Miller and his entourage lounged, I was more than a little nervous. I had played just three holes of "real" golf that day prior to coming to this tee and hadn't been entirely impressive (I think only one shot of mine had been used at that point).

I stood next to Johnny Miller and had the photo taken, then he asked me how my game was going. "Not bad for a beginner," I answered, and he motioned with his arm for me to take the tee. The tee box was elevated and the postage-stamp green below the hill of Utah sagebrush looked ten miles away. I dragged out a 4-iron and started toward the box.

"Hold it," Johnny said. He stepped up next to me and *sotto-voce* said, "Try an 8-iron." I schlepped back to my cart and retrieved the 8-iron. I spent roughly forty-five queasy seconds over the ball then, finally rushing at the swing, topping a one-hopper three feet into the sagebrush below.

I moved quickly away, hoping to get out of sight of the small gallery as quickly as possible. Johnny Miller had hopped down from his perch, and taking my club from my hand said to the group, "Now here's an example of what I was saying," and he proceeded to discuss fundamentals of the swing. As he finished he said, "Now remember, brush, brush, just brush the grass." He hit my 8-iron to within five feet of the hole.

He handed me my club and said, "Try another one. I think you can beat me."

I was shaking so badly I couldn't tee up the ball for an eternity. Finally, it stayed put. I stepped back to survey a green I'd never forget in a million years and Johnny stepped up and said, "Forget everything, just brush, brush." He turned and walked away.

I felt a calmness I'd never known descend over me. I was in a sort of weird watery realm where sounds were altered and light had a quality akin to sunlight filtered through seaweed. I could hear the breeze but nothing else. When I pulled the club head away from my address, I felt a strange new strength coursing through my entire body, yet I was so fluid, so relaxed, I could have wrapped myself into a golf bag.

The club head descended and "brush, brush" perfectly swept the ball away from the tee. As the ball began to rise, I realized that in my haste I had teed it up behind the silver iron ball denoting the tee-box boundary. No one had said a word.

My shot struck the iron ball—*klongggg*—and rebounded into the cart carrying Johnny Miller and the tournament organizer, who both managed to dive clear. By the time they'd been helped to their feet and dusted off, I was far below, disappearing on to the next hole.

Since that day, I've introduced a number of people I like and admire to the sport of golf. I never teach, only suggest that they begin with lessons from a pro. Well, occasionally I will share the concept of "brush, brush," then I'll duck and watch what happens next.

Steve Minnick

Zen and the Art of Getting
Over the Water Hazard

*Golf is a spiritual game. It's like Zen. You have
to let your mind take over.*

Amy Alcott

I have a brother-in-law who could have made it on the
Tour if fate and fortune had nudged him in that direction.
Instead, he married my sister and became a weekend
golfer, playing Saturdays and Sundays at a club called
Paradise in Fayetteville, Arkansas.

Heaven Paradise is not. It's a modest course designed
by someone whose imagination was not taxed. Unpos-
sessed of an oak-paneled Men's Grill to help brace the
athlete both at the turn and at the end of the 18-hole campaign, members are allowed to sign for a hot dog and a
beer at the snack bar. Nevertheless, Raul is a man who
wakes each morning convinced it's the best of all possible
days in the best of all possible places on Earth; and if work
lets out early enough he might get to play three holes in
Paradise before dark.

He's a cheery optimist. One of those people whose eyes

twinkle all the time except when closed for sleep; and who knows, maybe even then. Raul tells jokes. Jokes he makes up, and most of them are pretty funny. He likes to sing, but not as a soloist. Instead, he encourages all family members to sing along, apparently deriving great pleasure from this musical communion.

Something happened a couple of years ago that took the light out of Raul's eyes. The jokes flew out the window and the music stopped. He was at a crisis point. My sister couldn't figure it, couldn't drag out of him what was wrong. The moping around went on for a couple of weeks. If the attitude hadn't been so contrary to his nature, hadn't been 180 degrees away from the Raul we knew and loved, the condition might have lingered indefinitely. We decided to confront him as a family: to find out what was wrong, then immediately offer him our individual and communal support.

Surrounded, he felt compelled to answer, "I'm off my game," he said. It took some probing, but we learned more. "I've gotten in the habit of throwing my clubs in the water hazard." Apparently it was true, because my sister went in disguise and undercover to observe for herself the murderous drownings of golf clubs. "He behaved like a poor sport," she said, near tears.

Playing, as he always did, in a foursome, the threesome who stood watching her husband's out-of-control fit of temper did not come forward to offer use of their woods, irons or putters. Instead, each of the three took to riding in their carts with golf bags set between their knees. It was an ugly sight. And sad, said my sister.

Later that same day, Raul admitted he'd become addicted to throwing clubs in the water. He no longer even needed to be angry. He just threw them willy-nilly. It was as if he'd lost the power to govern not only his game but his reason.

He was a broken man. A broken man with a total of two clubs left in his bag.

It happens that we count among our family members a few persons of mystic leanings who have leaned so far over into spiritual revelation that they view the world reposed on their sides, propped up by elbows and revealed truth. One of these is a practitioner of Zen. Smiling benignly, which I'm given to understand is one of the requisites of the discipline, our Zen cousin gently took Raul aside and spoke with him for an hour and a half. At the end of the consultation, Raul returned into the warmth of the family circle, and we were amazed to see upon his face a smile of balanced alignment and peace.

Of course she had to crawl on her stomach into the rough to keep herself from view, but my sister did go out the following day to observe Raul's behavior on the golf course. At the first water hazard, she held her breath.

Even from a distance, she sensed a calmness in her husband. She saw him turn his head and say something to his golfing buddies. She saw the threesome laugh. Without apprehension, they laughed. They threw back their heads and laughed, prompting a party of four who were putting on the opposite green to chorus "Shhhhh!"

My sister then exhaled and sat up in the rough. Raul had obviously said something funny. Was he cured of the golf depression that had lapped over into real life, sinking his sunny disposition? Hope rode high.

Then she gasped again, for her husband had entered the lake. Dressed in golf shoes, Bermuda shorts, regulation golf shirt and souvenir cap that proved he'd once played St. Andrews, Raul strode into the snake-infested water. As this was northwest Arkansas and the season summer, snakes were not only proliferate but bold, lying in tangles upon the shore, wriggling into the pond at will.

Suddenly Raul dove beneath the water's surface and

disappeared. My sister ran screaming from the rough onto the fairway. Kicking coiled vipers aside, she stood wringing her hands at lake's edge. Up he popped. Arising triumphant from the baptismal waters, Raul held aloft his 9-iron.

Whenever she tells this story, my sister dramatizes the moment. "It was like Arthur emerging with Excalibur," she says.

We've never been privy to the exact words our Zen cousin said to Raul. One of the more prosaic among us speculates our mystical cousin merely suggested Raul get a grip, get in there and retrieve his clubs. Whatever happened to turn the tide, to this day his clubs remain sacrosanct, polished, hooded, safe and bagged.

Micki McClelland

Frank and Ernest

© 1997 Thaves.Newspaper distribution by NEA, Inc.

Reprinted by permission of Newspaper Enterprise Association, Inc.

More Help Than a Guy Needs

The dawn of my golfing debauchery was my last birthday, when my wife gave me a metal driver with a bright golden head the size of a cantaloupe. "Will turn your 200-yard drives into 250," said an advertisement that came in the box. "Whiplike shaft action." And, of course, that old saw "Greater sweet spot."

I tested the club with my two golfing buddies that very day. For six holes the results were inconclusive. Two of my drives failed to get airborne, two more sliced violently—"banana balls," my friends called them—and two of the holes were par-3s. But on the seventh hole I caught one just right, and my ball soared majestically in the air, landing dangerously close to a creek I had previously reached only in two. I was ecstatic; my friends were awed. While I can't say the new club lowered my score dramatically, it did create some magical moments: I reached a par-5 in two. I nearly drove the green on a short par-4. My friends started to call me Tiger, and I began to win our matches more often than before.

Step two in my moral downslide took place after the arrival of a mail-order catalog advertising a variety of items such as Swiss Army knives, CD players and pocket flashlights.

Thumbing through the pages I came upon a picture of a sleeve of golf balls called the Desperado. The accompanying text called the Desperado a "bandit ball," which didn't conform to USGA specifications and guaranteed that it would travel ten to fifteen yards farther than the ball I was using. Wow! The illegality of the ball bothered me not a whit. My friends and I are very rules lenient. We play lift, clean and place even if it hasn't rained in a month. Should a ball come to rest beneath a bush or even in the pines, we allow a drop of a full club length. Under conditions that tolerant, why should any of us care what name is printed on the cover of a golf ball? I couldn't wait to marry my golden-headed driver to a Desperado.

But there was more. On the very next page of the catalog was an ad for a bright orange plastic tee shaped like a goblet split down the middle, top to bottom. Hooks and slices, the ad copy pointed out, occur when the club face creates spin on the ball, but if a golfer used this tee, the driver would be hitting plastic, not the ball, eliminating spin. No hooks, no slices—hence, more distance. Each tee, the copy said, would last for several rounds.

I immediately ordered a dozen balls and a dozen tees. I began driving the ball even farther—smack into that creek one day—and thanks to my plastic tee, I rarely sliced. My scores, generally in the high 80s on our rinky-dink course, were several strokes lower, and I was beating my friends regularly.

By this time I was like a drunken sailor. I bought an Alien wedge guaranteed to get me out of any bunker. Greg Norman's Secret, a plastic brace with a Velcro strap to keep the wrist at the proper angle through the swing—mine! And, of course, I had to get the SmartGrip beeper with electronic sensors that signaled when I swung improperly, which was most of the time.

I'm not sure exactly when I realized that although my scores were lower, I wasn't having as much fun as I used to. My friends weren't wee Scots—as in "Play it as it lies, laddie"—nor were they using hickory shafts, but neither were they walking golf advertisements as I had become. I may have won three of four of our skins games, but was it me or my illegal ball, the plastic tee or the Alien? I had once taken great pride in my ability to play out of a bunker; now the Alien wedge did it for me. As my friends and I drove home, it seemed there were more silences among us, less camaraderie.

So one day I junked every one of the gadgets, saving only the golden driver as any considerate husband would. I'm back to slicing, and I don't necessarily out-drive my friends now, but our skins games are competitive again. When I hit a good shot, it's all mine, and I no longer leave the field of battle feeling guilty.

If anyone wants to buy an Alien wedge, hardly used, see me.

Walter Bingham

"You say on Thursday afternoon precisely at 3 o'clock
the defendant was with you on the seventeenth tee
hitting his usual 325-yard drive. Tell me, and remember,
you're under oath, how does he do that?"

The Clown Prince of Golf

A *man without a sense of humor is like a wagon without springs—he is jolted disagreeably by every little pebble in the road.*

Henry Ward Beecher

Pro-ams take two basic forms: the normal week-to-week events populated by local businessmen who fork over the fee to play with Greg Norman or Nick Price—or players far less famous but, they often find, just as much fun. Then there are the celebrity pro-ams that mix business people with actors, politicians and athletes. These tend to be major yuck-fests, personified in recent years by Bill Murray, who has become the dominant figure at Pebble Beach.

Several years ago, Jeff Sluman found himself in Murray's foursome. A big Murray fan, Sluman was looking forward to the experience. It was a memorable week for Sluman but, he admits, he had some trying moments. "On the first day I three-putted three holes on the front nine," he says. "I just kept missing short ones. We get to the eleventh hole (at Poppy Hills), and I hit my tee shot about forty feet above the pin. As we're walking off the tee, I hear Bill say to [partner] Scott Simpson, 'Now we're really going to find out about him.' I knew I was in trouble."

Sluman left his first putt about six feet short and could feel the yips coming on as he lined up his second putt. He got over the ball and was about to draw the putter back when he heard Murray say, "Ladies and gentlemen, I need some love for this man. Right now, can you all say 'love!'"

Sluman stepped back while the crowd, coached by Murray, yelled, "We love you, Jeff!" several times. Sluman put his hand over his heart to show how touched he was, then began lining the putt up again. Sure enough, just as he was about to start his stroke, he heard Murray's voice again. "This man needs more love. More! Can I hear you, now!"

By now, Simpson had all but dissolved into a puddle of laughter near the edge of the green. This time, as all the love washed down on him, Sluman pretended to cry. The third time, much to his surprise, Murray let him putt. And, even more to Sluman's surprise, the putt went in. "I think I got a bigger roar than on the eighteenth hole when I won the PGA [Championship]," he says.

He deserved it.

John Feinstein

Golf Carts Do Not
Have Four-Wheel Drive

The revelation that golf carts do not have four-wheel drive came to me one morning as I tried to find my ball in the mud, which I found out later was actually not part of the golf course at all but rather the site of a pending condo project, half a block away. I must have missed the out-of-bounds marker when I was crossing the freeway. It was just one more lesson in the complex world of golf.

I remember the first time I played. My twosome was paired up with another twosome. After my tee-off on the first hole went somewhat awry, landing on the clubhouse roof, one of the other players asked if I had a handicap. I thought his joke in poor taste and threatened him with my 9-iron. Now, of course, I realize that having a handicap is a good thing, even if it is 52.

Learning the rules and language of golf is crucial. It separates the obvious beginner from someone just having another bad day. Therefore, I have from experience compiled a few lessons that may help other novices.

If the instructor tells you to address the ball, do not take out a pen and write "to green" on the ball.

Try not to stand on asphalt in the summer while wearing golf shoes, unless you are with a very strong friend.

The easiest way to find a lost golf ball is to ask the guy limping in the next fairway.

Never insist that your spouse golf. It can lead to only two results. One, she/he plays really badly, complains for four hours and ruins your whole day. Or, he/she plays really well, offers four hours of suggestions on how you might do better and ruins your whole day.

A double bogey is not a strong drink from the movie *Casablanca*. It means two over par. And not a bad score at all. If they have a name for it it's a good score. There is no name for a fifteen.

A chip is not something left behind by a foraging cow. That's a flap. A chip is a carefully choreographed half-swing that often goes further than your original drive.

A divot is a lump of grass that flies up from where the golf ball used to be. A damnit is a lump of grass that flies up in your face as you hit two feet behind the ball.

A slice is a ball that curves to the right. A bad slice is a ball that lands behind you.

A tough lie has double meanings. It's when you have to come up with an excuse—for the umpteenth time—as to why it took six hours to play nine holes and why your breath smells like nacho chips and beer. It also refers to a difficult spot to have to hit your ball from. For instance, the base of a tree, the crook of a tree or the upper branches of a tree.

Heavy rough is the area along the edge of the fairway just before your ball is legally out of bounds. A good rule of thumb—if the guy beside you is barbecuing, you're probably out of bounds.

And finally, Club Rules imply that you are not penalized by foreign objects on the fairway. Therefore, if you knock out a tourist with your drive, you are allowed to move your ball one club's length from the body.

Now that you understand some of the basics, you should be able to better appreciate the game. And, you can focus on some of the more intriguing idiosyncrasies of golf, like if it's completely made out of metal, why do they call it a 3-wood?

Ernie Witham

Fifty Ways to Enjoy Golf More

1. Get there early enough to feel relaxed.
2. Leave all of your concerns in the car.
3. Take your watch off.
4. Turn off your cell phone.
5. Decide to let nothing bother you for eighteen holes.
6. Play like it's your first time.
7. Play like it's your last time.
8. Hit your favorite club off of the first tee.
9. Smile, or better yet, laugh, after a bad shot.
10. Play with someone who makes you laugh.
11. Compliment your partner every time he or she hits a great shot.
12. Repair someone else's ball mark on every green.
13. Let the group you're frantically trying to stay ahead of play through.
14. Become your partner's biggest fan.
15. Walk for a change. Or ride for a change.
16. Play it as it lies.
17. Golf with your spouse, and look only for his or her best qualities.
18. Give advice only when asked, especially with your spouse.

19. Take your child golfing on a weekday.
20. Really see and appreciate the beauty all around you.
21. Keep reloading until you clear that water hazard.
22. Slice one on purpose.
23. Pretend the objective is to hit in the sand on every hole—and see if you can for all eighteen.
24. Quit taking your game—and yourself—so seriously.
25. Remember: it may be business golf, but it's not work.
26. Recognize that if golf stresses you out, maybe you should just go back to the office.
27. Read a great golf book.
28. Keep a journal of your accomplishments and special moments on the course.
29. Caddie a round for a friend.
30. Play the course of your dreams with a favorite companion.
31. Play a round with your dog.
32. Play more often.
33. Lose attachment to the outcome stuck in your head.
34. Celebrate the balance between doing well and just being—in golf and in life.
35. Play in your bare feet.
36. Play an entire round as if you were an eight-year-old again.
37. Next time you sink a key putt, react as if you'd just won the U.S. Open.
38. Remember that in golf—as in life—you get what you focus on. Focus on the best parts.
39. Be respectful of other golfers.
40. Golf with strangers at every opportunity—you'll end up with more friends that way.
41. Aspire to be the best version of you on the course.
42. Play a round with the person who introduced you to the game as a tribute to them.

43. Do something to help make golf accessible for everyone.
44. Introduce a kid to the game.
45. Think of ten friends or relatives that could benefit from golf like you do, and then make it a goal to introduce them to the game.
46. Give that old set of clubs to a new golfer.
47. Play a record-breaking round entirely in your mind.
48. Take a moment to really appreciate the sunrise or sunset that you normally take for granted.
49. Think what a great world it would be if everyone golfed.
50. Thank God that this wonderful game exists, and that you have the ability to play it!

Mark and Chrissy Donnelly

De Profundis, Homo
(About Some Deep Stuff, Man)

It is not a matter of life and death. It is not that important. But it is a reflection of life, and so the game is an enigma wrapped in a mystery impaled on a conundrum.

Peter Alliss

Philosophers down through the ages have produced the concepts that have shaped all of our present governments, our societies and our very way of life. So, isn't it curious that the Yellow Pages list hundreds of golf instructors, golf stores and golf courses, but not one single philosopher? Absolutely none, zero, zilch, nada ... a totality of nothingness manifested in a positive universal absence, as a philosopher might say. I believe there would be more call for philosophers today if only more were known about their past statements and questions on the metaphysics of golf. I researched the subject (without a government grant) and unearthed a veritable strip mine of wisdom. Most basic perhaps was philosopher Ronnie Da Cart's famous pronouncement, "I golf, therefore I am."

Da Cart was trying to establish a starting point, a foundation of irrefutable truth upon which he could build a philosophy to cover all existence. His starting premise collapsed when it was challenged by the Mexican philosopher and publinks player Manuel Cant. Cant said that if golf were the basic truth about existence, then poor golf would prove a poor existence. Cant knew that was wrong because he had caddied for many rich Gringos who played very poor golf but had a very nice existence.

During the months when one can't be out on the course personally struggling with the existential mysteries of golf, it is a good time to exercise the mind with some of the following classic golf/philosophy conundrums:

"If a tree falls over in the middle of a forest and no one is around, does it count as a free drop if it comes down on top of a ball?" Yes, but nobody will hear about it.

"When an irresistible force meets an immovable obstruction, do you get line-of-sight relief?" No, because Einstein proved that light bends; golf rules do not. And since light bends, the line of sight must curve around the obstruction.

"Is heredity or environment more responsible for the development of a slice?" A predisposition to slicing is in the genes, although it becomes most pronounced when there is an environment of trees, water or out of bounds in the direction of the slice.

"How many angels can dance on the head of a pin?" Angels don't dance on the pin; they just hover over the green and keep track of bad language. There are other winged creatures that waddle around on some greens and are the cause of some of the bad language. In this vein it was India's great naturalist/philosopher, Washadurtee Ultrabalata, who stated, "Animal rights should be extended only to animals who are toilet trained."

"What is the sound of one hand clapping?" My friend Al

Van Dine solved this Zen puzzle when he said the sound of one hand clapping is the sudden joyous outburst of silence that comes from your opponent when you miss a short putt. Al has also written at length about dimpleness. Writes Al, "Dimples have perplexed philosophers because they represent intervals of non-ball and yet are presumed to be part of the ball whose absence defines their existence." How true. In closing, the question all children ask, and the appropriate answer: "Why is the sky blue?" Because it can't play golf even on the nicest days. Go in peace.

Frank J. Haller

He'd Give You the Shirt
Off of His Back

Caddying has long been a popular way to make a living for immigrants to this country, particularly in the large urban areas along the East Coast.

Winged Foot Golf Club outside New York City was one club that benefited from a ready pool of men new to this country. They might not have known much about the game, but they were willing to work hard and enjoyed being outside instead of in a factory.

One day a new caddie was walking up a fairway on the West course. As he approached the green, his golfer asked for his sand wedge. The caddie seemed to ignore him, walking stoically ahead with his head down. The man asked again for his sand wedge, and again got no reaction. After the third request the caddie stopped, laid the bag down, and reached inside one of the pockets, pulling out a brown bag.

"All right," he said in his heavily accented English as he reached inside the bag and pulled out a sandwich wrapped in paper. "But only half. I've got to eat, too."

Don Wade

The Secret

*It is a thousand pities that neither Aristotle nor
Shakespeare was a golfer. There is no game that
strips the soul so naked.*

Horace Hutchinson

It was a glorious May day and the air was filled with the
fragrance of a thousand magnificent blossoms. I was overwhelmed by the sights and sounds of spring as I slowly
walked the path to the practice range.

I stood on the practice range to prepare for my usual
Saturday match, but of more importance to me was finding a remedy for a snarling slice that had recently infected
my game.

I began as usual, lofting a few gentle sand wedges to the
red flag. Gradually, I worked my way down to the 7-iron,
striking fairly even-tempered shots to another flag. Even
with my particular collection of neurosynaptic connec-
tions I was able to play a fairly decent game—that is, until
I was pressed to hit the ball more than 150 yards. Then
suddenly it was a question of how far left I should aim.

I hit several passable shots with the 7-iron before it

happened. Then as quickly as it came, it slipped out of my consciousness and drifted away. What was I just thinking? I began to reconstruct my last five minutes of conscious thought. It wasn't easy. But there was something, and suddenly I felt an exhilarating impulse traveling up my right forearm as I neatly crushed another shot. My, that felt good. What did I do?

A voice inside spoke to me softly, very faintly. My thoughts played back again and again and I heard a faint sound over and over. Supinaaaaation. Supinaaaaation. Supinaaaaation.

Huh? Then I realized what it was. It seemed so hard to believe, but echoing in my head was Ben Hogan's famous word. This was particularly annoying since I, for one, had given up on supination a long time ago. Here I was, plagued all my life with a shot pattern that moved right to right, and I certainly didn't need to know how to supinate my left wrist. What I really wanted was a way to square the blade.

I smashed another 7-iron and watched with amazement as the ball flew high and landed well beyond the white flag. I began to sense that my body was reacting differently to the club. Something had changed, but what?

From the pile of balls I pulled another toward me. Then I noticed what, for me, was an amazing revelation: I was standing there like a duck. My right foot was not square to the line, but instead was pointed away from the ball. Taking the club back a few times, I could feel a difference in my right hip—that I felt coiled and poised behind the ball. As I swung down into the ball I sensed a tremendous leverage to hit down and through. I felt as though I could hit the ball as hard as I wanted. Finally, there it was—my secret.

I hit several dozen more balls. I turned and looked behind me and two smiling faces, old-lined faces, set a steady gaze on me. "You've got something there, son," one man finally said. "Lightning in a bottle. Better enjoy it."

I did. But at the same time I was frightened—afraid to let the 7-iron out of my hands.

I needed to know if the magic would work with other clubs in the bag, so I drew out a 4-iron. As I rehearsed my swing, the club sweetly sweeping across the top of the turf, I also rehearsed my disappointment, anticipating the return of my errant ways. I realized my objective—to feel a complete follow-through, with the right hand really delivering the blow—so I decided to just let it rip. The ball flew well beyond any I'd ever struck with the club. I hit another, and another; and after twenty more I swear they all could have been covered with a picnic blanket.

I pulled out the 3-iron, then the 2-, and suddenly I was in uncharted territory—knocking balls to the fence at the back of the range. I finished the practice session by hitting 9-irons to within ten feet of the sign marked 135; I think I hit the sign five or six times.

I met Ted in the locker room a few minutes before our Saturday match, where I said I was going to try some new strategies on the course today. "You really should try something new," he said, his sardonic smile meeting my confident grin.

Ted played first on the opening hole and cut his drive to the right edge of the fairway. Reiterating my intent to try something different, I announced my selection of a 3-iron. Instead, I drew a 5-iron and laced a beautiful shot that landed a mere fifteen yards behind Ted's drive. He acknowledged my effort with a quiet "good shot."

I hit a wedge to within eight feet and Ted again remarked, "Good shot." He hit up and matched my two-putt par.

We were both about 235 yards from the front edge of the green at No. 2, a medium-length par-5. I drew a 2-iron from my bag, set up, aiming slightly left of the flag, and fired. The ball soared down the fairway, landed softly at the front of the green, and rolled up neatly about twelve feet away for eagle.

Ted said nothing. I missed the putt but tapped in for a birdie and went to the third tee 1-up. Ted's play from that point on became decidedly lackluster, so for the rest of the day I was chiefly pitted against the golf course.

But everything was distorted. I was hitting the ball so far, my biggest problem became choosing the right club. Finally I resolved to hit two or three clubs less than usual, and that seemed to do the trick as I came home with a sizzling 30. Together with the 33 I shot on the front, I was suddenly the holder of the course record, a shocking feat considering my previous best score was a dozen strokes higher.

I was beside myself. I didn't know what to think. I played several rounds that week and shot in the 60s each time. In my locker someone placed a white Hogan cap with a note that read, "Enjoy it while you've got it." That was puzzling, but not as much as my new golf game was.

About two weeks later I hit my first slice. Three weeks after that I was shooting in the mid-80s again. Ted began taunting me, calling me "the greatest golfer that never was." I was powerless to respond. As quickly as the magic had come, it was gone.

In September the letter arrived. It was a simple white envelope with a return address that read, "The Hogan Company, Fort Worth, Texas." As I opened it I was amazed to find a handwritten note from the man himself. "I want to congratulate you for your recent success in breaking my course record," Mr. Hogan wrote. "I will always remember the round I played there in 1953. My score of 64 stood for all these years as one of my finest achievements, and I know just how well you must have played to break it. Best wishes, and enjoy it while you've got it."

I was shattered. The man who knew what it was like to

possess "the secret" knew also of its mercurial flight. He knew that I would lose it. He knew it was only temporary. My wife is just taking up the game. I've toyed with teaching her for several years, but I never wanted to push it. I wasn't sure, but I thought her recent enthusiasm may have been out of a desire to empathize with my shattering devolution as a player. She invited me out to the practice range to see her progress. She said she'd really enjoyed hitting balls lately, and attributed her success to a videotape she used to learn the swing. I was intrigued and questioned her about it. As she hammered a middle iron she slyly said, "Oh, it was just something I recorded one day when you were hitting balls on the range."

J. G. Nursall

Enjoy the Round

*You live more fully once you realize that any
time spent being unhappy is wasteful.*

Ruth E. Renkl

My old man was the original Silver Lining Guy. As a
teenager I dubbed him, not entirely kindly, Opti the
Mystic because of his crazy optimism, his relentless good
cheer and his imperturbable knack for seeing any problem or crisis as "an opportunity for growth."

For thirty years my father had been a senior rep for one
of the world's largest industrial publishing firms. He'd
transformed a sleepy advertising backwater into a thriving multi-million-dollar territory. To Opti, hard work was
a form of play because work involved solving problems.
This life view fit the philosophy of his favorite game—
golf—like a glove.

He first put a club in my hand when I was about ten. I
threw a lot of tantrums in the upland hills of North
Carolina, and clubs too. I was in such a rush to be good that
he would urge me to "relax and enjoy the round. The game
ends far too soon." I didn't have a clue what he meant.

The real joy of play, he said, was in solving the unique riddle of each golf shot—an unfair break, a horrendous lie in the rough. To him golf was also a character builder. For that reason, he was a stickler for the rules: you fixed dents in the green; you putted in turn; you congratulated an opponent on a good shot. He believed these courtesies were as essential to the game as oxygen, but I suffocated under their constriction.

Eventually when I calmed down and grew up, golf became much more than a game between my old man and me. It acted as my personal entry hatch to my father's cosmos—a means of seeing who this funky, funny, odd-ball philosopher really was, and who I needed to become. The golf course became the place where we sorted things out. No topic was out of bounds: sex, women, God, career, money. We debated without rancor, found common ground, competed like crazy and took each other's pocket change.

We played the day Neil Armstrong walked on the moon. We played the day before I got married and the day after my son was born. We played through the rain, the wind and the heat. We usually played late in the day, following our shadows in the last of the light.

But now Dad was pushing eighty, and he faced the unpleasant after-effects of a radical colostomy and a prostatectomy. His knees were weak, his hearing was going and he had a deteriorating cataract. He never mentioned these problems. And if I did, he merely laughed off my concerns.

On a wet and cold October day we played at Pinehurst, North Carolina, at one of Dad's favorite courses. He topped balls and missed putts he could once have made with his eyes shut. At one point I was passing a steep bunker when I heard him sheepishly ask me for a hand up. I took his hand. It was trembling ever so slightly. My heart almost broke. On the drive home I said, "Let's take the trip we always talked about."

The trip was to St. Andrews, Scotland, the Mecca of golf. We'd both been there before—I as a golf writer, Dad as a sergeant in the Eighth Army Air Force during World War II—but we hadn't played there together.

Two weeks before we were to leave, he called. "I had some bleeding," he said. The cancer had come back, spreading throughout his pelvic region, his back and stomach. He had a month, two at most, he said.

"They can pump me full of poison and buy a few more weeks, but who the hell needs that?" He said he planned to let nature take its course. I told him I admired his courage. He told me to save my lung power for the golf course. "I'm planning to whip your tail at St. Andrews," he said. "See you at the airport." Opti the Mystic had spoken.

We decided to play several courses in England before heading to St. Andrews. The first round would be at Royal Lytham, near the English village of Freckleton. For thirteen months during World War II my father had served as an Army Air Force parachute inspector on the outskirts of the village. On his days off he played golf.

As we rolled into Freckleton, schoolchildren jostled along the sidewalks. "We had kids just like that hanging around the base," my father said. "I took photos of a lot of them. We had one PX wall covered with their pictures."

On the course that day, Dad showed a discernible lilt in his step. I could picture him swinging a club in his staff sergeant's uniform.

We sat down to rest on the grass at the tenth tee. "Our scores are awful," I said.

"No matter. This is so delightful. Look at those birds."

I glanced up at several white birds darting over the peaked red rooftops. The moment really was delightful, proving, as someone once said, that golf is mostly about whom you choose to play with.

During an exchange with some locals the next evening, a woman spoke of a recent D-Day reunion at the former base. "There was quite a memorial service because of the bomber," she said.

"What bomber?" I asked.

"Why, the bomber that crashed," she replied.

I glanced at Dad. "Do you know the bomber they're talking about?"

His complexion had turned pale. "Yes." His voice was scarcely more than a whisper. "Come with me."

We walked to a burying ground at the rear of a church in the center of the village. I followed him to a large polished granite cross. I read some of the names inscribed on the stone border surrounding the plot: Gillian and June Parkinson. George Preston. Michael Probert. Annie Harrington . . .

Thirty-eight names in all. A mass grave.

"How did these folks die?" I asked.

"They weren't folks," he replied. "They were children. Four- and five-year-olds. They went to school here at the church. One of our bombers crashed into the school." He shut his eyes, and I wondered if he was playing or reliving scenes I couldn't begin to imagine.

"It was about 10:30 in the morning," Dad said. "I'd just stretched out on my cot to steal some shuteye when I heard a big roar overhead followed by an explosion. I was one of the first to reach the school. God, what a sight. Burning fuel was running down the street. I remember pulling away pieces of the plane, bricks and mortar, and all these precious little kids inside, buried alive. . . ."

I saw tears gathering in my father's eyes. I slipped my arm around him, and we stood that way for several minutes.

He cleared his throat and said, "There was one girl in

particular. She was always laughing. I called her Lady Sunshine. She was one of those killed."

Good Lord, I thought.

"A week after the crash, I found a note on the base bulletin board from her parents. They wondered if anybody had taken a photograph of her. I took them all I had, and we sat in their front parlor and cried. I don't think I've ever experienced anything quite so sad."

We left the burying ground, slowly closing the iron gate behind us. "I'm surprised you never told me this story," I said. He paused and looked back at the church.

"The war ended for me right here," he said. "I promised myself I would never speak about it again."

The night before, he had told me that when he'd joined the Army he was a cocky guy who thought he had everything figured out: But then "something happened," and he realized the only thing life really promises us is pain. It's up to us to create the joy.

Opti the Mystic had been born in that bomber's wreckage. That night, my prayer was simple:

I hoped that my own young children would never know the pain my dad had known. But if they must, I hoped the pain would make them little Optis.

There are six splendid courses in St. Andrews, but it is the Old Course, the most famous in the world, that draws golf's pilgrims. Demand for tee times is so fierce that there's a daily drawing to determine who will play. I knew a caddie who could get us on the course, but when I told Dad about my planned subversion he seemed puzzled. "Why would you want to do that?"

"We didn't come all this way not to play the Old Course, did we?"

"Do you think it's fair to ignore the rules?"

"That's not the issue, Dad." I felt as if I were twelve

years old, trying to explain why I'd used a crib sheet on a spelling test.

"So why do you want to play it? You've played it plenty of times," he asked.

We both knew why it was so important to play it, but I didn't want to say it, and I was sure he didn't want to hear it: that our outing on the Old Course would probably be our final round of golf together. It would be a fitting way to finish, but a finish is a finish and that's what I feared most.

"If that's how you want it," I said. "We'll put all our hopes on the ballot."

"That's the only way I want it," he said, "and you would, too, if you'd think about it."

We didn't make the ballot on the first two days. "Let's give it another day," he said.

"And then what?"

"Well, if we don't have any luck, it may be time to move along."

"You mean go home," I said evenly.

"I think it's time. I've got some things to do."

I went for a walk and found myself standing by the fence behind the first tee at the Old Course. Darkness was perhaps an hour away. I watched two players tee off, hoist their bags and march off to battle. I stood there feeling sorry for myself. We'd come all this way for naught.

Just then a voice behind me remarked, "I'm told golf has been played here for almost five hundred years and that anyone is entitled to walk these public grounds." It was my father.

We walked slowly and talked about golf, about days past, about Mom. Soon we were standing on the seventeenth tee, the Road Hole, regarded by many as the toughest par four in the world. The course lay almost fully in the embrace of a blue October twilight.

"I wish we had our clubs," I said.

"Aw, who needs 'em?" Dad said. "Let's play anyway." He pulled out an imaginary golf club, pretended to tee up his ball and swung. "There," he said. "Right over the sheds. Just like fifty years ago."

I outdrove him, as usual, by at least a hundred yards. From the fairway, Dad used his imaginary 3-wood to lay up short of the infamous bunker. Then he announced he was using a sand wedge, and lofted his ball sweetly to the green. We were playing magnificently.

We walked to the eighteenth tee, struck fine drives into darkness, then moseyed down the fairway. For weeks I'd been so fearful of this moment. But strangely, I was almost unnaturally happy.

"Call me sentimental," my father said, "but I think it's been a hell of a journey."

"The hotel showers were much worse than expected," I replied.

"You're talking about the trip," he said. "I'm talking about the journey."

Dad died the following March. Some time after that I was troubled by a dream in which I'd forgotten the sound of my father's voice. I woke up in a fierce sweat, weeping.

Three months later, I was on the Old Course once again. As my partners and I approached the Road Hole bunker, I pulled a small blue velvet satchel out of my golf bag. The others, who had been warned what was coming, watched solemnly. "You guys look like the three Horsemen of the Apocalypse," I said. "Please show a little proper disrespect." I told them my old man had said golf is a game that made you smile. "So please—smile." As they smiled, I slowly scattered my father's cremated ashes into the bunker.

After the round, a boy, maybe eleven or twelve, passed me heading home with his golf bag on his back. "Did you shoot a good one?" I asked.

"Not so good, sir. Me driver's a wee bit off."

"That's okay." I said. "Enjoy it. The game ends too soon, you know."

"Right. Thanks." He walked on and I walked on—and then I stopped. I'd heard it—my father's voice.

I smiled. Opti was back.

James Dodson

More Chicken Soup?

Many of the stories and poems you have read in this book were submitted by readers like you who had read earlier *Chicken Soup for the Soul* books. We are planning to publish five or six *Chicken Soup for the Soul* books every year. We invite you to contribute a story to one of these future volumes.

Stories may be up to twelve hundred words and must uplift or inspire. You may submit an original piece or something you clip out of the local newspaper, a magazine, a church bulletin or a company newsletter. It could also be your favorite quotation you've put on your refrigerator door or a personal experience that has touched you deeply.

To obtain a copy of our submission guidelines and a listing of upcoming *Chicken Soup* books, please write, fax, or check one of our Web sites.

Chicken Soup for the Soul
P.O. Box 30880 • Santa Barbara, CA 93130
fax: 805-563-2945
Web site: *chickensoup.com*

Just send a copy of your stories and other pieces, indicating which edition they are for, to any of the above addresses.

We will be sure that both you and the author are credited for your submission.

For information about speaking engagements, other books, audiotapes, workshops and training programs, please contact any of the authors directly.

You can also visit the *Chicken Soup for the Soul* site on America Online at keyword: chickensoup.

Supporting Golfers Everywhere

In the spirit of helping golfers and those who desire to take up the game, a portion of the proceeds from *Chicken Soup for the Golfer's Soul* will go to the following charities.

CaP CURE, the Association for the Cure of Cancer of the Prostate, was founded by Michael Milken shortly after his diagnosis of prostate cancer. Dedicated to finding a cure by rapidly funding promising research projects, CaP CURE was established with a single mission: To offer solutions to men facing prostate cancer—quickly and with a minimum of red tape. CaP CURE's SENIOR PGA TOUR FOR THE CURE program is co-chaired by Arnold Palmer and Jim Colbert, both prostate cancer survivors.

CaP CURE
1250 Fourth Street, Suite 360
Santa Monica, CA 90401
Phone: 800-757-2873
Fax: 310-458-8074
Web site: *www.capcure.org*

The **First Tee**'s mission is to create affordable and accessible golf facilities, with an emphasis on serving kids who have not had access or exposure to the game. It is a program of the not-for-profit World Golf Foundation that is overseen by Augusta National Golf Club, the LPGA, PGA of America, PGA TOUR and the USGA, and supported by many other golf and civic organizations.

The First Tee
170 Highway A1A North
Ponte Vedra Beach, FL 32082
Phone: 904-940-4300
Fax: 904-280-9019
Web site: *www.thefirsttee.com*

The **Shivas Irons Society** is a non-profit organization dedicated to enhancing golf's beauty and virtues. Through their Shivas Irons Scholarship Fund they give deserving at-risk girls and boys an opportunity to travel and attend some of the finest golf camps in the country.

The Shivas Irons Society
P.O. Box 222339
Carmel, CA 93922
Phone: 831-626-4566
Fax: 831-626-6701
Web site: *www.shivas.org*

Who Is Jack Canfield?

Jack Canfield is one of America's leading experts in the development of human potential and personal effectiveness. He is both a dynamic, entertaining speaker and a highly sought-after trainer. Jack has a wonderful ability to inform and inspire audiences toward increased levels of self-esteem and peak performance.

He is the author and narrator of several bestselling audio- and videocassette programs, including *Self-Esteem and Peak Performance, How to Build High Self-Esteem, Self-Esteem in the Classroom* and *Chicken Soup for the Soul—Live.* He is regularly seen on television shows such as *Good Morning America, 20/20* and *NBC Nightly News.* Jack has coauthored numerous books, including the *Chicken Soup for the Soul* series, *Dare to Win* and *The Aladdin Factor* (all with Mark Victor Hansen), *100 Ways to Build Self-Concept in the Classroom* (with Harold C. Wells) and *Heart at Work* (with Jacqueline Miller).

Jack is a regularly featured speaker for professional associations, school districts, government agencies, churches, hospitals, sales organizations and corporations. His clients have included the American Dental Association, the American Management Association, AT&T, Campbell Soup, Clairol, Domino's Pizza, GE, Hartford Insurance, ITT, Johnson & Johnson, the Million Dollar Roundtable, NCR, New England Telephone, Re/Max, Scott Paper, TRW and Virgin Records. Jack is also on the faculty of Income Builders International, a school for entrepreneurs.

Jack conducts an annual eight-day Training of Trainers program in the areas of self-esteem and peak performance. It attracts educators, counselors, parenting trainers, corporate trainers, professional speakers, ministers and others interested in developing their speaking and seminar-leading skills.

For further information about Jack's books, tapes and training programs, or to schedule him for a presentation, please contact:

Self-Esteem Seminars
P.O. Box 30880 • Santa Barbara, CA 93130
phone: 805-563-2935 • fax: 805-563-2945
Web site: *http://www.chickensoup.com*

Who Is Mark Victor Hansen?

Mark Victor Hansen is a professional speaker who, in the last twenty years, has made over four thousand presentations to more than two million people in thirty-two countries. His presentations cover sales excellence and strategies; personal empowerment and development; and how to triple your income and double your time off.

Mark has spent a lifetime dedicated to his mission of making a profound and positive difference in people's lives. Throughout his career, he has inspired hundreds of thousands of people to create a more powerful and purposeful future for themselves while stimulating the sale of billions of dollars worth of goods and services.

Mark is a prolific writer and has authored *Future Diary, How to Achieve Total Prosperity* and *The Miracle of Tithing.* He is coauthor of the *Chicken Soup for the Soul* series, *Dare to Win* and *The Aladdin Factor* (all with Jack Canfield) and *The Master Motivator* (with Joe Batten).

Mark has also produced a complete library of personal empowerment audio- and videocassette programs that have enabled his listeners to recognize and use their innate abilities in their business and personal lives. His message has made him a popular television and radio personality, with appearances on ABC, NBC, CBS, HBO, PBS and CNN. He has also appeared on the cover of numerous magazines, including *Success, Entrepreneur* and *Changes.*

Mark is a big man with a heart and spirit to match—an inspiration to all who seek to better themselves.

For further information about Mark write:

MVH & Associates
P.O. Box 7665
Newport Beach, CA 92658
phone: 949-759-9304 or 800-433-2314
fax: 949-722-6912
Web site: *http://www.chickensoup.com*

Who Is Jeff Aubery?

Introduced to the golf industry at an early age, Jeff was mentored personally and professionally by Nat C. Rosasco, the founder of Northwestern/Pro-Select Golf, Co., the world's largest manufacturer of golf clubs. Now an entrepreneur in his own right, Jeff founded and owns Tornado Golf Co., an industry-leading OEM golf bag manufacturing company. Committed to golf as a lifetime passion, Jeff is an active sponsor of junior golf programs and charity golf tournaments all over the world. An avid golfer, Jeff makes time for a round whenever possible, and has enjoyed playing with some of the greatest names in the sport at many of the world's most famous courses.

Perhaps his most memorable golf experience, he says, came from the people he met and the enthusiasm he encountered when working on *Chicken Soup for the Golfer's Soul*. Married to Patty Aubery, coauthor of *Chicken Soup for the Christian Soul* and *Chicken Soup for the Surviving Soul*, Jeff is no stranger to the *Chicken Soup* phenomenon. The couple and their two sons make their home in Santa Barbara, California. A dynamic and enthusiastic speaker and golfer, Jeff is available for personal appearances and can be reached at:

Tornado Golf, Inc.
4350 Transport Street, Suite 103
Ventura, CA 93003
phone: 800-GOLF-BAG
e-mail: *www.golfbags.com*

Who Are Mark and Chrissy Donnelly?

Avid golfers Mark and Chrissy Donnelly are a dynamic married couple working closely together as coauthors, marketers and speakers.

They are the coauthors of the *USA Today* bestselling and #1 *New York Times* bestselling book, *Chicken Soul for the Couple's Soul.* They are also at work on several other upcoming books, among them *Chicken Soup for the Father's Soul* and *Chicken Soup for the Friend's Soul*, as well as the sequel to *Chicken Soup for the Couple's Soul.*

As cofounders of The Donnelly Marketing Group, they develop and implement innovative marketing and promotional strategies that help elevate and expand the *Chicken Soup for the Soul* message to millions of people around the world.

Mark, currently CEO of the Donnelly Marketing Group, was introduced to golf at the age of three. He remembers following his father to the golf course and finding a four-leaf clover that he believes enabled his father to win a prominent local amateur tournament. As a result of this and other golfing experiences with his father, Mark developed an appreciation for the game, along with a respectable golf game. Mark grew up in Portland, Oregon, and unbeknownst to him, attended the same high school as Chrissy. He went on to graduate from the University of Arizona, where he was president of his fraternity, Alpha Tau Omega. He served as vice president of marketing for his family's business, Contact Lumber, and after eleven years resigned from day-to-day responsibilities to focus on his current endeavors.

Chrissy, COO of the Donnelly Marketing Group, is a recent convert to the game of golf. A quick learner, she shot her first 90 within a year of taking up the game. She already has Mark looking over his shoulder. Chrissy also grew up in Portland, Oregon and graduated from Portland State University. As a CPA, she embarked on a six-year career with Price Waterhouse.

Mark and Chrissy enjoy many hobbies together including golf, hiking, skiing, traveling, hip-hop aerobics and spending time with friends. Mark and Chrissy live in Paradise Valley, Arizona and can be reached at:

Donnelly Marketing Group, LLC
3104 E. Camelback Road, Suite 531
Phoenix, AZ 85016
phone: 602-604-4422 fax: 602-508-8912
e-mail: *soup4soul@home.com*

Who Is Golf Digest?

Golf Digest is America's oldest and most widely read golf monthly with a circulation of 1.55 million and six million readers. Since 1950 *Golf Digest* has advised golfers on how to play, what to play and where to play. It has won every major golf-writing award and twice in the last decade been named finalist in the prestigious National Magazine Awards.

Its contributing editors include the best writers and teachers in the country, including writers Dan Jenkins, Dave Kindred, Nick Seitz and Tom Callahan and teachers David Leadbetter, Jack Lumpkin, Hank Haney, Butch Harmon and Jim McLean, among many others. *Golf Digest* Schools, which serve as a laboratory to the magazine's highly-respected instruction content, are recognized as the leading golf schools in the country. *Golf Digest* has twenty-three affiliated publications around the world, offering the magazine's editorial content to some one million golfers in more than forty countries.

Golf Digest assisted *Chicken Soup for the Golfer's Soul* in the solicitation and selection of stories and cartoons for this book. Several of the stories here will be excerpted in the magazine and its writers are well-represented in these pages.

Contributors

Several of the stories in this book were taken from previously published sources such as books, magazines and newspapers. These sources are acknowledged in the permissions section. However, most of the stories were written by humorists, comedians, professional speakers and workshop presenters. If you would like to contact them for information on their books, audio- and videotapes, seminars, and workshops, you can reach them at the addresses and phone numbers provided below.

The remainder of the stories were submitted by readers of our previous *Chicken Soup for the Soul* books who responded to our requests for stories. We have also included information about them.

Todd Behrendt knows all too well the allure golf has for so many. He witnesses it almost daily during his duties as the golf writer for the *North Country Times* in Escondido, California. Perhaps that's why the traumatic event described in this passage hasn't kept him from teeing it up with his father-in-law again— thankfully, without further incident.

Patty Berg took up golf when she was thirteen and is known as one of the leading female golfers during the 1950s and 1960s. She won fifteen Majors and was a founding member of the LPGA in 1948. She became the LPGA's first president (1949-1952) and is one of the original inductees into the LPGA Hall of Fame. In all, Patty won fifty-seven tournaments on the LPGA tour. The LPGA honored her by establishing the Patty Berg Award in 1978 which is given to the female golfer who has made the greatest contribution to women's golf during the year. Her career sets an example to sportsmen and sportswomen everywhere. She is known for her great talent and lifelong dedication to the game.

Arthur Berk is a writer who has contributed to *Reader's Digest, Newsday* and *The Hampton Chronicle News*. At present, Arthur is preparing a one-man show in his hometown library in East Meadow, New York. He has taught writing and art at Westhampton Beach. At present, he is retired . . . on the golf course!

Greg R. Bernard, when not hacking his way around a golf course, is a college writing instructor, having taught at a small community college in Illinois before returning this past summer to his native northern Minnesota. He holds both a B.A. and an M.A. in English literature from Bemidji State University, and is currently teaching there on adjunct status. Susan, Greg's wife and life partner, provides him with encouragement, inspiration, and most recently, his latest muse—their daughter Madison.

Ken Bowden is currently president of Golden Bear Publishing, Inc., a division of Golden Bear International, Inc. Prior to his more than twenty-five-year association with Jack Nicklaus, Bowden was for three years editorial director of the world's leading golf periodical, *Golf Digest*, and prior to that the founding editor of the leading English-language golf magazine in London, *Golf World*. He has coauthored ten books with Jack Nicklaus that have sold over two million copies around the world. He has also coauthored bestselling books with John Jacobs, including *Practical Golf*. He has produced and co-produced more than 150 golf programs. His video productions include Nicklaus's top-selling "Golf My Way" series. He resides in Westport, Connecticut and Jupiter, Florida.

William M. Bowen, a retiree, has added anecdotal writing to his list of hobbies which include grandchildren, traveling with his wife June, working with the elderly, golf and fishing. The writing, which of course complements all of the above, quickly became his favorite of those activities. He motivates the "old folks" with whom he works to join in telling the stories from the past that will die if they are not passed on through their writing or recording. He says he can tell golf stories better than he can play the wonderful game!

Susan D. Brandenburg, born in Hollywood, California, the daughter of an Air Force Officer, has lived in Germany, Japan, California, Texas, Montana, Nebraska, New York and Florida. She now resides in Sawgrass, Ponte Vedra Beach, Florida. Her job as a coordinator at Blue Cross Blue Shield of Florida keeps her busy during the day, and her evenings are filled with interviewing exciting people and writing weekly feature articles for the *Beaches Leader* newspaper. The most exciting adventure of her life is a continuing one—being a mother of a fine son and daughter, and grandmother to two healthy, beautiful grandsons.

Brad Brewer is director of the Arnold Palmer Golf Academies. Brad joined Arnold Palmer's organization in 1984 after competing around the world. He is an internationally known and recognized golf instructor who is featured regularly on the Golf Channel and in many national magazines. Brad knows exactly what it takes to help amateur golfers improve their games while increasing their enjoyment.

Gina Bridgeman is a regular contributor to the devotional book *Daily Guideposts*. Her work has also appeared in several *Guideposts* publications and *A Second Chicken Soup for the Woman's Soul*. Her most memorable writing experience was collaborating with her father, broadcaster Joe Garagiola on his bestselling book *It's Anybody's Ballgame*. Gina lives in Scottsdale, Arizona, with her husband and two children.

Adam Bruns is a freelance writer and poet from Lexington, Kentucky. His work has appeared in *Golfweek, Golf Journal, Central Kentucky Golf* and *Greater Louisville Golf*. His features have also appeared in *American Libraries* and *The Lane Report*. Adam is a member of the Golf Writers Association of America.

Bob Brust is a native to Montana and an engineering graduate from the University of Washington. Bob spent thirty-two years with Chevron U.S.A., mostly in pipelining, and has recently traded in his old slide rule and calculator for a word processor. He and his wife, Harriett, live in Walnut Creek, California with a Siamese cat named Gato. He writes for magazines and periodicals and specializes in what he describes as a "slightly disjointed form of humor."

Tom Callahan is married with two children. He is a former *Time Magazine* senior writer, *Washington Post* sports columnist and a *Golf Digest* contributing editor. He coauthored *Around the World in 18 Holes* with Dave Kindred (Doubleday). He is recently back from seventeen months in Belfast and is at work on a book about "the Troubles," entitled *An Irish Thing*.

Jack Cavanaugh writes for the *New York Times*. He also has contributed to *Sports Illustrated, Reader's Digest, Golf Digest* and a number of other national publications. Cavanaugh is also the author of the book, *Damn the Disabilities: Full Speed Ahead*. He lives in Wilton, Connecticut.

Frank Christian and his family of photographers have been providing the official photos of the Masters Tournament for nearly sixty-five years. His recent book, *Augusta National and the Masters: A Photographer's Scrapbook* is one of the top-selling sports books. He lives in Augusta with his family.

Christine Clifford is CEO and president of The Cancer Club, a company that markets humorous and helpful products for people with cancer on an international basis. She is the author of two award-winning books, including *Not Now, I'm Having a No Hair Day: Humor and Healing for People with Cancer* and *Our Family Has Cancer, Too!*, especially for children. Christine is a professional speaker on how to use humor and exercise to recover from chronic illness. Her work has appeared in such publications as *Better Homes and Gardens, Coping* magazine, *MORE, American Health for Women, The Hindu in India* and *The Singapore Women's Weekly*. Recently she was featured on CNN Live as "one of the world's leading authorities on the use of therapeutic humor." Christine is also the host of the Christine Clifford Celebrity Golf Invitational, an event to raise money for breast cancer detection, research and awareness. Christine and The Cancer Club can be reached at 800-586-9062; fax 612-941-1229; 6533 Limerick Dr., Edina, MN 55439; e-mail at *canclub@primenet.com* or her Web site at *www.cancerclub.com*

Jan K. Collins is an editor at the University of South Carolina's business school and is also a freelance writer and columnist. A former award-winning newspaper reporter in Michigan, North Carolina and South Carolina, Jan was awarded a Nieman Fellowship at Harvard University. She coauthors two weekly columns, "Flying Solo"—on divorce and separation issues—and "Next Steps"—on issues involving the elderly—that are distributed nationally to more than 225 newspapers. She is a southern correspondent for *The Economist*, has been published in numerous national newspapers and magazines, and has contributed chapters to three books. She can be reached at 803-777-2510.

Betty Cuniberti is an award-winning journalist with a career spanning more than twenty years. She has covered collegiate and professional sports, profiled political figures in Washington, authored a humor column for the *Kansas City Star*, guest lectured at the University of Kansas journalism school and combined her twin passions of golf and writing for *Golf Digest* magazine. She became a fan of *Chicken Soup* books during her second bout with breast cancer in 1997, reading *Chicken Soup for the Surviving Soul*. She resides in St. Louis with her two golf partners/children, ten-year-old Angela and eight-year-old Oscar (originator of the left-handed, 360-degree, fall-on-your-face swing).

Gary D'Amato is an award-winning golf writer/columnist for the *Milwaukee Journal Sentinel*. He has coauthored two books: *The Packer Tapes: My 32 Years with the Green Bay Packers* and *Mudbaths and Bloodbaths: The Inside Story of the Bears-Packers Rivalry*.

A. J. Daulerio is from Ambler, Pennsylvania, and is a staff writer for Great Media Newspapers in East Brunswick, New Jersey, and a freelance journalist. He would like to thank his parents, Colleen, and his friend, Ernie.

Steve Densley is president and CEO of the Provo/Oren Chamber of Commerce in Provo, Utah. After working on the East Coast and in Chicago, he and his wife, Colleen, settled in Utah. He has written articles for several magazines and currently writes a weekly column for three Utah papers. He spends his free time doing amateur photography and playing with his six grandchildren.

Don Didio is a forty-five-year-old father of four, recently transplanted from Baltimore to the scenic mountains and valleys of central Pennsylvania. He has been writing since college as both a hobby and as a means of release. Most of his stories are taken from life's experiences, dreams, hopes, failures and successes. He believes that success is measured by what we overcome, not by what we acquire. He can be reached at 31 Winter Trail, Fairfield, Pennsylvania, or by calling 717-642-8598 or via e-mail *didiod@mail.cvn.net.*

James Dodson is an award-winning golf writer and author of the bestselling book, *Final Rounds*. James always felt closest to his father while they were on the links. So it seemed only appropriate when his father learned he had two months to live that they would set off on the golf journey of their dreams to play the most famous courses in the world. *Final Rounds* is a book never to be forgotten, a book about fathers and sons, long-held secrets, and the lessons a middle-aged man can still learn from his dad about life, love and family.

Tommy Ehrbar works at the University of Pittsburgh when not golfing. He is director of feature services, speech writer and steadfast contributor to university publications. He previously held a similar position at Kenyon College. He is a graduate of Notre Dame University, former congressional reporter for *The New Republic*, former TV weather forecaster, and freelance writer of pluck and vim.

Sondra Sue Ward Elder is a freelance writer and artist who claims she is a former West Virginia divot champion. "Can't hit a lick with a golf club," she says. However, she couldn't miss the wit and self-reliance of the parachutist she has dubbed the "world's greatest play-through champion."

John Feinstein spent eleven years on the staff of the *Washington Post* as well as writing for *Sports Illustrated* and the *National Sports Daily*. He is a commentator on NPR's "Morning Edition," a regular on ESPN's *The Sports Reporters*, and a visiting professor of journalism at Duke University. John's first book, *A Season on the Brink*, is the bestselling sports book of all time. *A Good Walk Spoiled* was a #1 *New York Times* bestseller.

David Field is the author of The Story of Happy. He has an A.B. from Colgate University and an M.A. from Ohio University. He retired as lieutenant colonel in 1962 after serving twenty years in the U.S. Army, service in Europe during WW II, service in Korea during the Korean War and on special mission in Vietnam. He has spent thirty years in education as a psychology professor at Emeritus Thomas Nelson Community College in Hampton, Virginia. He is currently a freelance writer with 277 articles published in regional and national periodicals on golf, religion, psychology, travel, history and military topics.

Leonard Finkel, together with artist Gary Max Collins, produced *The Secrets to the Game of Golf & Life*. He is a freelance writer and regular contributor to *Orlando Golflife* and *Atlanta Golflife* and writes for and appears on the TV show, *Links Illustrated*. Licensed products are being developed featuring the art and themes of the book. Information on books and products may be obtained from Leonard at 888-355-5179 or 800-621-1423, ext. 5631. Visit the Web site at *www.Golfandlife*.

Andrew Galanopulos is a fifteen-year-old sophmore at Daphne High School in Daphne, Alabama. In addition to being an avid writer and golfer, he is the editor of his school newspaper, a straight-A student and a member of the cross-country track team. He plans to become a doctor when he gets out of school.

Bud Gardner has been playing golf for fifty years. He was a member of the Fort Hays Kansas State University golf team in the mid-1950s, and later won many open tournaments in western Kansas. He won his hometown tournament in WaKeeney, Kansas, shooting a 92 for 27 holes on the old sand-green course. In the mid-sixties, he coached golf at American River College in Sacramento, California, guiding his team to a conference championship. He now lives in Del Web's Sun City in Roseville, California, where he plays Sun City's Billy Casper-designed courses. He is the coauthor of *Chicken Soup for the Writer's Soul*.

Jay Gearan is a freelance writer and a sports correspondent for the *Worcester Telegram and Gazette* in Worcester, Massachusetts. Jay also teaches English at

Gardner High School and Mount Wachusett Community College in Gardner, Massachusetts. A member of the Golf Writers' Association of America for several years, Jay has published several sports stories in New England newspapers and golf magazines. He is currently working with Bordalice Publishing in Delmar, New York on a book about the upcoming 1999 Ryder Cup Matches. Bordalice (*www.bordalicepublishing.com*) specializes in sports psychology books. Jay, his wife, Janice, and their two sons Jack and Mike, live in Massachusetts. You can e-mail him at: *jgearan@massed.net*.

Marc Gellman is the senior rabbi of Temple Beth Torah in Melville, New York. He holds a doctorate in philosophy from Northwestern University and a pretty decent handicap from the Metropolitan Golf Association. He has written for *Golf Digest* and the *Met Golfer* along with other important theological publications. He is the author of *Does God Have a Big Toe?*, *God's Mailbox* and *Always Wear Clean Underwear*. With his friend and golfing buddy Monsignor Thomas Hartman, he has written *Where Does God Live? How Do You Spell God?*, and most recently, *Lost and Found*, a kids book for living through loss. He appears regularly with Monsignor Hartman on ABC's *Good Morning America*, the "Imus in the Morning" radio program, and they have their own cable television program, *The God Squad*. He is the recipient of many awards, and is an honorary member of Old Westbury Golf and Country Club.

Jay Golden, PGA member, performs his golf comedy clinic entitled "THE FUN-damentals of Golf" across the U.S. He writes for several golf magazines, has appeared on TV hundreds of times, is a two-time quarter-finalist in the National Long Drive Contest and has produced a comedy and instruction video. For more information e-mail at *rjjjg1@aol.com*.

Adel Guzzo grew up in Lincolnshire, Illinois, and attended high school at Adlai Stevenson in Prairie View, Illinois. He loves golf, darts and writing music. Most of all, he loves his family and friends.

Frank J. Haller and his wife Julie reside in Scott Township, Pittsburgh, with their cat Max. They have four children: Jane, Nancy, Bob and Jim. Frank's main accomplishments are being a private to first lieutenant, U.S. Infantry, and working thirty-nine years in the ad agency business. The four most important things in his life are: God; family; friends; and his job—and not necessarily in that order.

Tracy Hanson has been playing golf on the Ladies Professional Golf Tour since 1995. She enjoys writing as a hobby. She can be reached through the LPGA Tour office at 100 International Golf Drive, Daytona Beach, FL 32124.

Scott Hipp resides in Mission, Kansas. He is a single accountant whose hobbies include: golf, Korean War history, and UFO and paranormal studies. He can golf both left- and right-handed and has broken 80 from both sides.

Jeff Kahler is president and CEO of Kahler & Company, a marketing communications agency located in Omaha, Nebraska. As a copywriter and creative director, he has won more than 150 creative awards on the local, regional, national and international level. A two-time club champion, he currently holds a 1 handicap.

John Keating is currently a wine consultant with a major interest in food, wine, travel and golf. He has a B.S. in political science from Georgetown University, Washington, D.C., and an M.A. in education from George Washington University, Washington, D.C. He was a fighter pilot in the U.S. Air Force for twenty years, a wine educator for eighteen years and a restaurant sales manager for a wine distributor for sixteen years.

Harrison Kelly is a freelance writer living in Memphis, Tennessee, with his wife, Lucretia, and their two children, Brad and Kristina. Some of his works have been published in *A Second Chicken Soup for the Woman's Soul* and *Stories for a Man's Heart*. He can be reached via e-mail at *dhk@sprynet.com*.

Dave Kindred is a columnist for *Golf Digest*. He says of Stuart and Renay Appleby: "The more I talked to Stuart, the more I wished I had known Renay. She lived in his every breath." Kindred and his wife, Cheryl, belong to four dogs who romp in the Civil War hills of central Virginia.

Bradley S. Klein, born in New York City in 1954, got his start in golf as a caddie, first at private clubs on his native Long Island then on the PGA Tour. He has caddied in half a dozen U.S. Opens. He is architecture editor/columnist for *Golfweek* for whom he also runs "America's Best," a national golf course ranking system of the top 100 classical and top 100 modern golf courses. He is also contributing editor to America Online's *GOLF*. His essays have appeared in nearly every major golf publication. He is a design consultant and frequent lecturer in the golf industry. Today, with a Ph.D. in hand, he teaches political theory and international relations at Clark University in Worcester, Massachusetts.

Michael Konik is well-known to frequent fliers as the west coast editor of Delta Airline's *SKY* magazine, where his monthly column Tee Time has been honored by the Golf Writers Association of America. Michael is also the gambling columnist for *Cigar Aficionado* and has been published in over 100 magazines and newspapers. He is the author of *The Man with $100,000 Breasts and Other Gambling Stories* (Huntington Press). Currently, he is working on his next book, *Good Shot, Mr. Nicklaus: Stories About the Game of Golf.*

Stephen Leacock (1869-1944), humorist, essayist, teacher, political economist and historian, was the recipient of numerous honorary degrees, awards and distinctions. He received The Lorne Pierce Medal, a postage stamp issued in his honor and the Leacock Medal for Humor established in his honor. Leacock was the world's best-known English-speaking humorist from 1915 to 1925.

Mitch Laurance is a passionate golfer, sports commentor (ESPN Championship 9-ball), television host ("On the Green" Golf Video Magazine, Myrtle Beach, South Carolina, and Infomercials), golf writer (*On the Green* magazine, *Golf Range* magazine), and actor ("Not Necessarily the News," "Matlock," "Dawson's Creek"). He can be contacted at 704-364-4864 or at *mitchewa@aol.com*.

Davis Love III has been on the PGA tour since 1985. He has won eleven Tour titles, including the 1997 PGA Championship and the 1992 Players Championship. He was a member of the last two United States Ryder Cup and Presidents Cup teams, and teamed with Fed Couples to win four consecutive World Cup titles. He lives in St. Simons Island, Georgia, with his wife, Robin, their daughter, Alexia, and their son, Davis IV.

Harvey Mackay is the author of *Pushing The Envelope* and four *New York Times* bestsellers, including *Swim with the Sharks*. The nationally syndicated business columnist is CEO of the $85 million Mackay Envelope Corporation based in Minneapolis. Toastmasters International named him one of the top five speakers in the world.

Carol Mann won thirty-eight LPGA victories in her twenty-one years on the tour, including a U.S. Open Championship. She is a member of the LPGA Hall of Fame, the International Women's Sports Hall of Fame, and was named one of the 100 heroes of the first 100 years of golf in America. Carol was the first female reporter for NBC's coverage of men's golf; she has also been the color analyst for ABC, PBS, ESPN and syndicated women's golf telecasts. Carol has served as president of the LPGA, and of the Women's Sports Foundation. She has written numerous articles for *Golf Magazine* and *Golf Illustrated*, and is an award-winning golf columnist for the *Houston Post*.

Micki McClelland has her fingers in an assortment of pies. A published poet and fiction writer, she is also a produced playwright of comedies and one musical. In recent years Micki has been a freelance writer for magazines, newspapers and for individual clients. In her spare time, she paints, although not formally trained in the art of knowing what to do with color, canvas and brush, Micki's style can be described as primitive and she tends to paint off the page. Currently senior editor of *MY Table: Houston's Dining* magazine, Micki pens essays on food and spirits for the publication, and her paintings have appeared as cover design for four issues.

Clint McCown, author of the golf novel, *The Member-Guest*, has twice won the American Fiction Prize. His stories, poems and essays have appeared widely. He is a professor of creative writing at Beloit College, where he also edits the *Beloit Fiction Journal*.

Alf McCreary is an award-winning journalist, author and broadcaster who lives and works in Northern Ireland, home to some of the best golf courses in the world.

Scott Medlock is one of America's foremost artists. His work is becoming legendary in the world of fine art, particularly through his fine art reproductions. Although he has recently concentrated on the world of golf, his past successes include portrayals of great athletes, abstract painting, children's book illustrations, magazine covers, book covers and paintings for major advertising campaigns. He was commissioned to be one of the official artists for the 1996 Olympic Games in Atlanta. Medlock has also created and "sold out" numerous limited edition reproductions. His paintings involve what art historians refer to as the "psychological moment," the inner world of a golfer setting up an important putt, the one-on-one competitiveness of Bill Russell and Wilt Chamberlain, the emotionally charged environment of Yankee Stadium as Babe Ruth bids farewell to his fans. Medlock's talent surfaced early; a graduate of the Art Center of Design at Pasadena, now just twenty-nine years of age, he has already received awards of excellence from the New York Society of Illustrators, Society of Illustrators of Los Angeles and the European Illustrators Society.

John Meyers is a writer of film screenplays and feature articles who lives and golfs to an 8 handicap in Maryland with his wife and two children ages six and nine. As a regular contributor to *The Washington Golf Monthly*, his essays span the whole spectrum of what makes the game of golf so unique in the grand scheme of the universe. At least he gives it a shot.

Steve Minnick has been involved in designing and managing computer systems for over twenty years. He divides his spare time writing the occasional screenplay and traveling with his wife Leanna, a composer and music teacher. How's his game today? "Much improved since his brush with Mr. Miller."

Rich Mintzer is the author of thirteen books including four golf books. In the past ten years he has also penned over 300 articles on a wide range of subjects for national magazines. Rich lives with his wife and two children in New York City where he doesn't get to play golf as often as he would like, but loves the serenity of the course when he gets out there.

Debra Moss combines a professional resume as a litigation paralegal and investment trader with a lifelong career as a freelance writer and photographer. During eight years living aboard a sailboat in Florida and the U.S. Virgin Islands, Debra wrote for fifteen boating publications, reporting on Florida, Bahamian and Caribbean yacht racing, as well as technical articles on maintenance and chartering for *Cruising World, Yacht Vacations* and *Yachting*. Her book credits include coauthoring a full-length biography on the life of rhythm-and-blues singer Jackie Wilson, and a novel in progress, *A Suspicion of Destiny*.

Carla Muir is a freelance writer of poetry and stories published in *More Stories for the Heart, Keepsakes for the Heart, Do Not Lose Heart* and *A Second Chicken Soup for the Woman's Soul*. Contact Carla through her agent, Susan Yates, at Yates & Yates, LLP at 714-835-3742.

Sam Murphy was born in Carlisle, Pennsylvania. He is sixty-two years old and is married to Marita. He has three children and six grandchildren. Sam is a retired insurance company general manager. Nowadays, he tinkers with making golf clubs and enjoys playing golf with his cronies at Bogie Lake Golf Club in White Lake, Michigan.

J. G. Nursall is a forty-five-year-old attorney living and working in southern California. Formerly an avid golfer, he writes to relax and to commemorate some of the valuable lessons learned on the links. His grandfather, the late Grant Halstead, was the formidable teaching pro who operated the Riverside Golf Club near Fresno, California. Regaled by Halstead's stories of his competitive days among the likes of Walter Hagen, Lawson Little, Harry "Lighthorse" Cooper and others, Nursall came to see his grandfather's "golfing world" as a richly heroic place, filled with characters and themes—suitable to muse upon, and to pass on to others.

David Owen is a contributing editor of *Golf Digest* and a staff writer for *The New Yorker*. His books about golf are *My Usual Game, Lure of the Links* and *The Making of the Masters*. Contact him at *david.owen@sent.net*.

Larry R. Pearson has held a variety of sales, marketing and management positions in the information-technology industry, is a high-handicap golfer and sports lover of all kinds. He and his wife Carolyn have been married for twenty-five years and live in Marietta, Georgia. Their two sons, Benjamin and Gabriel, are now twenty-one and eighteen years old, respectively. Until now, his poems and short stories have been used as gifts and expressions of love to family and friends.

Bill Pelham played on the PGA Tour from 1976 to 1980. Today, he owns a golf marketing company, specializing in promoting corporate golf events nationwide. He can be reached at Doubleagle, 8702 Stone Village Lane, Houston, TX 77040, or by phone at 713-937-3866.

Bob Phillips, who is now a local public relations executive in Memphis, Tennessee, was executive sports editor of the *Memphis Press Scimitar* and the *Nashville Banner*. The fifty-four-year-old native Memphian does extensive freelance sports writing in the southeast. Ironically, Bob does not golf, but loves to write about the sport and its participants.

Nick Price was born in South Africa, but moved to Rhodesia (Zimbabwe) at a young age. Growing up he enjoyed sports of all kinds including cricket, water-skiing and golf. He spent two years in the Rhodesian Air Force and obtained his pilot's license. As a family man, he believes in the importance of spending time together. His wife, Sue, and their three children often accompany him to his tournaments. Nick has been very generous supporting charities that benefit children and help protect wildlife. Because of his strong belief in giving back to his home country's youth, he actively supports Zimbabwe Junior Golf. For more information about Nick Price, please contact him at: 900 South U.S. Hwy. 1, #105, Jupiter, FL 33477. Phone: 561-575-6588; fax: 561-575-5420.

Rich Radford lives in Norfolk, Virginia, where he is a sports writer for *The Virginian-Pilot*, covering among other subjects, golf. He is a semi-regular contributor to *Washington Golf Monthly* and *The New York Mets Inside Pitch* magazine. He and his wife, Laurie, have two sons, Kevin and Alex.

Stan Reynolds is a freelance writer and security consultant. Now at work on his second novel, his articles have appeared in newspapers and journals. A former marine, Pinkerton detective, and president/owner of a security company, he also served as chairman of the Georgia State Board, Private

Detectives and Security Agencies. He can be reached at River Plantation, 8566 Sawyer Brown Rd., Nashville, TN 37221 or call 615-673-1207.

Jimmy Roberts is an Emmy-Award-winning correspondent for ESPN and ABC Sports. He is also a contributor to ABC News, where his work has appeared on *World News Tonight* and *Good Morning America*. On the print side, Roberts writes for *ESPN Magazine*. He also has a regular column on *ESPN.com* from which "An Embrace in the Bittersweet Middle" was taken.

Ken Robertson considers himself a rookie author and a veteran golfer. He began golfing in the Ottawa area in the 1930s. Since that time, he has gained quite a reputation as well as a low handicap, and earned himself a place in history in the local Cornwall Sports Hall of Fame. He is retired and lives with his wife, Anne. He has three sons, Bruce, Gordon and Mark.

Lorne Rubenstein is one of the world's best known and most respected golf writers. The author of half-a-dozen books, he has been the golf columnist for the *Toronto Globe* and *Mail* for more than fifteen years. He's won three first place awards in Golf Writer's Association of America writing contest, and one National Magazine Award in Canada. Lorne still carries a 3.1 handicap, and won the Golf Writers Association championship in 1984. He continues to maintain that his best days as a player are ahead of him.

Melissa Russell is the wife and mother of golfers, and an award-winning writer in her own right. Having her story published in *Chicken Soup for the Golfer's Soul* is her idea of a double eagle! Her essays have been published as back-page features in *Smithsonian* magazine and *ByLine*. One of her children's stories will appear in an upcoming issue of *The Flicker Magazine*. She can be contacted at 909 Country Club Circle, Grand Prairie, TX 75052, or *wedoma@aol.com*.

Nick Seitz resides in Rowayton, Connecticut, with his wife, Velma. He graduated from the University of Oklahoma, where he majored in philosophy. Before joining *Golf Digest* magazine, he was sports editor of the *Oklahoma Journal*, where he won several distinguished writing awards. In 1967, he became editor of *Golf Digest*, and in 1982 was named editorial director of *Golf Digest* and *Tennis Magazine*. He is presently editor-in-chief of *The New York Times* Company Magazine Group. Nick has authored many articles and several books on golf, and was coauthor on Tom Watson's *Strategic Golf with Watson*. His work has been included in the annual anthology *Best Sports Stories* numerous times.

Dave Sheinin, twenty-nine, loves chicken soup, golf and soul (music), which makes him feel peculiarly connected to this book. In addition to covering baseball for *The Miami Herald*, the Carrollton, Georgia, native and Vanderbilt University alumnus sings part-time for the Florida Grand Opera, which he thinks must be some sort of dubious first.

Alan Shepard was the first American launched in space in 1961. Ten years later, he commanded *Apollo 14* and became the fifth man to walk on the moon—and the first to play golf there. Alan passed away on July 21, 1998, following a battle with leukemia, at the age of seventy-four. His inspiration to many will not be forgotten.

Jerry Tarde, editorial director and vice president of *Golf Digest*, has been editor of the magazine for more than two decades. A graduate of Northwestern University, he started as an intern at the magazine in 1977 and since then has written hundreds of instruction and feature articles on golf. He is the co-author with Sam Snead of *Pigeons, Marks, Hustlers (and Other Golf Bettors You Can Beat)*. He now writes a monthly column for *Golf Digest*.

Giles Tippette the former rodeo cowboy, played college football, was a mercenary pilot in Africa, a venture pilot, has published fifty-four books with six major publishers and over 500 articles for major magazines. He has earned his living as a professional writer for thirty-four years. The most tired he has ever been in his life was when they got through hitting that golf ball for thirty-four miles.

Terry Todd is a professor in the kinesiology department at the University of Texas at Austin. He has published five books and over 500 articles in such magazines as *Sports Illustrated* and *Reader's Digest*. He is a former national champion in power-lifting and he has the world's largest collection of books and magazines about physical fitness.

Tom Turley is a former newsman, now retired on Cape Cod.

Don Wade, a former senior editor at *Golf Digest*, is the author of six bestselling collections of golf anecdotes. Covering professional golf since the 1970s, he has worked as a feature reporter for CBS Sports and NBC Sports and as a golf analyst for the USA Network. His writing has appeared in a variety of publications, including the *New York Times* and the *Boston Globe*. He has also written books with Ken Venturi, Sam Snead, Amy Alcott and Nancy Lopez.

Judy Walker is currently teaching seventh-grade language arts and has twenty-five years of teaching experience, which includes first through seventh grades. Her family includes her husband, Randy, and two sons, Greg and Jeff. She enjoys camping, golfing, cooking, reading, traveling, writing and scrapbooking. She would love to write a novel and be published.

Ernie Witham writes advertising copy for a living in Santa Barbara, California, but his real love is writing humor based on that ongoing adventure known as everyday life. His humorous essays have been published in the *Los Angeles Times*, the *Santa Barbara News Press*, *Santa Barbara Families* magazine and others. The moment he first stepped foot on a golf course, he knew he had discovered a new wealth of humor-writing opportunities.

Gordon W. Youngs has been playing golf for thirty-seven years, competitively in high school and college, and occasionally competitively (and always for pleasure) ever since. Golf has given him many enjoyable hours, and many allegorical lessons in life. He will always be thankful his father introduced him to the game. Gordon is a California native who is a human resources director for a local government; currently a single-digit handicap index, which varies with frequency of play; married to a non-golfer, but their eight-year-old son has shown some interest in the game. He enjoys trying new courses whenever and wherever they have the opportunity to travel.

Permissions *(continued from page vi)*

I Hate Golf—I Love Golf. Reprinted by permission of George Bush. ©1998 George Bush.

A Candle in the Wind. Reprinted by permission of Jack Sheehan. ©1998 Jack Sheehan and Peter Jacobsen.

Turning Back the Clock. Reprinted by permission of Betty Cuniberti. ©1998 Betty Cuniberti. Originally appeared in *Golf Digest Woman*.

Plimpton to the Fore. Reprinted by permission of George Plimpton. ©1998 George Plimpton.

There Is No "I" in Team. Reprinted by permission of Dave Sheinin. ©1998 Dave Sheinin. Originally appeared in *Golf Journal*.

The Magoo Caper. Reprinted by permission of Harvey Mackay. ©1998 Harvey Mackay.

Beat the Pro. Reprinted by permission of Susan D. Brandenburg. ©1998 Susan D. Brandenburg.

Golf Balls. Reprinted by permission of Sam Murphy. ©1998 Sam Murphy.

Walter Won the Honors. Reprinted by permission of Frank J. Haller. ©1998 Frank J. Haller.

A Special Rapport. Reprinted by permission of Paul Daugherty. ©1998 Paul Daugherty.

Life on the Back Nine. Reprinted by permission of Rich Radford. ©1998 Rich Radford.

Living the Dream. Reprinted by permission of Gary D'Amato. ©1998 Gary D'Amato.

Requiem for a Milkman. Reprinted by permission of Tom Callahan. ©1998 Tom Callahan. Originally appeared in *Golf Digest*.

Golf and the Caddie at Royal Troon. Reprinted by permission of Jeff Kahler. ©1999 Jeff Kahler.

The Day Mr. 59 Bottled Lightning. Reprinted by permission of Nick Seitz. ©1997 The New York Times Company Magazine Group, Inc. All rights reserved.

All the Good Things Any Man Should Be. Reprinted by permission of Nick Price Group, Inc. ©1998 Nick Price. Originally appeared in *Golf Digest*.

Ike, Mamie, Spiro and Me. Reprinted by permission of Clint McCown. ©1997 Clint McCown. Originally appeared in *Golf Digest*.

Every Shot I Take by Davis Love III and Michael Bamberger. ©1997 by Davis Love III and Michael Bamberger.

Payback. Reprinted by permission of Scott Hipp. ©1998 Scott Hipp.

Playing It Down. Reprinted by permission of Leonard Finkel. ©1998 Leonard Finkel.

We Play 'Em All. Reprinted by permission of William Bowen. ©1998 William Bowen.

A True Gentleman. Reprinted by permission of Hugh Baldwin. ©1998 Hugh Baldwin.

Play It as It Lies. Excerpted from *The Game I Love* by Sam Snead and Fran Pirozzolo. Copyright ©1997 by Sam Snead and Fran Pirozzolo. Reprinted by permission of Ballantine Books, a Division of Random House, Inc.

The Day I Cheated. Reprinted by permission of John Meyers. ©1998 John Meyers.

The Clutch Putt. Reprinted by permission of Ken Robertson. ©1998 Ken Robertson.

The Difference Between the Scots and the Americans. From *And Then Jack Said To Arnie* by Don Wade. Reprinted by permission of Don Wade. ©1991.

The Gentle Hustler. Reprinted by permission of Bob Brust. ©1998 Bob Brust. Originally appeared in *Golf Journal.*

The Compassionate Golfer. Reprinted by permission of Carla Muir. ©1998 Carla Muir.

Victory for Golf Rats. Reprinted by permission of Rabbi Marc Gellman. ©1998 Rabbi Marc Gellman. Originally appeared in *The Metropolitan Golfer.*

A Practice Round for Life. Reprinted by permission of Debra Moss. ©1998 Debra Moss.

The Collection Basket. Reprinted by permission of Jan K. Collins. ©1998 Jan K. Collins.

Remember When. Reprinted by permission of Bud Gardner. ©1998 Bud Gardner.

Being There. Reprinted by permission of Don Didio. ©1998 Don Didio.

Way Above Par. Reprinted by permission of Harrison Kelly. ©1998 Harrison Kelly.

Divorce, of Course. Reprinted by permission of Gordon W. Youngs. ©1998 Gordon W. Youngs.

The Ace Man. Reprinted by permission of Mitch Laurance. ©1998 Mitch Laurance.

Lightning Strikes Twice. Reprinted from *The Golf Nut's Book of Amazing Feats and Records* by Bruce Nash and Allan Zullo with George White. ©1994. Used with permission of NTC/Contemporary Publishing Group, Inc.

A Wing Grew Back. Reprinted by permission of Jay Gearan. ©1998 Jay Gearan.

The Healer. Reprinted by permission of Michael Konik. ©1998 Michael Konik.

Happy. Reprinted by permission of David Field. ©1998 David Field.

The Benefits of Being King. Reprinted by permission of Rich Mintzer. ©1998 Rich Mintzer and Peter Grossman.

A Humble Beginning. Reprinted by permission of William H. Grace for Patty Berg. ©1998 Patty Berg.

Putter Devotion. Reprinted by permission of *Guideposts* magazine. ©1998 by *Guideposts*, Carmel, NY 10512.

Riders. Reprinted by permission of Arthur Berk. ©1998 Arthur Berk.

The Man Whose Secret Was a Secret. Reprinted by permission of Jerry Tarde. ©1993 The New Times Company Magazine Group, Inc. All rights reserved.

Brush, Brush. Reprinted by permission of Steve Minnick. ©1998 Steve Minnick.

Zen and the Art of Getting Over the Water Hazard. Reprinted by permission of Micki McClelland. ©1998 Micki McClelland.

More Help Than a Guy Needs. Reprinted courtesy of *Sports Illustrated*, February 24, 1997. ©1997 Time Inc. All rights reserved.

The Clown Prince of Golf. Reprinted by permission of John Feinstein. ©1998 John Feinstein.

Golf Carts Do Not Have Four-Wheel Drive. Reprinted by permission of Ernie Witham. ©1998 Ernie Witham.

DeProfundis, Homo (About Some Deep Stuff, Man). Reprinted by permission of Frank Haller. ©1998 Frank Haller.

He'd Give You the Shirt off of His Back. From *And Then Fuzzy Told Seve* by Don Wade. Reprinted by permission of Don Wade. ©1991.

The Secret. Reprinted by permission of J. G. Nursall. ©1998 J. G. Nursall. Originally appeared in *Golf Journal*.

Enjoy the Round. From *Final Rounds* by James Dodson. ©1996 by James Dodson. Used by permission of Bantan Books, a division of Random House, Inc.

Books to Nurture Your Body & Soul!

Chicken Soup for the Surviving Soul

Heartwarming accounts of courageous people who found the power to battle cancer in their endless hope, unwavering faith and steadfast determination will inspire you to adopt a positive attitude, discover your faith and cherish every moment. Just what the doctor ordered for healing body, mind and soul. #4029—$12.95

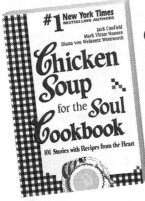

Chicken Soup for the Soul® Cookbook

In the spirit of *Chicken Soup for the Soul*, these inspiring stories revisit time-honored values such as love, loyalty and courage. Each story is paired with a kitchen-tested recipe providing nourishment for both body and soul. # 3545—$16.95

Chicken Soup for the Soul® at Work

This *New York Times* business bestseller is a timely addition to the ever-popular *Chicken Soup for the Soul* collection. This volume provides a much-needed spiritual boost for readers living in an age of global markets, corporate downsizing and unstable economies. #424X—$12.95

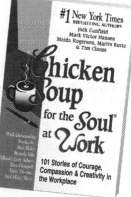

Selected books are also available in hardcover, large print, audiocassette and compact disc.

New for Kids

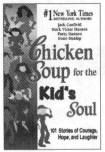

Chicken Soup for the Kid's Soul
Jack Canfield, Mark Victor Hansen, Patty Hansen and Irene Dunlap
Young readers will find empowerment and encouragement to love and accept themselves, believe in their
dreams, find answers to their questions and discover
hope for a promising future.
Code 6099, $12.95

Chicken Soup for the Teenage Soul II
Jack Canfield, Mark Victor Hansen and Kimberly Kirberger
The stories in this collection will show teens the
importance of friendship, family, self-respect, dreams,
and life itself.
Code 6161, $12.95

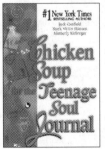

Chicken Soup for the Teenage Soul Journal
Jack Canfield, Mark Victor Hansen and Kimberly Kirberger
This personal journal offers teens the space to write their
own life stories, as well as space for their friends and par-
ents to offer them words of love and inspiration.
Code 6374, $12.95

The New Kid and the Cookie Thief
Story adaptation by Lisa McCourt
Illustrated by Mary O'Keefe Young

For a shy girl like Julie, there couldn't be anything worse
than the very first day at a brand new school. What if the
kids don't like her? What if no one ever talks to her at all?
Julie's big sister has some advice—and a plan—that just
might help. But will Julie be too scared to even give it a try?
Code 5882, hardcover, $14.95

Available in bookstores everywhere or call 1-800-441-5569 for Visa or MasterCard orders.
Prices do not include shipping and handling. Your response code is **CCS**.